RITSCHL
IN RETROSPECT

RITSCHL
IN RETROSPECT
History, Community, and Science

Darrell Jodock, Editor

Fortress Press • Minneapolis

Ritschl in retrospect : history, community, and science / edited by
  Darrell Jodock.
      p.   cm.
    Includes bibliographical references and index.
    ISBN 0-8006-2606-0 (alk. paper)
    1. Ritschl, Albrecht, 1822–1889.   I. Jodock, Darrell, 1941–   .
  BX4827.R5R55   1995   95-1016
  230'.044'092—dc20   CIP

Manufactured in U.S.A.   AF 1-2606

99   98   97   96   95   1   2   3   4   5   6   7   8   9   10

Contents

v

PART THREE: CHRISTIAN COMMUNITY
AND THE KINGDOM OF GOD

PART FOUR: THEOLOGY AND SCIENCE

Preface

The year 1989 marked the one-hundredth anniversary of Albrecht Ritschl's death. In itself such a centennial may have little intrinsic significance, but it can occasion a careful look at a theologian's contributions. In this case an assessment is needed, because the theology of the first half of the twentieth century was not always kind to Ritschl. He was often dismissed as but the culmination of a Liberal theology that should be consigned to the past, as a Kantian who championed Enlightenment philosophy and reduced Christianity to ethics, and as "the very epitome of the national-liberal German bourgeois of the age of Bismarck."[1] Whatever the strengths and weaknesses of his theology, Ritschl's contributions were too important to be dismissed. A number of dissertations[2] and studies during the second half of the twentieth cen-

---

1. Karl Barth, *Protestant Thought: From Rousseau to Ristchl* (New York: Harper & Brothers, 1959), 392.

2. Among those dissertations are the following:

- William Barnett, "Historical Relativism and Christology in the Thought of Wilhelm Dilthey and Albrecht Ritschl" (University of Chicago, 1976).
- Richard Busse, "The Implicit Metaphysical Scheme of Albrecht Ritschl's Theology" (Lutheran School of Theology at Chicago, 1984).
- Jonathan Draper, "The Place of the Bible in the Theology of Albrecht Ritschl" (University of Durham, 1984).
- Paul Jersild, "The Holiness, Righteousness and Wrath of God in the Theologies of Albrecht Ritschl and Karl Barth" (University of Münster, 1962).
- Darrell Jodock, "F. C. Baur and Albrecht Ritschl on Historical Theology" (Yale University, 1969).
- David Lotz, "Albrecht Ritschl's Interpretation of Luther's Theology: An Exposition, Analysis, and Critique" (Union Theological Seminary, 1971).
- Clive Marsh, "Albrecht Ritschl and the Problem of the Historical Jesus" (Oxford University, 1987).
- Gerald McCulloh, "Christ's Person and Life-Work in the Theology of Albrecht Ritschl: With Special Attention to *Munus Triplex*" (University of Chicago, 1974).
- Norman Metzler, "The Ethics of the Kingdom" (University of Munich, 1971).

tury have sought to interpret him more carefully, but the portrait that emerges from them is not widely known.[3] Thus a more adequate and more readily available assessment is still needed; for this a centennial can provide a fitting occasion.

The genesis of the present volume is linked directly to that anniversary. In 1986, during the Annual Meeting of the American Academy of Religion, Philip Hefner suggested that some observance of the upcoming centennial would be appropriate. Over a 6 A.M. breakfast (this *is* taking a task seriously!), he and I outlined a proposal for a two-year seminar on Ritschl's contributions to twentieth-century theology. William Barnett agreed to chair the steering committee for that Ritschl Seminar and to organize its program. The Seminar met twice, once during the Annual Meeting of the AAR in 1988 and again in 1989.

According to the nomenclature of the AAR a "seminar" involves a defined group of 15–20 scholars, working on a project oriented toward publication. From the very beginning we were in contact with the editors of Fortress Press, who (quite generously) expressed an interest in the project and throughout its development offered their advice and counsel. So it began.

The steering committee of the Ritschl Seminar selected two themes: "Christian community (including the Kingdom of God)" and "science and religion" (or, more broadly, "religion and culture" and "religion and philosophy"). Both are of contemporary interest and importance, and most brief treatments of Ritschl's theology have given neither theme the attention it deserves. Out of those Seminar sessions emerged the articles by McCulloh, Wall, Schwarz, Barnett, and Busse. In addition to benefiting from the discussions there, each was rewritten and subsequently revised several times before appearing here.

David Lotz, who had contributed a somewhat different paper to the AAR Seminar, was asked to draft an essay that would introduce the historical Ritschl—that is, seek to understand him in terms of his own concerns and the problems of his day. Lotz's essay appears in Part One.

Clive Marsh, who had participated in the Seminar but had not written a paper for it, was asked to discuss Ritschl's contributions to biblical theology, a topic largely (and unfortunately) overlooked by many Ritschl interpreters. Darrell Jodock, who presided at the second session of the Seminar and, along with Hans Schwarz, served on its steering committee, added an essay on Ritschl's concept of God, an essay not discussed by the Seminar.

Claude Welch, a lifelong student of nineteenth-century theology, cofounder in 1972 of the AAR Nineteenth Century Theology Working

---

• Michael Ryan, "The Role of the Discipline of History in the Theological Interpretation of Albrecht Ritschl" (Drew University, 1967).

3. See, for example, the monographs cited in the Abbreviations as Hefner, Lotz, Mueller, Richmond, and Schäfer.

Group, and in one significant way or another a mentor of all who work in this field, was asked to add a final chapter, where, in the light of these new studies, he could ponder again the ongoing significance of Ritschl's theology. This he did, in a chapter not begun until the other articles had been finished.

I am grateful to the authors of the several chapters for agreeing to participate and for responding so diligently to my requests, especially between 1989 and 1992. Their cooperation and commitment to the project made my role much easier and much more enjoyable than it otherwise would have been. Some of my work was done during a sabbatical in the spring semester of 1991; for that sabbatical and other forms of assistance I thank Muhlenberg College. My gratitude extends also to Timothy Staveteig for his excellent advice and his understanding of the importance of the topic and to Mrs. Elsie Schmoyer for her ever competent, cheerfully patient secretarial assistance.

The editor and authors of this volume are grateful to Philip Hefner for the original idea of a centennial observance reassessing Ritschl's significance, to the AAR for authorizing a two-year Ritschl Seminar, to the respondents and others who participated in those Seminar sessions, to Fortress Press, whose early commitment to the project encouraged continued work on the essays, and to all who contributed to the formation of this volume.

Darrell Jodock

Abbreviations

Barth	Karl Barth. *Protestant Theology in the Nineteenth Century: Its Background and History.* Valley Forge, Pa.: Judson Press, 1973.
DAR	Albrecht Ritschl. *Drei akademische Reden in Namen der Universität Göttingen gehalten von Albrecht Ritschl.* Bonn: Adolph Marcus, 1887.
EK	Albrecht Ritschl. *Die Entstehung der altkatholischen Kirche: Eine kirchen- und dogmengeschichtliche Monographie.* Bonn: Adolph Marcus, 1850; zweite, durchgängig neu ausgearbeitete Auflage, 1857.
GA	Otto Ritschl, editor. *Gesammelte Aufsätze von Albrecht Ritschl.* 2 vols. Freiburg i. B. and Leipzig: Akademische Verlagsbuchhandlung von J. C. B. Mohr, 1893 & 1896.
GP	Albrecht Ritschl. *Geschichte des Pietismus.* 3 vols. Bonn: Adolph Marcus, 1880, 1884, & 1886.
Hefner	Philip Hefner. *Faith and the Vitalities of History: A Theological Study Based on the Work of Albrecht Ritschl.* New York: Harper & Row, 1966.
Hök	Gösta Hök. *Die elliptische Theologie Albrecht Ritschls: Nach Ursprung und innerem Zusammenhang.* Uppsala: A. B. Lundequistska Bokhandeln, 1942.
HP	Albrecht Ritschl. "Prolegomena" to *The History of Pietism.* Translated by Philip Hefner. *TE,* 51–147. English translation from *GP,* 1, 3–98.
ICR	Albrecht Ritschl. *Instruction in the Christian Religion.* Translated by Philip Hefner. *TE,* 219–91. English translation of the third edition of *UCR.*

JR 1   Albrecht Ritschl. *A Critical History of the Christian Doctrine of Justification and Reconciliation.* Translated by John S. Black. Edinburgh: Edmonston and Douglas, 1872. English translation of the first edition of *RV 1.*

JR 2   Albrecht Ritschl. *The Christian Doctrine of Justification and Reconciliation: The Biblical Basis of the Doctrine.* Translated by Gerald W. McCulloh. Unpublished English translation of the third edition of *RV 2.* (No translation of *RV 2* has ever been published.)

JR 3   Albrecht Ritschl. *The Christian Doctrine of Justification and Reconciliation: The Positive Development of the Doctrine.* Translated by H. R. Mackintosh and A. B. Macaulay. Edinburgh: T & T Clark, 1900; reprinted, Clifton, New Jersey: Reference Book Publishers, 1966. English translation of the third edition of *RV 3.*

Leben   Otto Ritschl. *Albrecht Ritschls Leben.* 2 vols. Freiburg i. B. and Leipzig: J. C. B. Mohr, 1892 & 1896.

Lotz   David W. Lotz. *Ritschl and Luther: A Fresh Perspective on Albrecht Ritschl's Theology in the Light of His Luther Study.* Nashville: Abingdon Press, 1974.

Mackintosh   Hugh Ross Mackintosh. *Types of Modern Theology: Schleiermacher to Barth.* New York: Charles Scribner's Son, 1937.

MLK   Martin Luther King, Jr. *Stride Toward Freedom: The Montgomery Story.* New York: Harper & Row, 1958.

Moltmann   Jürgen Moltmann. *The Church in the Power of the Spirit: A Contribution to Messianic Ecclesiology.* Translated by Margaret Kohl. 1977. Reprint. Minneapolis: Fortress Press, 1993.

Mueller   David Mueller. *An Introduction to the Theology of Albrecht Ritschl.* Philadelphia: Westminster Press, 1969.

Niebuhr   H. Richard Niebuhr. *Christ and Culture.* New York: Harper Colophon Books, 1951.

Pannenberg   Wolfhart Pannenberg. *Theology and the Kingdom of God.* Philadelphia: Westminster Press, 1969.

PLK   Albrecht Ritschl. "Die protestantische Lehre von der Kirche." *Monatsschrift für die evangelische Kirche der Rheinprovinz und Westphalens* 9 (1851), 117–34.

Richmond   James Richmond. *Ritschl: A Reappraisal. A Study in Systematic Theology.* London: Collins, 1978.

Rupp   George Rupp. *Culture-Protestantism: German Liberal*

	Theology at the Turn of the Twentieth Century. Missoula, Mont.: Scholars Press, 1977.
RV 1	Albrecht Ritschl. *Die christliche Lehre von der Rechtfertigung und Versöhnung, Erster Band: Die Geschichte der Lehre.* Bonn: Adolph Marcus, 1870, 1882=1889.
RV 2	Albrecht Ritschl. *Die christliche Lehre von der Rechtfertigung und Versöhnung, Zweiter Band: Der biblische Stoff der Lehre.* Bonn: Adolph Marcus, 1874, 1882, 1889.
RV 3	Albrecht Ritschl. *Die christliche Lehre von der Rechtfertigung und Versöhnung, Dritter Band: Die positive Entwicklung der Lehre.* Bonn: Adolph Marcus, 1874, 1883, 1888=1895.
Schäfer	Rolf Schäfer. *Ritschl. Grundlinien eines fast verschollenen dogmatischen Systems.* Tübingen: J. C. B. Mohr, 1968.
SUK	Albrecht Ritschl. "Über die Begriffe: sichtbare und unsichtbare Kirche." *Theologische Studien und Kritiken 32* (1859), 189–226. Reprinted in *GA 1,* 68–99.
TE	Philip Hefner, editor and translator. *Albrecht Ritschl: Three Essays.* Philadelphia: Fortress Press, 1972.
TheoMet	Albrecht Ritschl. *Theologie und Metaphysik: Zur Verständigung und Abwehr.* Bonn: Adolph Marcus, 1881, 1887.
TM	Albrecht Ritschl. *Theology and Metaphysics: Towards Rapprochement and Defense.* Translated by Philip Hefner. *TE,* 151–217. English translation of *TheoMet.*
UCR	Albrecht Ritschl. *Unterricht in der christlichen Religion.* Bonn: Adolph Marcus, 1875, 1881, 1886=1890=1895.
Weiss	Johannes Weiss. *Jesus' Proclamation of the Kingdom of God.* Translated by Richard H. Heirs and David L. Holland. Philadelphia: Fortress Press, 1971. English translation of *Die Predigt Jesu vom Reich Gottes.* Göttingen: Vandenhoeck & Ruprecht, 1892.
Welch	Claude Welch. *Protestant Thought in the Nineteenth Century:* volume 1, *1799–1870,* and volume 2, *1870–1914.* New Haven: Yale University Press, 1972 & 1985.
WR	Walter Rauschenbusch. *Christianity and the Social Crisis.* New York: The Macmillan Company, 1907.

Contributors

William R. Barnett. Academic Vice President, Le Moyne College, Syracuse, New York.

Richard P. Busse. Lecturer in Christian Theology, Lutheran School of Theology at Chicago.

Darrell Jodock. Professor of Religion, Muhlenberg College, Allentown, Pennsylvania.

David W. Lotz. Washburn Professor of Church History, Union Theological Seminary, New York, New York. Author of *Ritschl and Luther: A Fresh Perspective on Albrecht Ritschl's Theology in the Light of His Luther Study* (Nashville: Abingdon Press, 1974).

Clive Marsh. Director of Studies and Lecturer in Christian Doctrine, Wilson Carlile College, Sheffield, England. Author of *Albrecht Ritschl and the Problem of the Historical Jesus* (San Francisco: Mellen Research Univ. Press, 1992).

Gerald W. McCulloh. Associate Professor, Department of Theology, Loyola University of Chicago, Chicago, Illinois. Author of *Christ's Person and Life-Work in the Theology of Albrecht Ritschl with Special Attention to* Munus Triplex (Lanham, Md.: University Press of America, 1990).

Hans Schwarz. Professor of Systematic Theology and Contemporary Theological Issues, Institute for Protestant Theology, University of Regensburg, Regensburg, Germany.

Rich M. Wall, Jr. Pastor of Mil-al Korean Presbyterian Church, Columbus, Georgia. Author of a Ph.D. dissertation at Union Theological

Seminary (New York), entitled "The Legacy of Liberal Protestantism: A Political-Theological Investigation of Albrecht Ritschl's Doctrine of Christian Community."

Claude Welch. Dean Emeritus and Professor of Historical Theology, Graduate Theological Union, Berkeley, California. Author of *Protestant Thought in the Nineteenth Century:* volume 1, *1799–1870,* and volume 2, *1870–1914* (New Haven: Yale Univ. Press, 1972 & 1985).

PART ONE

The Contemporary Situation and Ritschl's Context

1

Why Take Ritschl Seriously?

DARRELL JODOCK

Albrecht Ritschl (1822–89) was perhaps the most influential theological teacher in the second half of the nineteenth century. The son of George Carl Benjamin Ritschl and his second wife Auguste Sebald, Albrecht Ritschl was raised in a household with upper-class connections. His father, an advocate of the Prussian Union that brought Lutherans and Calvinists together into one church body, was from 1827 to 1854 the bishop of the Protestant Church and the general superintendent of the churches in Pomerania. Educated at Bonn, Halle, and Tübingen, Albrecht taught at Bonn from 1846 to 1864. In 1864 he moved to Göttingen, where he remained until his death in 1889. His earliest lectures and publications dealt with the New Testament. During the 1850s his research interests and teaching shifted from biblical studies to church history, especially to the sixteenth-century Reformation, and then gradually shifted again, this time to dogmatics. His mature theology integrated all three disciplines.[1]

Ritschl worked out his own distinctive theology—a theology that challenged the principal ecclesiastical parties of his own day. Like his father, he opposed the Confessionalists who worked against the unification of the Protestant Church and often also against the unification of Germany. When responding to the Confessionalists Ritschl often appealed back beyond the Protestant confessions and post-Reformation Orthodoxy to the earlier, more dynamic theology of the reformers—to Luther, Zwingli, and Calvin themselves, whose ideas could not easily be dismissed by those intent on preserving the Lutheran or the Calvinist tradition. Early in his student days he was attracted to the Hegelian under-

---

1. For a brief overview of Ritschl's life and thought, see Philip Hefner, "An Introduction," *TE*, 1–50.

standing of philosophy and theology, but during the 1840s he watched that school of thought disintegrate and never identified himself with it. For a number of years (in the 1840s and early 1850s) he was associated with the Tübingen School, led by Ferdinand Christian Baur. From Baur Ritschl learned a good deal about the importance of historical theology, but during the early 1850s Ritschl distanced himself from the interpretive framework favored by Baur and his associates.[2] Ritschl's emphasis on critical historical study distinguished him from the Supernaturalists, who called attention to the miraculous intervention of God in human affairs. Ritschl was deeply influenced by Schleiermacher but disagreed with his definition of religion and understanding of God and moved away from the subjectivism of Schleiermacher's followers. Ritschl disagreed vociferously with the pietists of his day (known more accurately as neo-pietists), because they appeared to him to lapse into a world-denying, pre-Reformation style of mysticism. He argued intensely against the Rationalists, insisting that Christianity involved a religious relationship with a loving God and God's forgiveness of sin, not just ethical obedience. Ritschl disagreed with the German proponents of the cultural significance of Roman Catholicism and challenged the exponents of secularism and materialism. Carefully he wove together a theology based on a critical rereading of the Scriptures and the reformers which to the Rationalists, the secularists, and the members of the Tübingen School appeared conservatively traditionalist but to the Confessionalists, the Supernaturalists, and the pietists appeared innovative and liberal. The positions he advocated were in touch with many of the major intellectual currents and theological issues of his day but were distinctive enough to be academically enticing, theologically invigorating, and highly controversial.

Ritschl's own thought was important,[3] but his historic significance does not rest in the legacy of a completed system endorsed and defended by his followers. Ritschl's vision was more suggestive than determinative. What makes him significant was the several ways in which he (1) inspired his followers to go beyond his own findings and (2) reconfigured the task of theology. Ritschl's theological outlook was comprehensive, but he also called for careful attention to all the specific, relevant data. The students he inspired tended to specialize; they made significant contributions in one or two of the several fields in which he himself worked: biblical studies (Johannes Weiss, Julius Wellhausen), church history (Karl Holl), historical theology (Adolf von Harnack), systematic theology (Wilhelm Herrmann), or ethics (Ernst Troeltsch). (Such a list itself indi-

2. For a more detailed analysis of Ritschl's relationship with Baur and the Tübingen School, see Darrell Jodock, "F. C. Baur and Albrecht Ritschl on Historical Theology" (Ph.D. diss., Yale University, 1969).

3. For a good summary, see the chapter entitled "Albrecht Ritschl: Faith, History, and Ethics in Balance," in Welch 2:1–30.

cates the remarkable breadth of Ritschl's own scholarly endeavors.) His followers tended to extend his research and, in so doing, made discoveries that led them to disagree in one way or another with their mentor. Those he influenced exhibited little uniformity; what they shared was a loyalty to Ritschl's vision of a theology deeply rooted in the particularities of history and rooted in the practical and to his vision of a personal (rather than a metaphysical) God, of a reformed and revitalized Protestantism, and of an ethical vocation within the kingdom of God. The vigor with which he appealed to the Scriptures (understood historically and critically), to the central Protestant principle of justification by grace through faith, and to the legacy of Martin Luther and the other reformers inspired his followers to pursue themes that had previously been less prominent on the theological agenda.

How does one assess the contributions of a gifted teacher whose own students so quickly make his conclusions seem dated? In Ritschl's case, the second generation—that is, the students of his students—more often than not felt they could safely and profitably leave Ritschl behind. But did they in fact do so? Some of the major Protestant theologians of the twentieth century can be found among this "second generation." Can evidence of distinctively Ritschlian themes be discerned in their thought? Moving beyond those theologians, can one identify some major issues with which Ritschl wrestled that are still on today's theological agenda? What are these issues, and what can we learn from the shortcomings and strengths of Ritschl's own attempts to resolve them? These are some of the questions that will be addressed in this volume.

A deeper question should perhaps be voiced: Why bother? During the Annual Meeting of the American Academy of Religion in 1989, a member expressed surprise that enough people were taking Albrecht Ritschl seriously to fill a seminar room. For many, Ritschl has been consigned to the nineteenth century for safekeeping. Surely additional study of the Bible and research into the history of Christian thought has rendered much of what Ritschl said out of date, in some cases by following avenues of study that he himself initiated. And surely the limitations of his thought are evident to any careful student who does not share his nineteenth-century, middle-class, male European outlook. So why bother? What difference does it make? Why seek to reassess Ritschl's contribution? Let me suggest three answers.

The first does not reach very far, but it needs to be mentioned. Ritschl's contributions deserve to be reassessed simply to set the record straight. So often Ritschl has been blamed for things he did not endorse, and not credited for ideas he did propose, that an elemental sense of justice can inspire another look. Just as with any other historical figure, he deserves appropriate praise and appropriate blame.

A second response is more significant. The closer we get to the end of the twentieth century, the more evident it becomes that the relationship between nineteenth-century theology and twentieth-century theology needs to be reconceived. Neoorthodoxy tried to draw a line between the two centuries, claiming that nineteenth-century theology focused on human beings and their religion while theology in the twentieth century needed to focus on the Word of God, or (stated differently) that the nineteenth endorsed culture while the twentieth needed to critique it. Neoorthodoxy called for a new beginning; it recommended discontinuity with its own immediate past. For several decades such voices seemed persuasive, but the 1960s, 1970s, 1980s, and 1990s have brought back into view questions for which neoorthodoxy provides little assistance. During these more recent decades the *continuity* between the theology of the nineteenth and the theology of the twentieth centuries has become increasingly evident.

Once this continuity has been recognized, Schleiermacher and Hegel retain their significance as the pioneers of the entire enterprise, but Ritschl looms ever larger as the historic bridge between early nineteenth-century idealism and the kind of theology practiced in the twentieth century. As Claude Welch puts it, "Ritschl was representative of a new kind of mediation, cutting loose from the speculative and metaphysical and turning to the practical and historical as a new foundation and form for theology."[4] Wilhelm Herrmann, one of Ritschl's earliest followers, developed Ritschl's theology in one direction, in turn influencing his own pupils, Rudolf Bultmann and Karl Barth, and through them dialectical theology and neoorthodoxy as a whole. This one Ritschl-inspired line was prominent from the 1920s through the 1950s. Ernst Troeltsch, who had been a student of Ritschl's at Göttingen, developed and revised Ritschl's theology in another direction, wrestling much more forthrightly than did the Herrmann line with pluralism and modernity, with the interaction between religion and culture, and with the relationship between theology and the social sciences. This second Ritschl-inspired line has become increasingly significant during the last half of the twentieth century. For many, Troeltsch—more than Herrmann, Barth, or Bultmann—now speaks as a contemporary.

Even in matters not so easily traced by means of this two-branched lineage, Ritschl functioned as a bridge between idealism and the twentieth century. For example, he critiqued what has come to be known as "classical theism." This critique set the stage for the penetrating and far-reaching reconsideration of the doctrine of God that has been so characteristic of the last half of the twentieth century.

Reassessing Ritschl's significance is an important step in the larger task of reconceptualizing the relationship between nineteenth-century and twentieth-century theology and ascertaining the contribution made by each of the various theological movements that have arisen during these last two hundred years.

4. Welch 2:2.

A third response to the questions raised above is that theology still has things to learn from Ritschl. For none of the authors in this volume does learning from Ritschl mean endeavoring today to reproduce or repristinate his theology. Each readily acknowledges that Ritschl's theology is in some ways out of date. But if a historical theologian ends the analysis with such observations, the verdict is incomplete. That theologian can (and should) go on to identify those significant themes in Ritschl's thought which deserve attention yet today. As the authors of this volume seek to show, Ritschl remains a valuable partner in contemporary theological reflection.

The stance assumed in this book is thus dialogical. We ask: What can be learned by probing the strengths and weaknesses of Ritschl's theological accomplishments? And what can be learned by allowing his priorities to challenge our own? This dialogical stance means, first, that Ritschl must be evaluated in his own context. He deserves to be understood in terms of what he was trying to accomplish in his own time and place, not in terms of how he agrees or disagrees with some later consensus. And this dialogical stance means, secondly, that the reciprocal relationship between then (the issues of his day and his response to them) and now (the issues of our day and our response to them) must be carefully explored. Ritschl's theology must be recontextualized carefully and then listened to, as well as critiqued, if it is to be taken seriously.

Why bother to reassess Ritschl's contribution? Because we can learn some important things from Ritschl, and a careful reassessment opens the doors for this learning to occur. He can become again for us a seminal teacher, instructing us in ways that enable and inspire us to move beyond him.

From the distance of one hundred years, Ritschl's theology remains a fascinating piece of constructive thinking, based on a critical interpretation of the Bible and of church history, intended as an alternative to the major schools of thought in his day, and dedicated to the edification of the Christian community living within a modern society. It deserves to be taken seriously, to be assessed carefully, and to be recontextualized appropriately. We can then be instructed by his insights, and he can receive whatever credit is rightfully his.

2

Ritschl in His Nineteenth-Century Setting

_____ DAVID W. LOTZ

Albrecht Ritschl was the luminary of the theological faculty at the University of Göttingen from 1864 until his death in 1889. During this immensely productive quarter-century he completed two monumental works: *The Christian Doctrine of Justification and Reconciliation* (3 vols., 1870–74) and *History of Pietism* (3 vols., 1880–86). To these were joined an impressive series of monographs: *Christian Perfection* (1874); *Schleiermacher's "Speeches on Religion" and Its Effects on the German Evangelical Church* (1874); *Instruction in the Christian Religion* (1875); *Theology and Metaphysics* (1881); and *Fides implicita* (1890). He also published *Three Academic Addresses* (1887), among them his important "Festival Address on the Four-hundredth Anniversary of the Birth of Martin Luther" (1883). Earlier in his career, while teaching at the University of Bonn (1846–64), Ritschl had produced a seminal book on early Christianity: *The Origin of the Old Catholic Church* (1850; 2d rev. ed., 1857). Fourteen of his essays, originally published in learned journals, were later reissued in two volumes edited by his son (and biographer), Otto Ritschl: *Collected Essays of Albrecht Ritschl* (1893, 1896). These writings included a memorable treatise on "The Origin of the Lutheran Church" (1876) and three weighty articles entitled "Historical Studies on the Christian Doctrine of God" (1865, 1868).[1]

---

1. See "Abbreviations" for bibliographic information regarding *RV 1, RV 2,* and *RV 3; JR 1* and *JR 3; GP* and *HP; UCR* and *ICR; TheoMet* and *TM; EK; GA; DAR;* and *Leben.* See also *Die christliche Vollkommenheit: Ein Vortrag* (Göttingen: Vandenhoeck & Ruprecht, 1874, 1889); *Schleiermachers Reden über die Religion und ihre Nachwirkungen auf die evangelische Kirche Deutschlands* (Bonn: Adolph Marcus, 1874); and *Fides implicita: Eine Untersuchung über Köhlerglauben, Wissen und Glauben, Glauben und Kirche* (Bonn: Adolph Marcus, 1890). [A translation of Ritschl's "Festival Address on the Four-hundredth

This magisterial body of work accorded Ritschl an influence as a Protestant systematic theologian, during the last three decades of the nineteenth century, comparable to that of Friedrich Schleiermacher in mid-century. It also secured his standing among the century's premier historians of Christianity, in company with Ferdinand Christian Baur and Adolf von Harnack. (Baur had been Ritschl's teacher and mentor at the University of Tübingen in the mid-1840s, while Harnack, though not having studied with Ritschl, allied himself with the latter's theological program in the mid-1870s and became a leading member of the so-called Ritschlian School.) Ritschl's writings, moreover, and those of his many illustrious students and associates (the chief of whom, besides Harnack, were Wilhelm Herrmann and Ernst Troeltsch) made "Ritschlianism" a powerful and pervasive force in Protestant academic circles from the 1880s to the 1920s, not only in Germany and Continental Europe but also in Great Britain and North America. In this light, then, it has justly been said that "in the century between the death of Schleiermacher in 1834 and the death of Harnack in 1930 the most imposing figure in Continental Protestant theology was Albrecht Ritschl."[2]

By the early 1930s, however, Hugh Ross Mackintosh—himself a cotranslator of the third volume of *Justification and Reconciliation*—could judge that "Ritschl at the moment belongs, like Tennyson, to the 'middle distance,' too far for gratitude, too near for reverence. He is behind a passing cloud today."[3] That cloud was remarkably long in passing! In 1968 Rolf Schäfer published a pathbreaking book on Ritschl that bore the striking subtitle *Outline of an Almost Vanished Dogmatic System*.[4] The fact is that from the 1920s to the 1960s Ritschl and Ritschlianism (and nineteenth-century Protestant theological Liberalism as a whole) were subject to relentless attack—and effectively put in the shade—by Karl Barth and Emil Brunner and their neoorthodox allies.

Much of this criticism was by catchword, even by caricature. Barth, for example, declared that "Ritschl has the significance of an episode in more recent theology and not, indeed not, that of an epoch." Ritschl's main contribution (and egregious failing) was that he "energetically seized upon the theoretical and practical philosophy of the Enlightenment in its perfected form." That is, by going "back to Kant," and specifically to Kant interpreted as "an antimetaphysical moralist," Ritschl's theology marked the actual fulfillment, not the overcoming, of the Enlightenment's preoccupation with the autonomous rational self. The Christian religion was now presented as a bulwark of human self-confidence, as "a great confirmation and strengthening" of the view

Anniversary of the Birth of Martin Luther" has been made by David W. Lotz as an Appendix to Lotz, 187–202; hereafter cited as "Luther Address."]
  2. Jaroslav Pelikan, "Editor's Preface" to Hefner, ix.
  3. Mackintosh, 141, n. 1. (This book was based on lectures delivered in 1933.)
  4. Schäfer.

that "modern man wishes above all to live in the best sense according
to reason." Ritschl himself, accordingly, was "the very epitome of the
national-liberal bourgeois of the age of Bismarck."[5]

That Ritschl's antispeculative "back to Kant" could actually mean,
in substance, "back to Luther"; that the interpretive construct best
warranted by the textual evidence is not "Ritschl and the Enlightenment" but "Ritschl and the Reformation"; that the liberty that Ritschl
ever had in view was not the freedom of autonomous human reason, of
the Kantian noumenal self, but the evangelical liberty of the Christian
to live before God in freedom from sin and guilt, owing to one's unconditional faith in God's own unconditional forgiveness for Christ's sake,
and so to live in freedom from the world's oppressive weight and in
freedom for loving service to humankind in keeping with the law of the
kingdom of God revealed by the Son of God; that Ritschl's vision,
therefore, was focused not on the Second German Reich, the creation
of Bismarck, but on the universal, world-encompassing kingdom of
God, the self-end of the world's creator and so the destined end of
God's creatures: none of this found its due articulation in the Ritschl
interpretation of Barth and company.

Such was the sway of this neoorthodox historiography that between
1922 and 1964 only one book devoted exclusively to Ritschl's theology
was published in any language: that of the Swedish scholar Gösta Hök.[6]
Since the mid-1960s, however, there has been a "Ritschl renaissance,"
owing to the development of a far less polemical and much more text-
based historiographical tradition. This newer literature, impressive in its
quantity and quality, has served to rehabilitate Ritschl's theological reputation through its dispassionate exposition of his animating concerns
and leading themes, and through its patient endeavor to locate Ritschl's
texts in their immediate historical context and thus to illumine his work
"from within."[7]

The present volume of essays is itself a product of—and a substantive contribution to—this reappraisal and revisionist interpretation of

5. Barth, 655–56.
6. Hök. In 1922 (the centenary of Ritschl's birth) was published Carl Stange's *Albrecht Ritschl: Die geschichtliche Stellung seiner Theologie* (Leipzig: Dieterich'sche Verlagsbuch-handlung, 1922); in 1964, Paul Wrzecionko's *Die philosophischen Wurzeln der Theologie Albrecht Ritschls* (Berlin: Alfred Töpelmann, 1964). Individual essays, chapters of books, and (unpublished) dissertations on Ritschl continued to appear, of course, during the inter-vening years. For extensive listings of the literature through the 1960s, see the bibliogra-phies in Hök, Schäfer, and Lotz.
7. In addition to the aforementioned books by Wrzecionko (1964), Hefner (1966), Schäfer (1968), and Lotz (1974), the newer literature includes: Hermann Timm, *Theorie und Praxis in der Theologie Albrecht Ritschls und Wilhelm Herrmanns* (Gütersloh: Gerd Mohn, 1967); Mueller; Richmond; Ueli Hasler, *Beherrschte Natur: Die Anpassung der Theologie an die bürgerliche Naturauffassung im 19. Jahrhundert (Schleiermacher, Ritschl, Herrmann)* (Berne: P. Lang, 1982); Stephan Weyer-Menkhoff, *Aufklärung und Offen-barung: Zur Systematik der Theologie Albrecht Ritschls* (Göttingen: Vandenhoeck & Ruprecht, 1988); and Joachim Ringleben, ed., *Gottes Reich und menschliche Freiheit: Ritschl-Kolloquium (Göttingen 1989)* (Göttingen: Vandenhoeck & Ruprecht, 1990).

Albrecht Ritschl's theology. Its chief purpose, as the editor's Preface makes plain, is to consider some important lines of continuity (and discontinuity) between Ritschl's theological enterprise and post-Ritschlian theology and religious thought. This much-needed and long overdue attention to Ritschl's posthumous influence, however, presupposes a reasonable measure of clarity and consensus about *what Ritschl himself intended and achieved* in his system of theology. I propose, therefore, to examine the central impulses and main components of this system, doing so, perforce, in a very summary fashion and building on my own earlier scholarship. My approach, in short, is more retrospective than prospective, primarily moving back to Ritschl in his nineteenth-century setting rather than forward from Ritschl to his twentieth-century heirs. Where possible and pertinent, however, especially in my concluding section, I will make some connections between Ritschl and his successors, between "then" and "now."

RITSCHL'S SYSTEM OF THEOLOGY

Scholars have not yet given a definitive answer to the question: What, precisely, was Albrecht Ritschl "up to" during his Göttingen years, that is, in the voluminous writings that composed his mature literary corpus? The standard answer, correct so far as it goes, is that Ritschl was engaged in constructing a system of church doctrine—a Christian dogmatics—based on the biblical-Reformation teaching of justification (by God) and reconciliation (with God), and on the idea of the kingdom of God, which formed the core of the teaching of Jesus as recorded in the New Testament (Synoptic Gospels). Not surprisingly, then, the great majority of interpreters have focused on the third volume of *Justification and Reconciliation,* the subtitle of which is *The Positive Development of the Doctrine.* Hence relatively little attention has been directed to the two foundational volumes of Ritschl's magnum opus: the critical-historical recounting of the doctrine's development since the Middle Ages (volume 1) and the critical-exegetical unfolding of the doctrine's biblical content (volume 2). Further, Ritschl's multivolumed *History of Pietism,* the bulk of his essays and addresses, and the larger number of his monographs routinely receive but cursory notice.

In effect, then, Ritschl's "theological system" has been virtually identified with his "systematic theology," as exhibited in *JR 3* and as further elaborated in *Instruction in the Christian Religion.* Usually one also includes *Theology and Metaphysics* as a commentary on Ritschl's methodological canons and philosophical prolegomena. On this threefold textual basis one then proceeds to give an account and appraisal of his main systematic-theological topics: religious epistemology, phenomenology of religion, doctrine of God, Christology, kingdom of God, church, sin, justification and reconciliation, the Christian ideal of life, and so on.

This traditional approach to Ritschl is misleading because it is much too narrow in scope. It fails to emphasize that the Ritschlian system of theology includes, in principle, the totality of his mature corpus: all of his major writings since the publication in 1857 of the second edition of *The Origin of the Old Catholic Church*. Although diverse in method and content, this body of work forms a coherent whole and so requires to be studied as a whole. It is a system of thought animated by historical, exegetical, and constructive impulses and is itself a complex structure of tradition-historical, biblical, and dogmatic matter. Failure to take due account of each of these impulses and of each of these material components, and then to display their intricate linkage, has resulted in a one-sided reading and truncated presentation of Ritschl's theology, even on the part of his most sympathetic interpreters. Specialized studies of Ritschl as historian or exegete or dogmatician are, of course, indispensable; but such study of the parts cannot be taken for articulation of the whole. In sum: "The theology of Albrecht Ritschl" includes far more than the familiar themes of *JR 3,* the *Instruction,* and *Theology and Metaphysics.*

In this connection one recalls that Ritschl himself, in the preface to the third edition (1888) of *JR 3,* warned that a lack of knowledge of the preceding two volumes would only increase the difficulty of understanding volume three. This caveat may seem self-evident, yet the course of Ritschl scholarship shows that it has not been given due weight. (Ritschl's warning suggests that even his contemporary critics were disposed to regard *JR 1* and *JR 2* as "excess baggage"!) Still, one can see how it happened that *JR 3* became the focus, almost the exclusive focus, of scholarly concentration.

Ritschl is primarily regarded and remembered as a dogmatician, as a leading figure in the grand tradition of modern Protestant systematic theology from Schleiermacher to Barth and Paul Tillich (and beyond). Since *JR 3* is Ritschl's chief dogmatic text, it invariably attracts the attention of students of this modern development, who forthwith assimilate it to the model, say, of Schleiermacher's *The Christian Faith.* What drops from sight, however, is that *JR 3* is the "positive development" of a single doctrine and so is not a full-scale systematic theology or dogmatic textbook in the usual sense. Hence one also overlooks the unique character of Ritschl's "dogmatics": that it is the elaboration of a cardinal Christian doctrine on the ground of massive historical and biblical research and, as such, calls for deliberate investigation of its historical and biblical foundations.

Most of the many books and essays on Ritschl, moreover, have been written by systematic or philosophical theologians rather than by historical or biblical theologians. And even the latter scholars, in their relatively infrequent literary encounters with Ritschl, normally treat his theology as coterminous with the doctrinal formulas of *JR 3.*[8] One also

---

8. This is the case with Ernst Haenchen's "Albrecht Ritschl als Systematiker," in his *Gott und Mensch: Gesammelte Aufsätze* (Tübingen: J. C. B. Mohr, 1965), 409–75. Likewise, Norman Perrin's two pages (14–16) on Ritschl in *The Kingdom of God in the Teach-*

suspects that most students in theology and religious studies have been and still are introduced to Ritschl—if, in fact, such introductions continue to occur—by a reading of *JR 3* or, more likely, the much briefer and seemingly more luminous *Instruction* (both of which have long been available in reliable English translations).[9] All these circumstances help to account for the persistent failure to give Ritschl the critical church historian and serious biblical exegete his due.

If this failure is to be rectified, then it is incumbent upon present-day scholars to show that Ritschl's methodological canons and doctrinal formulations (*JR 3* and related writings) were the precipitate of his long-term, painstaking study of Scripture (*JR 2*) and of Reformation and post-Reformation theology and spirituality (*JR 1, History of Pietism,* and related writings). One would thus retrace, as it were, Ritschl's own course of research and reflection since 1857 (when he began intensive work on the doctrine of justification): from historical study through biblical exegesis to dogmatic formulation—or, as Ritschl himself would have said, from "analysis" to "synthesis."[10]

In so doing, one must be mindful that Ritschl's entire system was in motion from 1870 onward; that is, the first main stage of dogmatic formulation (the first edition of *JR 3* in 1874) promoted fresh biblical and, especially, historical study, whose results were then taken up into the subsequent editions of all three volumes of *Justification and Reconciliation* (above all, the second edition of *JR 1* in 1882 and the third edition of *JR 3* in 1888). Synthesis thus generated new analysis and the latter, in turn, generated new (or revised) synthesis.

My remarks in the preceding paragraphs require this qualification: While granting the constitutive importance of Ritschl's biblical scholarship for his dogmatics, I consider historical inquiry, not New Testament exegesis as such, to be the mainspring of his total enterprise. For that matter, any attempt to play off history against exegesis would be foreign to Ritschl's thinking. As was befitting an heir of Schleiermacher, Ritschl viewed biblical theology as a subdivision of historical theology. Hence the study of early Christianity, including the New Testament documents, must be conducted in accord with the same canons of critical-historical inquiry that obtain in the study of all other eras of the church's history, even if one maintains (as Ritschl did most emphatically) that the Bible

---

ing of Jesus (London: The Westminster Press, 1963) are based exclusively on (a misreading of) the opening pages to *JR 3*, with not a single reference to *RV 2*: a most curious procedure, since this book originated as a 1959 dissertation under the direction of Joachim Jeremias at the University of Göttingen!

9. Philip Hefner's translation of *ICR* is a revision of Alice Mead Swing's translation, originally published in Albert T. Swing, *The Theology of Albrecht Ritschl* (New York: Longman's, Green and Co., 1901), 171–286. One is best advised to begin study of Ritschl—as Otto Ritschl counseled a century ago—with his "Prolegomena" to *The History of Pietism.*

10. Ritschl's personal motto, a variation on an axiom of the medieval scholastics, was *Qui bene distinguit et bene comprehendit bene docet:* "One teaches well who divides rightly and combines correctly." See *Leben* 2:167–68.

possesses an authority superior to that of the postbiblical tradition, by which the latter must always be judged. Hence Ritschl's biblical study must be regarded as an integral part of his historical study, not as an independent or self-contained undertaking. Moreover, as was befitting a student of Baur and the mentor of Harnack, Ritschl began and ended his career by publishing seminal historical works. By conservative estimate, at least two-thirds of his literary corpus falls under the rubric of church history or historical theology in the narrower sense, not including the lengthy historical excursuses in *JR 3*. Ritschl, however, did not simply write historical texts, but made historical inquiry the basis and dynamic of his entire system. In sum: "History"—meaning historical modes of thinking and the concrete findings of historical research—is the Ritschlian theology's system-shaping force.[11]

THE IDEA OF THE UNFINISHED REFORMATION

What, precisely, does it mean to say that historical inquiry is the driving and shaping force of Ritschl's comprehensive system of theology? In a previously published essay I addressed and answered this question by using the interpretive construct of "the unfinished Reformation."[12] This construct was adumbrated in various of Ritschl's essays dating from the 1860s. It came to prominence in the two editions of *JR 1* (1870, 1882); in the essay "The Origin of the Lutheran Church" (1876); in the lengthy "Prolegomena" to *History of Pietism* (1880); and (in its most concentrated statement) in the "Festival Address" that Ritschl delivered at Göttingen commemorating the quadricentennial of Luther's birth (10 November 1883). The idea of the unfinished Reformation was thus a product of Ritschl's intensive historical study.

The leading features of this construct may be summarized as follows:

1. The sixteenth-century Reformation was an epoch-making event in the history of the Christian religion and church. It was also an event of world-historical significance for modern culture and society.

2. Considered as a *theological-doctrinal phenomenon,* however, the Reformation must be judged unfinished, owing to serious theological deformations of biblical-Reformation religion at the hands of the reformers themselves. Luther, Zwingli, Melanchthon, and Calvin all shared the same "practical root ideas," which they had derived from the Bible (New Testament) and from the loftiest spirituality (the Augustinian "grace alone" piety) of Western Catholicism. These religious ideas and insights—all centering on the thought of God's free forgiveness of sinners for Christ's sake—constituted "the principle of the Reformation" by which the four leading reformers jointly accomplished

---

11. This was demonstrated, in a pioneering way, by Hefner (see "Abbreviations").

12. David W. Lotz, "Albrecht Ritschl and the Unfinished Reformation," *Harvard Theological Review* 73 (July–October 1980): 337–72. The reader is referred to this long essay for a detailed exposition of each of the seven points summarized in the text. Also relevant is Lotz, esp. 25–87.

their epochal reform of the late medieval church. Yet each reformer, in his own way, failed to carry out the necessary reformulation of traditional Christian doctrine in keeping with the original Reformation principle. Luther, for example, reappropriated alien medieval-scholastic theological constructs, such as the nominalist concept of a hidden and "arbitrary" God of absolute power and the Anselmic idea of the Atonement as Christ's vicarious satisfaction of God's penal justice. Melanchthon reintroduced a scholastic-Aristotelian dogmatic method, allowed for a natural no less than a revealed knowledge of God, and transformed the church into a type of school: an assembly of "pure doctrine" or "orthodoxy." Calvin, likewise, intellectualized the Christian faith by insisting that it must be "scholastically precise." Most fatefully, he reverted to a medieval-monastic life ideal of ascetic sanctity: a world-renouncing piety that also distinguished Anabaptism and that later gave rise to Pietism in the Calvinist-Reformed church of the Netherlands and Germany. The sixteenth-century reform of the Christian religion, in short, did not bring with it a corresponding reform of Christian theology. At least it did not articulate a system of church doctrine that was fully consistent with the religious ideas that occasioned the church's renewal. Viewed in respect of its formal theological productions, then, the Reformation is seen to be incomplete: it was a "stunted growth."[13]

3. Far from being overcome in later Protestantism, these early theological deformations of biblical-Reformation Christianity have been perpetuated, indeed intensified, by post-Reformation patterns of thought and piety: by Lutheran and Reformed Orthodoxy (neoscholasticism); by a half-Catholic mysticism and asceticism; by a sectarian Pietism that flourished in both Lutheran and Reformed circles; by the rationalistic and eudaemonistic theology of the German Enlightenment; by a repristinating Lutheran Confessionalism erected on a neo-pietistic base; and by the speculative theology of Hegel and the Hegelians. To be sure, both Kant and Schleiermacher made notable contributions to the overcoming of these deformations by their own recovery of essential elements in biblical-Reformation Christianity. Their gains, however, were soon surrendered by their epigones and were, in any case, not adequately safeguarded in their own writings. The history of Protestantism, therefore, is one of persistent failure to construct a homogeneous doctrinal system informed throughout by the Reformation principle.

4. This continuing theological deformation of biblical-Reformation religion and the attendant atrophy of Protestant piety and church life have relegated Protestantism to a state of perpetual immaturity. They have also prompted leading representatives of modern intellectual cul-

---

13. See *HP* in *TE*, 134: "The distinctiveness of Protestantism is still sufficiently discernible that almost all who count themselves as its adherents recognize that its original manifestation was stunted [eine Verkümmerung] or deformed [eine Missbildung]."

ture to deny the world-historical importance of the Protestant Reformation and have emboldened Roman Catholic critics to proclaim the "end
of Protestantism."

5. The exigent task confronting the serious-minded heir of the
Reformation, therefore, is the reconstruction of Evangelical theology
through the creative reappropriation of the reformers' practical root
ideas, inasmuch as one can show, by biblical exegesis, that these ideas
are congruent with the religion of the New Testament. The latter-day reformer of Protestant theology will also gratefully take up the leading
ideas of that handful of Protestant thinkers who brought Reformation
Christianity to new expression in new historical contexts, albeit incom-
pletely. In consequence of this comprehensive critical-historical, biblical-
exegetical, and systematic-theological enterprise, churchly Protestantism
will at last attain a mature independence and self-assurance and will become what it has ever claimed to be: the *ecclesia reformata*, the church
reformed on the basis of the Word of God.

6. This reformed Protestantism will also be vindicated before its traditional and newly resurgent Roman Catholic foes and before its many
cultured despisers.

7. Finally, and not least, the theological reconstruction of Protestantism through the recovery of the authentic heritage of biblical-
Reformation religion will demonstrate the continuing relevance of the
sixteenth-century Reformation to some of the most pressing problems
confronting the modern world.

These findings, generated by my historical study of Ritschl's historical
writings, have led me to the following conclusion and contention: The
key to understanding Ritschl's entire undertaking during his Göttingen
years (after 1857, in fact) is to be found in his endeavor to bring the theologically unfinished Reformation to completion through the re-formation
of Protestant dogmatics on the basis of original Reformation Christianity
and its normative principle of "Scripture alone." I have thus located the
central impulse of Ritschl's system in the historical-critical dynamic of return to biblical-Reformation religion, not to Reformation theology as
such or as a whole, nor to a post-Reformation tradition of theology and
spirituality.

For Ritschl, plainly, any simple repristination of "the Protestant tradition"—including the sixteenth-century confessions of the Lutheran and
Reformed churches—was out of the question, since this tradition was no
homogeneous, internally coherent phenomenon. Wheat and chaff had
grown up together over the centuries, from the Reformation era itself
down to the present day. Hence a critical sifting of the entire heritage
was imperative, to be carried out on the basis of the Reformation principle, in the light of which one could confidently distinguish between "essential" and "deformed" Protestantism. As is also plain, however, and as
bears repeating: this return to and revalidation of biblical-Reformation
Christianity was not an end in itself. It was required for the urgent con-

temporary tasks of restructuring Protestant doctrinal theology, reforming Protestant church life (religious-moral praxis), and demonstrating the abiding importance of the Protestant Reformation for the modern world.

Even so, for Ritschl himself, the historical construct of the unfinished Reformation was a mandate to ongoing theological polemic and apologetic no less than to fresh biblical interpretation and new dogmatic formulation. Likewise, for the Ritschl scholar, this interpretive construct has the value of approaching Ritschl's mature literary corpus as a coherent whole and of disclosing the form and the substance of that coherence. Thereby it treats his *total* system of theology precisely as *system* and so serves to explain what Ritschl was "all about" in his great undertaking.

This perspective finds wide support in the older (pre-Barth) literature, at least as regards the pivotal importance for Ritschl of Luther's Christianity (and Reformation religion as a whole). The closest parallel to my view that I have come across is the following passage from a 1913 essay by Arthur Titius on "Albrecht Ritschl and the Present":

> If out of the multitude of valuable stimuli that Ritschl brought to the theology of his time, one attempts to expound the decisively central impulse, then—according to Ritschl's own testimony—this must be construed as follows: the new factor was not formed by isolated theological propositions of a systematic or historical sort, but rather by Ritschl's belief that amid later excrescences he had newly discovered the original type of Christian, i.e., biblical-Reformation piety, and had given it new currency as a solution to the religious problems even of his own day. When in the course of his Reformation studies the awareness first ripened that the authentic essence of the Reformation becomes evident in Luther's Christianity, not in the doctrinal formulations of the later confessions; and when this Christianity of Luther's flowed together with that of Paul and the New Testament to compose one homogeneous magnitude: then for the first time there developed in Ritschl that imposing self-awareness which characterized him, that conviction that he was able to give something new to the theology and the religious life of his age, something normative and definitive.[14]

Titius and I clearly concur in our mutual identification of "the decisively central impulse" in Ritschl's system of theology. I have located this impulse, however, in Ritschl's overarching endeavor to bring the theologically unfinished Reformation to completion through the systematic articulation of biblical-Reformation religion in a new Evangelical dogmatics. This doctrinal system, averred Ritschl, cannot be deduced, in Hegelian fashion, from a single speculative principle or idea (such as the Incarnation understood as the "absolute identity" of finite and infinite

---

14. Arthur Titius, "Albrecht Ritschl und die Gegenwart. Ein Vortrag," *Theologische Studien und Kritiken* 86 (1913): 67.

spirit). It must, rather, revolve around the *historically demonstrable foci* of biblical and Reformation Christianity. It would thus be centered on *Jesus Christ* as the prophetic revealer of merciful God and of God's royal rule or kingdom, and as the priestly representative before God of the new covenant community that Jesus himself had founded through his calling of disciples to repentance, faith, and love. And so this dogmatics would be no less centered on the *believing community* as the immediate object of God's unmerited pardon or justification of sinners for the sake of Christ, who ever remains the community's head, redeemer, and advocate, and as the immediate locus of the individual's appropriation of divine forgiveness and entrance into the new life of reconciliation with God characterized by trust in God's providence, by patience in suffering, by humble submission to God's beneficent will, and by prayer. Accordingly, this dogmatics would also be centered on *personal faith* as lively trust or confidence, amid all circumstances of worldly existence, in the God of pure love revealed by Christ, and as active in obedience to God and love for the neighbor, whereby God's kingdom is progressively extended and will ultimately be realized in the moral unification of all nations and peoples.

This perspective on Ritschl's total theological system is much broader than the one adopted by Titius (though he hints at it). Titius, furthermore, did not take directly into account that, for Ritschl, "the authentic essence of the Reformation" was not only lacking in the "later [Protestant] confessions" but also did not find consistent expression in Luther's own theology and in Reformation and post-Reformation theology as a whole. One well understands, then, what Ritschl meant and intended when he declared in 1883:

> Until now the practical root idea of Luther's Reformation has not been employed in all clarity and vigor for the regulation of Protestantism's many tasks, i.e., it has still not been directed to the ordering of theology and its demarcation from all useless forms. Therefore Protestantism has been forced to rely on instruments of thought that are alien to its character, and to pursue an uncertain course that cannot be circumvented by reliance on foreign support so long as an independent sense of direction is lacking. I should like to advance the thesis that to date Protestantism has not yet emerged from its age of teething problems, but that its independent course will begin when—on the basis of a thoroughgoing comprehension of its practical root ideas—it reforms theology, fructifies churchly instruction, shores up the moral sense of community, and achieves political resoluteness for the actualization of those spiritual riches which one of her greatest sons once acquired for [the German] nation.[15]

Albrecht Ritschl applied himself to these multiple tasks for over thirty years. His mature literary corpus was his many-sided instrument for at

---

15. "Luther Address," in Lotz, 200–201.

last bringing about, within a Protestantism not yet come of age, "the ordering of theology and its demarcation from all useless forms . . . on the basis of a thoroughgoing comprehension of [the Reformation's] practical root ideas."

THE CONTEXTUAL SIGNIFICANCE OF
RITSCHL'S THEOLOGY

What, in particular, were some of the concomitants and consequences of Ritschl's history-based system of theology, itself centered on the project of re-forming the Protestant doctrinal tradition and of thereby bringing the theologically unfinished Reformation to completion? Viewing this system in its own historical context, and without any pretension to completeness of statement, one can identify a number of Ritschl's main contributions to late nineteenth-century theology and religious thought and, in some cases, to the more recent theological enterprise. To this end I will focus on the significance of Ritschl's theology for the pivotal theme of "Christianity and history."

With the work of Friedrich Schleiermacher, especially *The Christian Faith* (2d ed., 1830), Protestant theology took what Claude Welch has aptly termed "a decisive Socratic turn to the self, to an understanding of religious truth that may rightly be called 'existentialist,'" inasmuch as all discourse about God necessarily entails talk about the self and its relationship to God and to the world (as the creation of God).[16] Ritschl fully approbated this methodological recourse to Christian religious experience—to the activity (knowing, feeling, willing) of the believing subject within the community of faith—as the proper object of theological cognition. Said Ritschl:

> If what is wanted is to write theology on the plan not merely of a narrative of the great deeds done by God [the method of Protestant Orthodoxy], but of a system representing the salvation God has wrought out, then we must exhibit the operations of God—justification, regeneration, the communication of the Holy Spirit, the bestowal of blessedness in the *summum bonum* [the "highest good" or kingdom of God]—in such a way as shall involve an analysis of the corresponding voluntary activities in which man appropriates the operations of God. This method has already been adopted by Schleiermacher.[17]

Ritschl thus hailed his great predecessor's epoch-making break with the sterile objectivism of neoscholastic orthodoxy and his attendant return to the foundational religious idea of the reformers, above all Luther, that God and faith belong inseparably together—that in order to say who the God revealed in Jesus Christ truly *is,* one must ever say who this God is *for me.* Such, in fact, was Ritschl's own emphasis on uncondi-

16. Welch, 1:59–60.
17. *JR* 3:34.

tional trust in God as the indispensable condition of valid assertions about God that Walther von Loewenich was moved to assert: "Luther's endeavor to understand all biblical proclamation of redemption as pronounced *pro me* has found here in Ritschl's thought a reverberation which, to my knowledge, exceeds that in any earlier theologian."[18]

In Ritschl's judgment, however, Schleiermacher's existentialist or (in nineteenth-century terminology) "ethical" viewpoint, proceeding from a consideration of Christian personal and communal experience, finally gave way to a neo-pietistic subjectivism because it did not accord equal weight to the "dogmatic" viewpoint that proceeds from a consideration of the divine activity as manifested in the person and work of Jesus Christ, i.e., on the transsubjective plane of *history*. Hence, for Ritschl, the specific meaning of a divine operation (such as justification or the unmerited forgiveness of sins) is to be determined by constant reference to the historical life course of Christ: "In dogmatics, his person must be regarded as the ground of knowledge to be used in the definition of every doctrine."[19] Again: "In Christianity, revelation through God's Son is the *punctum stans* [the Archimedean point] of all knowledge and religious conduct."[20]

Schleiermacher, accordingly, failed to unite (correlate) the Christ of present Christian experience with the Jesus of past history as known by critical-historical study of the New Testament Gospels (preeminently the Synoptic Gospels rather than the Gospel of John, on which Schleiermacher chiefly relied for his delineation of Christ's "archetypal" nature as the Second Adam, the model of authentic personhood). Moreover, in declaring that "Christian doctrines are accounts of the Christian religious affections set forth in speech," Schleiermacher primarily had in view the faith (religious experience) of the individual member of the contemporary church rather than the corporate faith of the earliest church as attested in the apostolic kerygma (the New Testament epistles). Ritschl, by contrast, announced his fidelity to the reformers' "Scripture alone" by elevating the *original* faith of the church to normative theological status. Christian doctrine, therefore, must be both established and tested at every point by the data of Christian history: the history of Jesus himself (his teaching and, above all, his sacrificial death) and the history of the primitive church's experience or appropriation of his message and redemptive work.

Critical-historical exegesis of the New Testament writings, undertaken with the aid of Old Testament hermeneutical principles and constructs, is thus the fundament of Evangelical dogmatics. This biblical literature con-

---

18. Walther von Loewenich, *Luther und der Neuprotestantismus* (Witten: Luther-Verlag, 1963), 96. Cf. the 2d ed. of Ritschl's *RV 1* (1882), 219: "A judgment concerning God that is not effected by complete trust in him has no cognitive value, and half-knowledge is not worthy of the name."

19. *JR* 3:331.

20. *JR* 3:202.

tains the earliest (most historically reliable) and the purest (least influenced by Hellenistic syncretism) records of *the career of Jesus* and of *the community's original faith,* which, taken together, constitute the normative Christian revelation.[21] Furthermore, notwithstanding the many distortions of the intellectual content of Christianity over the ages, beginning with the rise of early Catholicism in the second century, critical-historical inquiry also demonstrates that much of *the post-apostolic tradition*—above all Reformation Christianity and the Western-Augustinian piety of "grace alone" on which the reformers built and by which they legitimated their cause before their opponents—is continuous with New Testament Christianity and so may be accorded both regulative and constitutive importance for Protestant doctrinal theology. Thus biblical religion and Reformation religion flow together to form one great stream of normative Christian truth (belief and practice). It is this latter magnitude that Ritschl proposed to "systematize" in *JR 3.*

In this light, then, one can fairly claim that Schleiermacher's theology of Christian experience was transformed by Ritschl's massive "historification" of Evangelical dogmatics. The legacy of Schleiermacher was mediated to the later nineteenth and the twentieth century in a new "Ritschlian" form that made historical investigation of both Scripture and tradition much more central to the enterprise of dogmatic theology—to a determination of "the Christian faith"—than had been the case with Schleiermacher himself and his mid-century heirs. In effect, Schleiermacher's "Socratic" turn to the self was now matched, and signally modified, by Ritschl's "Baurian" and "Rankean" turn to history, in that Ritschl here displayed the continuing influence of F. C. Baur and the Tübingen School, in which he had been trained, as well as the pervasive influence of German historical scholarship in the line of Leopold von Ranke.

To be sure, the problem of "faith and history" proved to be an inordinately complex and difficult one, issuing in both a confident "quest for the historical Jesus" (as with Ritschl himself) and a categorical rejection of that quest on source-critical grounds (as, finally, with Rudolf Bultmann). Today, in the last decade of the twentieth century, one can scarcely claim that this problem has achieved definitive resolution; it remains a matter of ongoing contention and widely divergent approaches. It should be noted, however, that Ritschl's insistence that one has access to the Jesus of history only *through* the New Testament kerygma, through the apostolic preaching and the post-Easter faith of the first Christians, was to become, within fifty years, a hermeneutical axiom in Protestant theology and biblical studies. In any case, Ritschl's general approach to the faith and history issue—his rejection of radical historical criticism à la Baur and David Friedrich Strauss; his assertion of the New Testament's basic credibility, including most of its miracle accounts and Resurrection narratives; hence his sur-

---

21. See *ICR,* 1–3, *TE,* 221–22.

prisingly conservative doctrine of biblical authority—was soon subject to
intense criticism, not only by his former Tübingen associates, but by his
leading students and disciples as well.

Herrmann, for example, concluded that Ritschl was "the last great
representative of the orthodox dogmatics," because he had again made
Scripture into a binding doctrinal norm (*Lehrgesetz*), in the manner of
the old Protestantism.[22] Harnack styled him "the last Lutheran church
father" on the ground that "in Ritschl's theology the old Protestant
doctrinaire element comes to the fore" along with the original-
religious element of biblical-Reformation Christianity.[23] And Troeltsch
roundly criticized Ritschl, "the last great dogmatician," for his biblicism and supernaturalism and, not least, for his inattention to the history of religions, to the impact on primitive Christianity of Jewish
apocalypticism and Hellenistic religious ideas.[24] It is striking, indeed,
that in the half-century after Ritschl's death the Protestant dogmatician
who most nearly replicated Ritschl's conservative "theology of revelation"—Bible-based, oriented to the Reformation tradition, Christ-and
church-centered, antispeculative, antimystical, antipietistic—was none
other than Karl Barth![25]

Still, whatever Ritschl's perceived limitations as an exegete and dogmatician on the part of friend and foe alike, his impetus to critical-historical study of the entire Christian tradition, from the New Testament to the
present, bore abundant and abiding fruit. Great importance attaches, in
particular, to his establishment of a discipline of Luther and Reformation
scholarship that must be deemed a genuine innovation in the annals of
nineteenth-century Protestant thought. Bernhard Lohse, a dean of contemporary Luther research, has rightly remarked: "Luther, before Ritschl, was
a church father whose writings were reverently cited but hardly ever read.
After Ritschl, Luther was a theologian who had decisive contributions to
make to the situation of the later nineteenth century—even though this
was quite different from the situation of the sixteenth."[26] In his own
unique way the sober-minded Ritschl conveyed to his hearers and readers—to a rising generation of young Protestant theologians—a sense of excitement, a vision of new possibilities for a theology based on the classic

---

22. Wilhelm Herrmann, "Die Lage und Aufgabe der evangelischen Dogmatik in der
Gegenwart" (1907), in *Gesammelte Aufsätze*, ed. F. W. Schmidt (Tübingen: J. C. B. Mohr,
1923), 118–19.

23. Adolf Harnack, "Zur gegenwärtigen Lage des Protestantismus" (1896), in *Reden
und Aufsätze* 2 (Gieszen: Alfred Töpelmann, 1906), 139.

24. Ernst Troeltsch, "Adolf von Harnack and Ferdinand Christian von Baur 1921,"
trans. Wilhelm Pauck as an Appendix (97–115) to his *Harnack and Troeltsch: Two Historical Theologians* (New York: Oxford Univ. Press, 1968), 104.

25. Cf. Dietz Lange, "Das Verständnis von 'Offenbarung' bei Albrecht Ritschl und
Karl Barth," in J. Ringleben, ed., *Gottes Reich und menschliche Freiheit*, 40–59. Carl
Heinz Ratschow, *Gott existiert* (Berlin: Alfred Töpelmann, 1966), 64, could even designate
Barth "Ritschl's disciple"!

26. Bernhard Lohse, *Martin Luther: An Introduction to His Life and Work*, trans.
Robert C. Schultz (Philadelphia: Fortress Press, 1986), 220.

statements of Reformation faith (such as the 1520 treatise *On Christian Liberty*, which was Ritschl's favorite Luther text). It is not surprising, therefore, that his leading disciples invariably traced the power with which his theology gripped them to his creative reappropriation of Luther's religious root ideas. For example, Julius Kaftan (professor at Berlin from 1883 to 1920) maintained: "Albrecht Ritschl was the first to raise the fundamental demand to take up and set about the theological task in the way Luther had originally proposed, in that he bestowed pride of place upon the faith-principle as the only possible way to knowledge of God. Due to this he has become a leader and teacher for me and others."[27]

Ritschl's own Reformation research was distinguished by its mastery of all the primary theological and church-historical texts. His knowledge of the available documentary sources "exceeded by far" that of Schleiermacher, Baur, and Richard Rothe.[28] This scholarship was subsequently appropriated, extended, and often deepened by his pupils. A survey of publications on Luther's theology and Reformation history during the years 1875–1918 discloses substantive contributions by the following Ritschlians: Ferdinand Kattenbusch, Paul Drews, Karl Thieme, Johannes Gottschick, Martin Rade, Karl Müller, Karl Benrath, and Theodor Brieger.[29] To these one should add the magisterial works in the history of dogma (including, of course, the history of Reformation thought) by Adolf Harnack, Friedrich Loofs, and Otto Ritschl.[30] One also recalls that Wilhelm Herrmann's most influential book, *The Communion of the Christian with God* (1886), bore the revealing subtitle *Described on the Basis of Luther's Statements.*[31]

This Ritschlian tradition of scholarship, which too often has been passed over in accounts of modern Luther–Reformation research, came to fruition in the work of Karl Holl. Though he is not reckoned a member of the Ritschlian School, Holl had studied with Harnack and, in 1906, became his faculty colleague at Berlin. Holl's remarkable volume of col-

27. As quoted in Otto Wolff, *Die Haupttypen der neueren Lutherdeutung* (Stuttgart: W. Kohlhammer, 1938), 139. Cf. *TM* in *TE*, 209: "In what I have written here, I have shown that the epistemology which I use in theology corresponds to the actual intention of Luther, in particular, his aim to break with [scholastic theology]. He was not able to perform this task. Melanchthon, for his part, was not equal to it either."

28. According to Loewenich, *Luther und der Neuprotestantismus*, 92. I have discussed Ritschl's textual scholarship in "Albrecht Ritschl and the Heritage of the Reformation," in *Revisioning the Past: Prospects in Historical Theology*, ed. Mary Potter Engel and Walter E. Wyman, Jr. (Minneapolis: Fortress Press, 1993), 237–56.

29. For bibliographical details, see Lotz, 55, n. 82.

30. A. Harnack, *Lehrbuch der Dogmengeschichte*, 3 vols. (Tübingen: J. C. B. Mohr, 1886–89; 4th rev. ed., 1909–10; 5th ed., 1931). F. Loofs, *Leitfaden zum Studium der Dogmengeschichte* (Tübingen: M. Niemeyer, 1889; 6th ed., 1959). O. Ritschl, *Dogmengeschichte des Protestantismus*, 4 vols. (Leipzig and Göttingen: J. C. Hinrichs, 1908–27).

31. Cf. Wilhelm Herrmann, *The Communion of the Christian with God*, trans. from the 4th German ed. of 1903 by J. Sandys Stanyon (London: Williams and Norgate, 1906); reprinted with a most informative historical introduction by Robert T. Voelkel (Philadelphia: Fortress Press, 1971).

lected essays on Luther, published in 1921, is usually credited with having inaugurated the so-called Luther renaissance of the twentieth century, that is, the taking up of Luther's basic religious ideas into the very fabric of Protestant systematic theology, predicated on intensive historical study.[32] While granting that Holl's work marked a new stage in this enterprise, especially in respect of fresh perspectives, independent judgments, and text-critical precision, one observes, however, that just such a "renaissance" had *already* occurred in the joint historical-theological labors of Ritschl and the Ritschlians. Holl's scholarship, for all its originality and immediate reliance on the definitive critical edition of Luther's works launched at Weimar in 1883, was both methodologically and materially indebted to Ritschl's Luther interpretation.[33] One thus understands why Gustav Aulén, a central figure in mid-twentieth-century European (Scandinavian) Luther study and systematic theology, was prompted to declare: It is to the lasting credit of the Ritschlian theology that it "called into being an intensive Luther research" and "could scarcely have undertaken any other work which, in the existing situation, could possess more decisive significance for theology."[34]

As already noted, the comprehensive history of Christian doctrine was another academic discipline that became the special (if not exclusive) preserve of the Ritschlian School. In December 1885, Harnack sent Ritschl the first printed copy of the initial volume of his great *History of Dogma,* adding that "without the foundation you have laid, [this book] would never have been written."[35] Harnack's famous "Hellenization" thesis—that the trinitarian and christological dogmas of the fourth and fifth centuries were "a work of the Greek spirit on the soil of the gospel"—was at once a reformulation and radicalization of Ritschl's thesis that early Catholicism was the result of a gradual "de-Judaization" of primitive Christianity. What is often overlooked is that neither Ritschl nor Harnack denied that this dogmatic Christianity, however speculative in substance and dependent on Hellenistic philosophy, was an expression of the deepest religious interests of the early church. Ritschl, for example, held that "the Nicene form of the doctrine of the person of Christ was originally of direct practical consequence for the Greek church and was a vehicle for the soteriology that was distinctive to that church." Changing historical circumstances, however, required a changed attitude toward dogma. The old Greek-metaphysical Christianity "no longer corresponded to the vital interests of medieval piety" nor, above all, to the religious concerns of the reformers, especially Luther, who simply "interpolated his understanding of the love and the grace of God in Christ into

32. Karl Holl, *Gesammelte Aufsätze zur Kirchengeschichte,* I: *Luther* (Tübingen: J. C. B. Mohr, 1921). The essays collected here date from the years 1903–20.

33. See Lotz, 153–61 ("Ritschl and Twentieth-Century Luther Research [Karl Holl]").

34. As quoted in Wolff, *Die Haupttypen der neueren Lutherdeutung,* 127–28.

35. As quoted in Agnes von Zahn-Harnack, *Adolf von Harnack* (2d ed., Berlin: W. de Gruyter, 1951), 135. See E. P. Meijering, *Theologische Urteile über die Dogmengeschichte: Ritschls Einfluss auf von Harnack* (Leiden: Brill, 1978).

the [Chalcedonian] formula concerning the two natures," even though this ancient dogmatic construct was not adequate to Luther's religious root idea that in Christ one has to do with the loving God himself, not merely with a divine nature conjoined with a human nature.[36]

One should also emphasize that Harnack's most popular and widely published book, *What Is Christianity?* (1900), exemplified Ritschl's distinctive mode of doing theology out of historical inquiry, which involved the identification of an original "essence" of the Christian religion in whose light one could then distinguish between authentic and inauthentic developments in theology and spirituality. Here, in Harnack, one witnesses the typical Ritschlian distinction between religion (piety) and theology (doctrine), with the parallel insistence that an adequate theological formulation must always subserve and be entirely congruent with the underlying religious interests of which it is a vehicle. This position further implied that Christian doctrine must perforce change in keeping with significant changes in Christian piety. And this perspective, in turn, could lead to a boundless historical relativism unless such extreme relativizing were somehow held in check; by appeal, for example, to a historically based standard of essential (perennially valid) Christianity.

The latter strategy was adopted not only by Ritschl and Harnack but also by most of the Ritschlians, though they differed (often widely) among themselves in their specific identification and interpretation of this normative essence, and despite the fact that this very notion of what amounted to a *timeless* "core" of Christian truth was at root metahistorical and so at odds with a strictly historical-empirical approach.[37] Nonetheless, since nineteenth-century German historicism was decisively informed throughout its course by a philosophy of history rooted in German idealism, in a metaphysics of time-transcending *Geist* or "Spirit," this latent contradiction between an empirical and an idealist historiography usually went unremarked and, in any event, was left unresolved.[38]

No doubt it was Troeltsch, himself a member of the so-called left

---

36. *HP* in *TE*, 127.

37. Cf. Harnack, *What Is Christianity?* (= *Das Wesen des Christentums*), trans. Thomas Bailey Saunders (London: Williams and Norgate, 1900; reprinted, New York: Harper & Row, 1957), 149: "I have tried to show what the essential elements in the Gospel are, and these elements are 'timeless.' Not only are they so; but the man to whom the Gospel addresses itself is also 'timeless,' that is to say, it is the man who, in spite of all progress and development, never changes in his inmost constitution and in his fundamental relations with the external world." In short: an essentially timeless gospel for an essentially timeless humanity.

38. See Georg G. Iggers, *The German Conception of History: The National Tradition of Historical Thought from Herder to the Present* (Middletown, Conn.: Wesleyan Univ. Press, 1968); and Maurice Mandelbaum, *History, Man, and Reason: A Study in Nineteenth-Century Thought* (Baltimore: Johns Hopkins Univ. Press, 1971), esp. 41–138 on "Historicism." I judge that Harnack's understanding of historical thought was much more indebted to German Romanticism (Goethe) and philosophical idealism than was Ritschl's, as is evident in Harnack's very un-Ritschlian idea of "pure inwardness" as constituting the human essence which lies beyond change, and to which the timeless Christian gospel ever addresses itself ("God and the soul, the soul and its God").

wing of the Ritschlian School, who wrestled most strenuously, even ago-
nizingly, with the problem of Christian faith and historical thinking. His
chief concern was to uphold a consistently historical and thus relativizing approach to Christian faith and life without giving way to an utter
relativism, to a despair of ever arriving at religious norms and ethical
values whose validity could be defended on empirical-historical grounds
and that would serve the vital contemporary interests of the Christian
cult and community as well as those of Western (Christian) civilization.
This exigent historical-theological project, Troeltsch insisted, must be
carried out without recourse to a metahistorical "essence of Christianity" (in the manner of Ritschl and Harnack), or to a no less metahistorical and quasi-mystical notion of personal religious encounter with the
"inner life of the historical Jesus" (in the manner of Herrmann), or to an
ahistorical body of Christian doctrine, of eternal truths divinely revealed
"from above" (in the manner of Roman Catholicism, Eastern Orthodoxy, and traditional Protestantism).[39]

To be sure, this general program of "overcoming history [boundless
relativism] by history [modern historical consciousness]," *not* by dogma
(a premodern, antihistorical, intellectualist idea of the Christian revelation), was common to all the Ritschlians: a program that Ritschl himself
had set in motion by way of his inheritance from Baur and Ranke.
Troeltsch, however, was the most consistent historicist in the Ritschlian
camp, perhaps because he was the thinker most receptive to—and best
informed about—the Western European (British) tradition of empiricism, as well as the thinker who was most profoundly aware that "history" and "relativity" are synonymous. And so it was Troeltsch, also,
who most distanced himself from Ritschl's theology of revelation (of
Christianity as "the perfect religion within which the perfect knowledge
of God is possible") and from Harnack's determination of Christianity's
essence by abstracting a perennially valid "simple gospel" from the
teaching of Jesus and Apostle Paul.[40] Yet Troeltsch, too, readily granted
that "in that part of my knowledge which is related to church history

39. For Troeltsch's critical judgments and his own conceptually sophisticated
standpoint, see *Ernst Troeltsch: Writings on Theology and Religion,* ed. and trans.
Robert Morgan and Michael Pye (London: Gerald Duckworth & Co. Ltd.; Atlanta:
John Knox Press, 1977), esp. "Half a Century of Theology: A Review" (1908), 53–81,
and "What Does 'Essence of Christianity' Mean?" (1903, 1913), 124–81. I judge that
Troeltsch's solution to the problem of unlimited relativism involved both an existentialist decision for certain normative values, a creative act of the interpreter based on a
comprehensive historical-empirical induction, and a metahistorical confidence, based
on an idealist philosophy of history (and on the Christian faith!), that the course of
human history has engendered values that are connected to the Absolute, to the divine
ground which both transcends and is immanent in the historical process. Thus
Troeltsch, too, remained materially indebted to a metaphysics of Spirit. To be sure, he
was, I think, far more aware of, and explicit about, this synthesis of "history and metaphysics" than was either Ritschl or, in particular, Harnack.

40. Ritschl's assertion of Christianity's "perfection" is from his *ICR,* in *TE,* 221 (paragraph 2). Cf. Troeltsch, *The Absoluteness of Christianity and the History of Religions,*

and the history of doctrine, I am most deeply indebted to him [Harnack]; indeed, I have derived it from his and Ritschl's infinitely productive works."[41]

Troeltsch's testimony stands as a fitting summary reminder that Ritschl's masterly impulse to critical-historical study of the total Christian tradition continued to work as a leaven in the labors of his students and disciples, and, through them, in the shaping of Protestant theology well into the twentieth century—down, in fact, to the present day. Alongside Troeltsch's testimony, therefore, should be placed that of Rolf Schäfer, who has published the fullest and finest treatment to date of Ritschl's dogmatics. Writing in 1968, at the outset of the Ritschl renaissance, Schäfer concluded that "Ritschl's theology is at one and the same time forgotten and present," adding in explanation:

> His writings are scarcely read any longer—though now and then one remembers him as the consummate heretic-father of all the perversities of his century. Yet whoever undertakes the labor of reading his works finds displayed under the light covering of antique expression the most precious wares of contemporary theology. Not a little that impresses us as the most up to date was both formed and informed [*gebildet und gelehrt*] by Ritschl.[42]

The present volume of essays, appearing a generation after Schäfer's pioneering book, gives ample evidence that Albrecht Ritschl is no longer forgotten, that his writings are no longer scarcely read, and that his posthumous reputation is no longer that of nineteenth-century heretic par excellence. So also, in their respective ways, these essays show that Ritschl's system of theology—for all its rhetorical quaintness and material failings—may justly be regarded (and has been so regarded in wide circles during much of the past century) as a worthy dialogue partner in the continuing conversation about the requisite form and content of the Christian witness in the modern world.

---

trans. David Reid (Richmond, Va.: John Knox Press, 1971), esp. 80–83. Regarding Harnack, see *What Is Christianity?* 275: "Protestantism reckons . . . upon the Gospel being something so simple, so divine, and therefore so truly human, as to be most certain of being understood when it is left entirely free, and also as to produce essentially the same experiences and convictions in individual souls." (This passage is italicized throughout.)

41. Troeltsch, as quoted in Pauck, *Harnack and Troeltsch*, 115.
42. Schäfer, "Vorwort."

PART TWO

Theological Approach
and the Bible

3

A Historical Bible, A Reasonable Faith, A Conscientious Action

The Theological Legacy of Albrecht Ritschl

 GERALD W. McCULLOH

On the occasion of the centennial of Albrecht Ritschl's death, and at a time when the possibility of mediation between conservative, fundamentalist, and liberal theology is again in question, the theological legacy of Albrecht Ritschl may offer the opportunity to set aside party labels and consider the resources for the life of faith. Ritschl's contribution may be considered in terms of his efforts in three areas: the interpretation of the Bible, a systematic articulation of the Christian faith, and a description of the content of the Christian life. These areas are of importance today to those who seek insight into the historical sources, conceptual organization, and ethical application of the Christian faith as a meaningful lifestyle. This essay will explore each of these emphases in turn.[1]

---

1. The three areas in terms of which this essay is structured, Albrecht Ritschl's contributions to biblical, critical-historical, and constructive systematic-ethical theology, correlate with the involvement of Ritschl himself in the three principal stages of his own life-work as represented by his publications. In addition, the movement from biblical sources, critically received, to a reconstruction of the understanding of traditional Christian thought, and, finally, to the application of these ideas in a constructive statement of the Christian life in the midst of history appears to me to be consistent with Ritschl's own work in the preparation of his major work, *The Christian Doctrine of Justification and Reconciliation.* I believe that this is consistent with David Lotz's attempt in "Ritschl in His Nineteenth-Century Setting" (see chapter 2), to describe Ritschl's "endeavor to construct a total theological system—historical, exegetical, and dogmatic" in this volume. The biblical basis for the doctrine appeared in the second volume of the study, but it referred to materials published earlier in Ritschl's career (done before he undertook the "critical history" of the doctrine in volume 1). My sense is, however, that Ritschl's concern about avoiding the limitations of metaphysical systems of the past would make Ritschl somewhat chary of the claims for system invoked by Lotz, preferring perhaps to regard his work as a sustained historical effort of practical reason and not a tour de force of pure reason. See Albrecht Ritschl, *Das Evangelium Marcions und das kanonische Evangelium des Lucas* (Tübingen:

A HISTORICAL BIBLE

Throughout his career Ritschl gave his attention to the use of the Bible as a resource for the Christian community's knowledge of God and knowledge of the person and life-work of Jesus. The critical study of the Bible brings the believer to Jesus and Jesus to the believer. Critical biblical study was not an attack upon faith but an exercise of good faith, particularly in the Evangelical tradition in which Ritschl emerged. Christians today have an opportunity to reappropriate the Bible as source for mutual encounter and understanding of the richness of the Christian faith.

Ritschl's concern not only set the agenda for his early work on the historical setting of the Gospels of Marcion and Luke and his account of the rise of the ancient Catholic church, but remained an important feature of his later work. The biblical basis of the doctrine of justification and reconciliation occupied the second, pivotal volume of his study of systematic theology, *The Christian Doctrine of Justification and Reconciliation.* The biblical materials constituted both a source and a regulative norm for further doctrinal statements, a position that he developed in his *Instruction in the Christian Religion.* The historical account of the Jerusalem church that he found in the biblical texts provided Ritschl with his understanding of what the early Christian church was and continued to be through the second century. Against this pattern he could measure the characteristics of later medieval and Protestant Christianity. This frame of reference allowed him to point out the contradictory claims on the authority of the holy Scriptures represented by the Anabaptists and by Zwingli and still to find a basis for overcoming Protestant and Catholic differences in defining the Christian faith.[2]

In order to gain a clearer sense of the significance that Ritschl placed on the Bible as a positive historical source for knowledge of Jesus by later Christianity, we will consider Ritschl's early work on the Bible in greater detail. First we will examine what Ritschl's position was in re-

Osiander'sche Buchhandlung, 1846) and *EK.* For Ritschl's biography see *Leben;* Mackintosh, 138–80; Hefner, 1–50; Richmond; and Welch 2:1–30. For Ritschl bibliography see *Leben,* 1:438–50, 2:526–32; Hök, xiii–xxxiv; Hefner, 187–90; also Richmond, 32, for mention of Gerhard Ruhbach's record of works on Ritschl to 1965, and Welch 2:303–4. For Baur, see Peter Hodgson, *Ferdinand Christian Baur on the Writing of Church History* (New York: Oxford Univ. Press, 1968) and *The Formation of Historical Theology: A Study of Ferdinand Christian Baur* (New York: Harper & Row, 1966).

2. *HP* in *TE,* 74. Ritschl distinguishes between the stage of Christianity from the second century onwards, described as the Catholic stage of Christianity, and the Reformation of Luther and Zwingli. He finds that the Anabaptists do not represent the earliest biblical patterns of Christian life, but rather are closest to the medieval age. Zwingli's position is traced forward through Conrad Grebel. Ritschl acknowledges that the educated people of the Reformation and post-Reformation periods restricted themselves to general principles, but the actual applications among uneducated adherents looked only at the letter of Scripture. One may then share with other Christians profound reverence for the continuity of the biblical witness without surrendering a critically nuanced appreciation of that continuity.

spect to Baur, his mentor, explore Ritschl's own judgment of the historical value of the texts to help provide a context for their interpretation, illustrate Ritschl's interpretation, and finally (*a*) reflect on the broader implications of Ritschl's approach to the biblical materials about Jesus with respect to later ecclesiological and dogmatic concerns, and (*b*) suggest the contemporary significance of Ritschl for understanding Norman Perrin and James M. Robinson.

The important accomplishment of Ritschl's mentor in the Tübingen School, Ferdinand Christian Baur, was the development of a comprehensive historical theology. This approach to theology aimed at a critical investigation of Christianity in order to grasp the dynamic life of the early Christian community by recognizing the concerns and achievements of the different groups within the community. With this comprehensive understanding in place it was possible to evaluate the role played by a particular biblical text as it expressed the point of view of its author(s) in the developing history of the community. Evidence of these different parties and their self-understandings was, Baur and Ritschl agreed, preserved in the midst of the surviving biblical texts. Any significant doctrine or teaching would have to be related to the formative process of the community, from Jesus onwards. For Ritschl, Baur's approach avoided a dualism in which religious history was separated from world history and instead regarded religion as an object suited for rational inquiry and interpretation. The texts of the Bible could be regarded as the results of thoughtful decisions made by the writers and later editors of the various works, and their writings preserved evidence of the communities of persons whose lives constituted the earliest stages of the historical movement. The modern reader could, then, recover the significance of these decisions when the order of their writing and the setting of their creation were understood. This understanding linked the lives of contemporary Christians with the lives of those who preceded them. However, it placed great responsibility on the scholar-theologian as exegete and critic. To read the Bible uncritically would be to sacrifice its value as a historical source, while to read the Bible without exegetical insight would be to lose its importance for the Christian community and Christian theology.

In order to receive the full import of the Christian Gospel, the scholar-exegetes attempted to identify with greater precision the historical sequence in which the documents of the early church were written. Historical investigations and critical discussions, it was thought, would allow a reconstruction of the process whereby the books of the New Testament were formed.[3] The various points of view that existed in the earliest

---

3. On the American scene "Ritschlianism" was sometimes used in a pejorative sense to represent the entire enterprise of higher and historical biblical criticism. James Orr's *The Ritschlian Theology and the Evangelical Faith* (London: Hodder and Stoughton, 1897) at times also preserves a denunciatory tone. Some conservatives felt that the authority of Scripture was undermined by placing its formation in a historical context for interpretation

Christian community could be seen as continuing influences, borne along in the canonical texts of the Bible.

When Baur was skeptical that the apostles or their immediate associates were responsible for the origin of some biblical documents, Ritschl argued that the books should be dated earlier and that they reflected more unity than Baur admitted. The interpretation that Ritschl offered entailed a more complex understanding of Jewish and Gentile structures than Baur presented.[4]

As Baur portrayed the struggle between Jewish Christianity and Hellenistic-Gentile Christianity, it issued in a synthesis represented by the Johannine materials and the emerging Roman papacy. Ritschl disagreed. He argued that the Catholicism that Baur described was not the true Jewish-Gentile synthesis but a departure that ignored the Hellenistic-Jewish heritage of early Christianity. The corrective for Ritschl was to find in the Old Testament the most valuable source for understanding the significance of the New Testament message.[5] At the same time, Ritschl was conscious of wanting not to claim to have constructed yet another philosophically shaped and doctrinally dominated system. Ritschl had shied away from Baur and from Hegelian idealism in the direction of a commitment to the historical evidence of the early community present in the texts.

The elements at work in the development of Ritschl's own critical point of view can be found in his report of his research. In the introduction to *The Gospel of Marcion and the Canonical Gospel of Luke,* dedicated to his father, the Protestant bishop and general superintendent of Pomerania, Ritschl began with a reference to David F. Strauss. Strauss believed that the task of the historical critic was to determine the value of the Gospel as a source of history, apart from dogmatic considerations. Ritschl agreed with Strauss that the Gospel participated in the formation of the larger Christian myth, which came to represent the consciousness of the early Christian community. He likewise agreed with Bruno Bauer that the influence of the Gospel needed to be defined. These critical perspectives informed Ritschl as he examined the character of Marcion's Gospel and related it to what he thought was the earliest form of the Gospel of Luke, in order to characterize and distinguish the interpolations.

Ritschl saw a similarity between the various critical perspectives on Christianity in his own time and the different groups of thinkers in the

and understanding rather than affirming in wholesome terms the inerrancy of Scripture and a particular, often highly dogmatic, view of its meaning.

4. Ritschl published a study of the Gospel of Marcion and the Gospel of Luke in 1846, shortly after becoming associated with Baur and the Tübingen School. Ritschl later dropped the defense of an earlier date for Marcion's work and joined other scholars in the acceptance of the Gospel of Mark as the earliest Gospel.

5. Jonathan Lee Draper discusses Ritschl's exegetical effort in critical detail in "The Place of the Bible in the Theology of Albrecht Ritschl: With Special Reference to Christology and the Kingdom of God" (Ph.D. diss., University of Durham, 1984).

early Christian community. He sought to identify the influence of these groups on the presentation of the life and person of Jesus found in the canonical Gospels. When discussing the words of Jesus, questions of the historical origin of the Jesus materials and their authenticity needed to be considered. The proper historical ground for interpreting Jesus would emerge, in Ritschl's judgment, from increased attention to the correspondence between his teachings and the Mosaic Law. The later approaches to understanding Jesus, offered in turn by Paul, Nazarene and Pharisaic Ebionites, Essenes, and the Hellenistic Greek churches that faced gnostic and Montanist heresies, could then be assembled as they derived from the earlier material.

According to Ritschl, Baur had not been sufficiently faithful to the evidence of the diversity within early Jewish Christianity. Baur had also moved too quickly to his characterization of a false opposition between the Hellenistic and Jewish components of the early church. These judgments led Ritschl to dissent from his mentor and take up his own position.

Through a historical-critical interpretation of the canonical New Testament, Ritschl felt, one could closely approximate the ideas that represented the mind of Jesus. To the extreme rationalist, Ritschl still placed too much emphasis on the actual historical value of the Sermon on the Mount or the Lord's Prayer. To the Confessional theologian, Ritschl insisted too strongly on finding the Old Testament passages that informed the testimony preserved in the New Testament texts for him to be faithful to consistent dogmatic standards.[6] For Ritschl, both the Rationalist and the Confessionalist were themselves guilty of a subjectivism that ignored the objective historical character of the Christian community brought into being by the life of Jesus.

The exegete must develop a critical understanding of the apostolic and post-apostolic period in order to help interpret the partial and inconsistent record found in each individual source and to allow the Christian believer to perceive in the Bible the effects of Jesus' life. Baur had provided a start in this direction. A consideration of the movement from the New Testament church to the post-apostolic church helped Ritschl provide a dynamic model that could in turn help the critical scholar to reach beyond the mere assembly of scattered parts to grasp a sense of the whole. While the specific details of Ritschl's position may no longer be accepted by New Testament scholars, his insight into the dynamic process by which the thoughts of the earliest Christians were preserved in the production of the New Testament documents still continues to guide critical discussion.

6. David Lotz's emphasis, in "Ritschl in His Nineteenth-Century Setting," on the necessity of regarding Ritschl's "theological system" in broader terms, including earlier historical and biblical theology as a part of a mature corpus, is, I believe, correct. I would see Ritschl's earlier work on Marcion as part of an exegetical preparation for the historical work, consistent with the self-acknowledged intention of going back to the Bible.

Indeed, many of the broader assumptions of his position still prevail. The relative values of the Synoptic Gospels and the Johannine materials as historical sources for the early strata of tradition still have to be weighed critically. Within the Synoptics, Ritschl came to accept the priority of Mark and traced the influence of Mark and Matthew upon Luke. Ritschl emphasized the close bond between the Old Testament and the New. His conviction that the Bible is the primary source for commentary on itself has significance for a broad spectrum of Christian believers. Ritschl had limited patience with the ultraconservatives who sought to impose later dogmatic categories upon older historical texts. At the same time, Ritschl could also try to avoid the stereotypic conflict between the liberals and conservatives by sticking close to Scripture as the standard for belief and practice in the authentic Christian community. Ritschl knew that the character of Jesus preserved within the witness of the Christian community and its Scripture would always seem strange to those who ignored the critical task of informed interpretation in favor of party lines.

While the extent to which Weiss, and later Schweitzer, emphasized the distance between the conventional portrayals of Jesus in the nineteenth century and those of the first century went beyond Ritschl, it would have been no surprise to him to find another set of dogmatic presuppositions overturned by a careful study of historic texts.

His interpretation of Mark's account of Jesus feeding the disciples on the sabbath illustrates his exegetical approach. Ritschl finds in the Old Testament distinctions in the kind and use of religious laws which illuminate the role of the Law in the New Testament. In this passage (Mark 2:23) the details of the sabbath law were not considered binding, but neither was the Mosaic Law itself overturned. The needs of the kingdom of God and the authority of the Son of Man justify it (Mark 2:28; Matt. 12:8; 11:27; John 5:1-18).[7] Placed in the context of other reflections on the Law, it was possible for Ritschl to feel that he had reached the meaning which Jesus had intended, because he was able to isolate the controlling idea, which he identified as the criterion used by Jesus in dealing with questions about the sabbath law. The controlling idea was present, Ritschl thought, in Mark 12:28-34, where the scribe approves Jesus' response about the first commandment, and Jesus indicates that the scribe is not far from the kingdom of God. For Jesus the motive of loving God and the neighbor justifies an action. The exception to the law here is based on the authority of the Messiah and counts only for those who believe in him. Distinctions made between ceremonial laws and moral laws are not part of later dogmatic concerns to distinguish Christianity from Judaism, but are already a part of the prophetic tradition in the Old Testament—a tradition that has a different emphasis than the sources associated with the Mosaic cultus.

7. *EK*, 28–51.

In the Gospel of Matthew, the central feature is the Sermon on the Mount and the interpretation of Jesus' teaching in relation to the Mosaic Law (Matt. 5:3-12; 5:17-20).

> If Jesus distinguished with the Law between the portions which determine the highest purpose of mankind, that is the command to love God and one's neighbor, and such requirements which are only concerned because of men, which he is directed to overthrow, that is specifically sabbath keeping and divorce, then we have the standard which we seek. The complete development of the highest purpose of love, which the Law itself expressed, is itself only able to be complete through the overthrow of the decrees and arrangement of the Law, which does not serve these but other purposes.[8]

The formula concerning the Law and the Prophets (Matt. 7:12 and 22:40) is also used to set off two other related ideas, that one should do to others as one wishes they would do in return and that the love of God and neighbor is righteousness. This interpretation, Ritschl finds, captures the meaning and value of the Law and the Prophets as a unity, and this, he believes, is the sense intended by Jesus. The result, gained by proper historical exegesis of the central texts of the tradition, is an enhanced appreciation of the person and work of Jesus within the early community. Ritschl takes the results of his work as the basis for the second volume of *The Christian Doctrine of Justification and Reconciliation.*[9]

His first observation is that the historically determined words of Jesus do not yield a uniform theological system. By grasping the ideas of Jesus encountered in a critical reading of the Gospel materials, a reading informed by the appreciation of the several levels of law preserved in the Old Testament, Ritschl understands that the individual participates in determining the significance of Jesus' thoughts.

> One will have to calculate the special significance of his [Jesus'] thoughts individually if one wants to relate them without contradiction. The clearest indication that his proclamation of truth is of a religious and not a scientific kind is the consideration given to the special connection of the speeches of Jesus by different groups.[10]

The standards of authority that control various theological positions need to be identified and disclosed in order that their presuppositions be known and accounted for. The exegetical process does have its own place in history.

> For as there is in the Catholic Church no unanimous tradition, so too the symbolic concepts of doctrine in the Lutheran and Reformed Churches are

8. *EK,* 45.
9. The translation of volume two is my own, hereafter *JR* 2.
10. *JR* 2:42.

not without gaps and important points which are disputed interpretations, even as much as there are disputed places in Scripture. . . . For the evangelical (Protestant) theologian it can only concern the task of *the interpretation of Scripture from itself* and the approximation of the completion of this task. It is not simply the grammatical knowledge or logical completeness that can comprehend the significance of the particular in relation to the unity of the whole. It is related to the aesthetic application of art: to the range, the connection, the lofty placement of the religion of the Old Testament in order to reproduce the correct view and to understand accordingly the documentation of Christianity in its original and historical sense. . . . Biblical theology in its historical sense strives for the goal of using Scripture to interpret Scripture.[11]

Ritschl's presentation of the life of Jesus seeks to avoid the overlay of later ecclesiological or dogmatic concerns.

Jesus appears with the quality of an Israelite prophet, not only because he himself proclaims the fulfilled kingdom of God at hand while his followers do the same (Mark 1:15; Matthew 10:17), but even more because he announces that the actual, final purpose of the divine covenant will be realized, and gives the impression that his speech belongs to the immediately imminent experience and that it has the character of action done on the expressed order of God (Mark 1:22). The proclamation that the kingdom of God is at hand and that this highest good will finally occur in the life of Israel has in the mouth of Jesus the sense that the time is fulfilled (Mark 1:15) in which the kingdom of God will be effective over the covenant people called to him. It does not have the sense that the kingdom is somewhere in the future and may be expected eventually to occur.[12]

Ritschl found that the ideas of Jesus brought together forgiveness of sins and the kingdom of God.

The ideas of Jesus then come to the following. He proclaims the present coming of the kingdom of God in the covenant people while he represents it as the bearer or lets it be known. He understands the realization of the kingdom of God in terms of a community of disciples who recognize him as the bearer of the kingdom of God. He proves the correctness of this identification as he, through assurance of the forgiveness of sins and the call to repentance, separates those who join themselves with him in faith from the rest of the unworthy and redeems them from being lost in sin.[13]

The life of Jesus, then, provides evidence of the validity of his claims.

As the kingdom of God comes into being while his disciples carry out the will of God, the claim of Jesus to have founded the kingdom of God is

11. *JR* 2:29–30.
12. *JR* 2:43.
13. *JR* 2:57.

demonstrated. It is the very food of life for Jesus, that is to say, the provision of his self-preservation or the delight of his personal self-consciousness to complete the will and work of God which forms his calling (John 4:34). This solidarity with God as his Father is not defined but demonstrated as he speaks of the mystery of his life; that is, that he knows God, and reveals the ground on which God in turn knows him as his Son (Matthew 11:27). The works which he does in God's service are the works of God himself (John 9:3,4; 10:14). Jesus presupposes the love of God as the ground of his individual personality and his conforming work (John 15:9; 17:26). He demonstrates as evidence the fact that he observes the command of God, especially in so far as he is prepared to offer his own life in God's service (John 15:10; 10:17).[14]

The value of Scripture for the proper understanding of the Christian religion is summarized by Ritschl in his *Instruction in* (or *Institutes of*) *the Christian Religion,* paragraph 3.

Any understanding of Christianity can do justice to its claim to perfection only when undertaken from the point of view of the Christian community itself. But because this point of view has often been shifted in the course of history, and because the intellectual horizon of the community has been clouded by outside influences, it stands as the fundamental principle of the protestant church that Christian doctrine is to be obtained from the Bible *alone.* This principle refers explicitly to the original documents of Christianity gathered together into the New Testament, for the understanding of which the original documents of the Hebrew religion gathered together in the Old Testament serve as an indispensable aid. These books are the foundation of a competent understanding of the Christian religion from the point of view of the community, because the gospels set forth in the work of its founder the immediate cause and final end of the community's religion, whereas the epistles make known the original state of its common faith.[15]

The connection between the work of Ritschl and the present may be seen in several ways. His colleague Adolf von Harnack pursued the question of the measure of Jewish Christian and Greek Christian influence on the teaching traditions of later Christianity in his *History of Dogma.*[16] Ritschl's son-in-law, Johannes Weiss, explored the strangeness that Ritschl had referred to when considering Jesus' own words on the kingdom of God. In *Jesus' Proclamation of the Kingdom of God* (1892), Weiss identified apocalyptic thought as the proper context for under-

14. *JR* 2:59.
15. *ICR,* §3, 222.
16. Adolf Harnack, *Lehrbuch der Dogmengeschichte* (Freiburg, 1886–90). English translation of third edition by N. Buchanan, *History of Dogma* (London: Williams and Norgate, 1896–99).

standing Jesus' words.[17] Among Ritschl's students at Göttingen was Julius Wellhausen, who went on to join the faculty after Ritschl's death. Wellhausen sought greater precision in understanding the various sources of tradition present in the Old Testament materials. He went beyond the distinctions that characterized Ritschl's understanding of the components of the biblical corpus, that is, the Mosaic Law, the prophets and poets, and the concerns of the priestly tradition. Wellhausen pursued further the reconstruction of the historical formation of the different strands of tradition present in the biblical text and provided an account of the multiple sources to be found in the Hexateuch. With Graf he shared credit for providing the structure of Old Testament criticism to the present day. In addition, Wellhausen also published commentaries on the New Testament Gospels, which laid down lines for the later development of form criticism. Norman Perrin, in *What Is Redaction Criticism?*, recognized that Wellhausen provided the characteristic emphases of twentieth-century Synoptic scholarship and form criticism, which he enumerated in the following way:

> (1) the original source for the material in the Gospel is oral tradition in which that material circulated in smaller units; (2) this material has been brought together and redacted in various ways and at various stages, only one of which is that of the evangelist; and (3) such material gives us information about the beliefs and circumstances of the early church as well as about the ministry of Jesus.[18]

The residual emphasis of Ritschl on the importance of the historical context of the biblical texts, the engagement of these texts with a variety of points of view in both the Old Testament and New Testament historical periods, and the ability of this critical process to provide information about Jesus is still present here.

Finally, the titles of Norman Perrin's major works, *The Kingdom of God in the Teaching of Jesus* and *Rediscovering the Teaching of Jesus*,[19] reflect the persistence of Ritschl's focus on critically studying the salient themes in the New Testament in order to understand the ideas of Jesus.

---

17. Weiss. Although many commentators emphasize the discontinuity between Weiss and Ritschl with respect to their views of Jesus, in this case Ritschl is presenting Jesus as challenging the accepted cultural form of religion. It might be said that Ritschl was prepared to accept that Jesus was somewhat strange at times, while Weiss was confident that Jesus was quite strange when judged by the cultural expectations of first-century Pharisaic Judaism or nineteenth-century Liberal Protestantism.

18. Norman Perrin, *What is Redaction Criticism?* (Philadelphia: Fortress Press, 1969), 14. Also "Wellhausen, Julius," in F. L. Cross, *The Oxford Dictionary of the Christian Church* (London: Oxford Univ. Press, 1958), 1444.

19. Norman Perrin, *The Kingdom of God in the Teaching of Jesus* (Philadelphia: Westminster Press, 1963) and *Rediscovering the Teaching of Jesus* (New York: Harper & Row, 1967).

The importance of historical-critical methodology for the study of the historical Jesus, a concern Ritschl had in distinguishing himself from rationalism and pietism in general, and Baur and Francke in particular, is present in James M. Robinson's account of the procedure for "a new quest of the historical Jesus." Ritschl believed the Bible, understood from the historical-critical perspective, to be a public source of historical evidence for the life and work of Jesus. Despite some attempts to distance the followers of the new quest from their nineteenth-century forerunners, the debate returns to struggle with the method for identifying the authentic sayings of Jesus in terms of those that fit the historical-critical tests and address the understanding of existence occurring in history.[20]

> For such research has as a legitimate goal the clarification of an understanding of existence occurring in history, as a possible understanding of my existence. Hence the purpose of a new quest for the historical Jesus would be to test the validity of the *kerygma*'s identification of *its* understanding of existence with *Jesus'* existence.
>
> As a purposeful undertaking, a new quest of the historical Jesus would revolve around a central problem area determined by its purpose. . . . In the case of a new quest, this focal problem would consist in using the available source material and current historical method in such a way as to arrive at an understanding of Jesus's historical action and existential selfhood, in terms which can be compared with the *kerygma*.[21]

Ritschl's caveat to the new quest might be to encourage them to continue to emphasize the historical context of Judaism for interpreting the emergence of Christianity on the one hand, and to correct the individualism of existential selfhood by reasserting the understanding of the kingdom of God as a community. For those who detach texts from their original historical setting, there is Ritschl's challenge to pietism and subjectivism. Ritschl's legacy to us, received directly from his own work and mediated by his students and colleagues, is to preserve the recognition of the Bible as the historical source that brings us faithfully to Jesus as the historic founder of the Christian community and encourages us to be renewed and restored in that knowledge.

A REASONABLE FAITH

While Ritschl's theological work began with the problems of New Testament interpretation, it led to the development of a critical history of the ancient church and to a broader consideration of the history of Christian

---

20. James M. Robinson, *A New Quest of the Historical Jesus* (London: SCM Press, 1959).
21. Ibid., 94.

doctrine. The result of his effort is to provide us with a sense of the responsibility of faith to be a reliable and coherent witness to the experience of God's grace and forgiveness present in Christ. Ritschl was conscious of the tension in Catholic and Protestant communions and within the branches of Protestantism. He realized that different philosophies had informed and perhaps misinformed different ages in the statement of the Christian faith.

Ritschl's encounter with the ideas of Jesus provided him with a basis from which to view the development of later Christian thought. Ritschl makes a valuable contribution to the lives of Christians who follow his steps in seeking to distinguish authentic Christian teaching from the special concerns of intervening ages. Ritschl does not leave us the complete critical system of Christian thought; he leaves us his contribution to the continuing critical task. This legacy remains an enlightening and humbling challenge. Possession of the ideas of Jesus has an effect on the moral lives of Christians. The dynamic expression of this takes place in justification and reconciliation.

Ritschl was on guard not to let later dogmatic concerns of parties within the Christian tradition distort the testimony of Jesus preserved in the life of the Christian community as a whole. He felt that his task was to make the basis of the Christian faith and its development clear to those who would follow him.

Beginning in 1857, Ritschl directed his attention to the doctrines of justification and reconciliation. The result unfolded into a major critical and systematic effort. In 1872 two of Ritschl's Scottish students, J. S. Black and W. Robertson Smith, produced an English translation of volume 1, *A Critical History of the Christian Doctrine of Justification and Reconciliation*. In the introduction Ritschl offers his thoughts on the task.

> The Christian doctrine of Justification and Reconciliation, which I propose to unfold in a scientific manner, constitutes the real centre of the theological system. In it is developed the determinate and direct result of the historical revelation of God's purpose of grace through Christ—the result, namely, that the Church founded by Christ has freedom of religious intercourse with God, notwithstanding the fact of sin, and that at the same time, in the exercise of that freedom, directs the workings of its own will in conformity with God's expressed design. To the religious discernment this implies in itself the moral restoration of man and all religious blessedness.[22]

The religious discernment needed to grasp the ideas of Jesus from the collection of texts is also involved in the application of these ideas as a standard for further conduct. Ethics, spirituality, and cognition are not separate abstractions but aspects of the Christian faith.

22. *JR* 1:1.

Ritschl eschews as metaphorical the traditional discussion of the person and life-work of Christ associated with the threefold office, *munus triplex*.[23] He argues that neither Jesus nor the New Testament writers made use of the offices as comprehensive and exclusive forms for expressing the saving operation of Christ and warns that this practice was not introduced until the Reformation period. Such inharmonious and strange impressions are created by these titles as to suggest that they ought to be avoided. The proper task is "a survey of *the moral effects of the Life, Passion, Death and Resurrection of Christ towards the founding of the Church.*"[24] Following the Reformers, particularly Melanchthon, Ritschl connects justification and reconciliation directly with the actions and suffering of Jesus. The development of Christian doctrine beyond this basis is established by means of close examination of successive schools of thought. The changes in consciousness must involve not just the individual believer but the whole society and culture. Ritschl charges that both Baur's and Ritschl's predecessor at Göttingen, I. A. Dorner, failed to provide a satisfactory basis for the historical investigation of doctrine by uncritically reducing theology to philosophy.

> [A]lthough it may be useful for finding one's bearings at the beginning of the investigation to assume in the alternation of periods such variations as that in the seventeenth century that the factor of the authority of Scripture has a preponderating weight over the doctrine of justification by faith, which had previously stood in equipoise with it, yet it is the task of the historian to trace to all its sources the error into which people at that time universally and "unwittingly" fell, which assuredly is not sufficiently accounted for by the intellectual striving after a firm basis for systematic theology; for certainly every change in theology presupposes changes in the religious and church consciousness. Although these influences may have been hidden from people then, it is the business of history to reveal them to us now.[25]

Returning to a Kantian position that reason is properly used within the limits of human experience, Ritschl sought to demonstrate how Christian doctrine could be understood to have developed without entailing a fall into any abstract rational system, despite the distorted formulations that were attempted. In this case Ritschl struggled to provide a critical account that would unravel the misconstructions and allow the reader to appreciate the real historical record. In this attempt he tried to distinguish the development of historic Christianity from Neoplatonic, Aristotelian, or other metaphysically controlled representations. Ritschl bent to the task and produced his critical history of the doctrine of justi-

---

23. Gerald W. McCulloh, *Christ's Person and Life-Work in the Theology of Albrecht Ritschl: With Special Attention to Munus Triplex* (Lanham, Md.: University Press of America, 1990).
24. *JR* 1:4.
25. *JR* 1:18.

fication and reconciliation, locating the development of the doctrine as a phenomenon of the Western church. He noted the range of opinions that Thomas Aquinas found in the medieval church and observed that the intensification of feeling that occurred in the Reformation period could not tolerate the range of understanding of doctrinal formulations in the church that had characterized the earlier era. The theories of Anselm and Abelard in respect to atonement had been, in Ritschl's view, improperly set against each other rather than allowed to stand in juxtaposition. Undue emphasis, in Ritschl's opinion, was placed by the pietists on the side of Anselm. Neither Thomism nor the "repristination" of Luther could prevent the distortions of doctrine by scholastic or pietist. The Reformation did not intend new churches or a different religion, nor did it introduce into the church a new polity or new themes not already present in the biblical period, if its documents were understood critically. Only the Anabaptists claimed a break with Christendom.

Although his critical history addressed an overemphasis on sacramentalism and merit in the Catholic tradition, addressed the inconsistency and individualism in Lutheran theology, and traced the independent tendencies of Calvinism, locating the continuity between the Anabaptist movement and the common Christianity of state and church was most difficult for Ritschl.

The decline of church authority in the Enlightenment period allowed the rise of philosophical systems that appeared to be sympathetic with church Christianity but that, in fact, led to indifference and a speculative interest in natural religion. According to Ritschl, English deism contributed to the development of German rationalism, but idealism prevailed over the empiricism imported from England, allowing Kant to emerge as a critical idealist who preserves the moral dimension in spite of skepticism.

In reviewing the modern period, Ritschl provides an ironic judgment that Schleiermacher marks an epoch as a theological lawgiver in regard to the general culture of his age (a Moses in his own time), notwithstanding Schleiermacher's familiarity with all fields of theological study except the Old Testament. Alongside of Kant's distinction between the power of nature and the power of the will, Schleiermacher demonstrated the social character of all activities of the spirit.[26] That these activities possess moral value follows from his presupposition that moral science includes the mutual relations between purpose and result as well as the inner region of virtue and dutiful purpose.[27]

---

26. Schleiermacher's aesthetic of absolute dependence as the basis for knowledge of God represents a less historically grounded position than Ritschl's appreciation of the transcendent encountered in the moral teaching of Jesus and Ritschl's consciousness of being a part of the moral organization of humanity that resulted from Jesus' life-work.

27. I am indebted to Darrell Jodock for this insight and his editorial encouragement throughout.

The existence in the late nineteenth century of schools of thought devoted to pietistic orthodoxy and philosophical radicalism represents, for Ritschl, evidence of departure from the influence of Schleiermacher. The modern form of pietism, in Ritschl's eyes, is to be distinguished from the older roots in Halle. The "new" pietists seek to control church theology rather than to practice ascetic isolation. Philosophical radicalism, Ritschl observes, is heir to the efforts of Schelling, Hegel, and Goethe to achieve a resolution of the absolute idea and individual poetic consciousness, but it fails to transcend, exhaust, or surpass Christianity, providing only abstractions and symbols.

Ritschl concludes his critical history of doctrine with the belief that he has charted the particular history of Christian doctrine and disclosed its historical course, not its necessary development. His constructive statement of the doctrine of justification and reconciliation, which forms volume 3, acknowledges that where thinkers have departed from the idea of the forgiveness of sins called into existence by Jesus as founder of the Christian church and maintained by the apostles, they should not be followed. The statements of Jesus become intelligible when seen in the light of the consciousness of those who believe in him and trace their forgiveness back to him, his action, and his passion. This principle reappears in the opening paragraph of the *Instruction in the Christian Religion* and illustrates Ritschl's concern to demonstrate the effect of the words of Jesus upon the consciousness of the community. A reasonable faith, as Ritschl has envisioned it, involves the use of biblical texts as records of the faith of the early community; these texts provide the basis for articulating the consciousness present in individuals and in the community of faith, both past and present. A historical consideration of opposing points of view allows a clearer understanding of this consciousness than does any attempt to limit its presentation to a neutral orthodox formula. The task of systematic theology, then, is to formulate the faith of the community; it does this through the orderly reproduction of the thought of Jesus and the apostles and the influence of their thought on the later positive history of the religion.

Ritschl defined Christianity as

the monotheistic, completely spiritual, and ethical religion, which, based on the life of its Author as Redeemer and as Founder of the Kingdom of God, consists in the freedom of the children of God, involves the impulse to conduct from the motive of love, aims at the moral organisation of mankind, and grounds blessedness on the relation of sonship to God as well as on the Kingdom of God.[28]

Ritschl's historical and theological work influenced many. Indeed, as Hefner reports, one of Ritschl's students or supporters could be found

28. *JR* 3:13.

on each German theological faculty, except for the one at Heidelberg University.[29] Wilhelm Herrmann, Adolf von Harnack, Julius Wellhausen, William Robertson Smith, Friedrich Loofs, and Ernst Troeltsch offered leadership in systematic theology, the history of doctrine, biblical studies, and the philosophy of religion. Ritschlian scholars exercised additional influence by publishing the *Journal for Theology and Church* and *The Christian World.*[30] However, Ritschl's students did not form an identifiable school. His focus on the historical manifestations of Christianity and his renunciation of metaphysical systems left them free from his patronizing stamp.

In the broadest sense, Ritschlianism could mean concern for higher criticism of Scripture as a key to further historical knowledge of Jesus and the apostolic community, skepticism about the value of metaphysics for theology and epistemology, and interest in the kingdom of God and the moral organization of humanity. In narrower terms the legacy of Ritschl stands for the connection between the knowledge of a loving God shared by Jesus and today's Christian believer encountered in the everyday world of human experience. In these terms, Ritschl encourages us to view the Christian faith as the reasonable and intelligent response to history.

The wider assessment of Ritschl's influence on twentieth-century thought can be found in recent discussions of some of the century's major figures. The similarity of Ritschl to Tillich is noted by Livingston and his affinity to Bultmann by Mueller, while his influence in ethics is present as a factor in the work of Paul Lehmann and H. Richard Niebuhr.[31]

A CONSCIENTIOUS ACTION

The third aspect of Ritschl's legacy relates to his appreciation of the ethical character of the Christian life. His systematic expositions in the *Instruction* and in *Justification and Reconciliation* conclude with a dis-

29. "Albrecht Ritschl: An Introduction," in *TE*. Hefner's assessment of Ritschl's influence on 16–47 is the background for this discussion. Other measures of Ritschl's influence in terms of his students are in Robert Mackintosh, *Albrecht Ritschl and His School* (London: Chapman and Hall, 1915), 30ff.; Mueller, 9–10, 15–19; and Richmond, 266–310. Richmond is of particular interest here for his treatment of Orr's *The Ritschlian Theology,* in which the list of Ritschl's students has a negative connotation, and for his ability to find positive continuity between Ritschl and later neoorthodox theologians who were otherwise self-avowedly anti-Ritschlian, principally Karl Barth!

30. Cf. *Zeitschrift für Theologie und Kirche* and *Die christliche Welt.*

31. James C. Livingston, *Modern Christian Thought: From the Enlightenment to Vatican II* (New York: Macmillan, 1971), 252. Paul Tillich identifies Ritschl most strongly for his moral and anti-ontological emphasis. See Paul Tillich, *Perspectives on 19th and 20th Century Protestant Theology* (New York: Harper & Row, 1967), 215–19. Mueller, 41. Mueller shares with Richmond the impression that there is much also in common with Barth, an affinity not welcome to Barth. Paul Lehmann, *Ethics in a Christian Context* (New York: Harper & Row, 1963). H. Richard Niebuhr, bibliography of Paul Ramsey, *Faith and Ethics: The Theology of H. Richard Niebuhr* (New York: Harper & Row, 1957).

cussion of the Christian life, public worship, Christian perfection, and action in one's moral calling. The task that occupied the last years of Ritschl's life and work was a critical study of Pietism and an evaluation of the authentic Christian life and its claims to perfection. For Ritschl the individual believer in the Christian tradition is empowered by experiencing the effects of grace as impulses for personal action. The wholistic character of Ritschl's involvement with the Christian faith has gone from the encounter with Jesus in Scripture to understanding the significance of the Christian faith in history to a concern with the future.

Everything good, in turn, is recognized as the effect of grace on the believers. These effects of grace are, in Ritschl's view, a sense of freedom that involves spiritual dominion over the world and a sense of fellowship with God in which one's sins are forgiven through faith in Christ. The result is the feeling of religious and ethical perfection. The aesthetic and moral are related.

> Faith in the fatherly providence of God is the Christian world view in an abbreviated form. In this faith, although we neither know the future nor perfectly comprehend the past, yet we judge our momentary relation to the world on the basis of our knowledge of the love of God and on the basis of what we derive from this knowledge, namely, that every child of God possesses a significance greater than the world which God directs in accordance with his final purpose, i.e., our salvation. From this faith there springs that confidence which in all its gradations is equally far removed from the gnawing anxiety which might arise from our relation to the superior power of nature, as it is from dull indifference or bold recklessness or from stoic imperturbability, since none of these are an expression of ongoing spiritual freedom. More specifically, faith in providence furnishes a standard by which the first impression of evils as limitations of freedom or as divine punishments is transformed into an interpretation of them as blessings, i.e., as means of education or testing.[32]

The more limited contexts in which the Christian life is engaged required the perspective of the whole but involvement in the particular. Ritschl helps us see that loving humanity is accomplished by loving our neighbors, person by person. Each willing action of the Christian, in the love of God, brings life and faith together.

> The ethical imperative of the kingdom of God is performed as the most universal imperative of the Christian community, but only when the ultimate motive for all conduct is love for one's neighbor. We carry out this action in naturally conditioned moral communities which are narrower in scope (marriage, family, civic and social life, the nation), and we do so according to the specific principles that govern each. For the universal is always realized only in the particular.[33]

32. *ICR*, §51, 242–43.
33. *ICR*, §56, 245.

We can trace this trajectory from Ritschl's time to our own. Ritschl's emphasis on the real character of the Christian life experienced within the limits of ordinary human experience continued in the work of his student Ernst Troeltsch. One of those who learned from Troeltsch's extension of Ritschl's concern for historical methodology and restraint of metaphysical speculation was H. Richard Niebuhr.[34] The echoes of Ritschlian concerns can be heard in Niebuhr's own words as he concludes *The Responsible Self* with an appendix on "Responsibility and Christ."

> For we note that the human problem is this: how can we interpret all actions upon us, especially the decisive action by which we are, and all things are, by which we are destroyed and all things are destroyed, as divine actions, as actions of affirmation and reaffirmation rather than as actions of animosity or of indifference? How is an ethos of universal responsibility possible, even in modest measure, to human beings? That one power is present in all the powers to which we are subject is a presupposition of our lives which we may question intellectually but do not question in our action. We entertain pluralistic hypotheses about the world in various metaphysical speculations yet we continue to seek to know as those who have a universal intent. We seek a knowledge that will be universally true, though all our propositions are known to be only approximations to universal truth. We have the inconquerable conviction that we confront a oneness behind and in and through all the many-ness in which we live and which we know.[35]

For Christians, this oneness is present in Jesus Christ. Responsible participation in a pluralistic world fulfills, not negates, personal commitment.

> However adequate or inadequate our theories of atonement or reconciliation may be, the fact remains: the movement beyond resignation to reconciliation is the movement inaugurated and maintained in Christians by Jesus Christ. By Jesus Christ men have been and are empowered to become sons of God—not as those who are saved out of a perishing world but as those who know that the world is being saved. That its being saved from destruction involves the burning up of an infinite amount of tawdry human works, that it involves the healing of a miasmic ocean of disease, the resurrection of the dead, the forgiveness of sins, the making good of an

34. H. Richard Niebuhr, *The Meaning of Revelation* (New York: Macmillan, 1941, 1960), x, 22–34. In *The Meaning of Revelation* Niebuhr acknowledged both Troeltsch and Barth as his teachers and cited Ritschl as an example of the continuing influence of Kantian ethical theory in the history of Christian thought. Ritschl served as a point of departure in Niebuhr's discussion of Walter Rauschenbusch and the kingdom of God movement in *Christian Ethics* (with Waldo Beach) (New York: Ronald Press, 1955) and in his study *Christ and Culture* (New York: Harper & Row, 1951).

35. H. Richard Niebuhr, *The Responsible Self* (New York: Harper & Row, 1963), 175.

infinite number of irresponsibilities, that such making good is not done except by suffering servants who often do not know the name of Christ though they bear his image—all this Christians know. Nevertheless, they move toward their end and all endings as those who, knowing defeats, do not believe in defeat.[36]

Niebuhr is more chastened than Ritschl, perhaps, by the apparently infinite extent of irresponsibility and tawdry human works, but he nonetheless finally views the Christian as empowered by reconciliation to know hope and not despair.

For Ritschl the moral organization of mankind to act from the motive of love provides participation in the kingdom of God available to ordinary human beings living in history. In a world newly troubled by the collapse of ideological regimes and challenged by ethnic diversity and religious strife, the recovery of hope at the level of the individual with implications for humanity is essential.

CONCLUSION

Finally, one should not fail to consider the resonance of Ritschl's work with the structure of contemporary university theological faculties in which distinctive and complementary attention is given to biblical studies seeking to explore further the intimate historical connection between Old and New Testaments; to historical and systematic theology in the continuing critique of the tradition above the sectarian interests of denominationalism, seeking to sustain the coherence of the faith; to the practical concerns of ethics, church, and society in dealing with the area in which the Christian life and its influence in the world is experienced. These areas of concern in Ritschl's work, which we have been able to suggest only briefly, continue as areas of increased specialization and research in the ongoing discipline of theological investigation. Renewed interest in the doctrine of God, contemporary Christology, and the liberation of the church are occasions to consider once again what Ritschl discerned as the basis for pushing the critical horizons further.

History, reason, and action are united in the Ritschlian legacy in the heritage of the Bible, knowledge of the history of Christian thought, and participation in Christian ethics as part of the kingdom of God. The evidence of their power and their validity is their ability to transform our experience and bring us together in the presence of God. We are grateful to Ritschl for his focus on these truths and his labor in their behalf as we continue the task of living the Christian life, responding to its witness, interpreting its texts, understanding its significance, and sharing in its

36. Ibid., 177.

achievement as part of the kingdom of God. Where we ignore the breadth of Ritschl's efforts, we risk the impoverishment of our own understanding; where we fail to progress beyond his age, we fall short of his self-critical consciousness and the legacy he has left us; where we succeed, our participation in the life of Jesus and the moral organization of humanity is enriched and extended.

4

Christocentricity and Community as Norms for Biblical Theology

CLIVE MARSH

> Logically, the rejection of natural religion means, at the same time, a rejection of all universal concepts which one might possess prior to the particular structures of revealed religion or apart from the actuality of those structures in the founder and in the community.
>
> (*Theology and Metaphysics*)

I

What understanding of "biblical theology" is possible today? Christian theologians will always attempt to establish a single, unified biblical theology that crosses the Old and New Testaments or, at least, they will try to pinpoint a thread that runs through both Testaments and forms the theological core of the biblical material. It seems, however, more honest and accurate to point to the sheer richness, complexity, and diversity of the biblical texts. Historical, literary, religious, and theological enquiries conducted into the biblical writings over more than two centuries have far from destroyed the power of the Bible to "speak" in all sorts of ways in new situations. But such enquiries have made it difficult to talk of the Bible in a general way. Josipovici's description of the Bible as "the Book of God" may well be the best common denominator available.[1]

So what sense can "biblical theology" possibly have? Are we left with a history of religious traditions, a record of past theologies, a resource book that may or may not be theologically useful? If so, what right has such a collection of texts to function as an authority for current attempts to construct Christian theology? These are perennial questions. In this

---

1. Gabriel Josipovici, *The Book of God* (New Haven and London: Yale Univ. Press, 1988).

article, I conduct a conversation with Ritschl in order to clarify the extent to which any Christian theology in the present must be said to be biblical.

I argue, with Ritschl's support, that any Christian theology must be construed biblically. I concur with Ritschl that in this task Christocentricity and a communal focus for biblical interpretation are primary concerns. Against Ritschl, I argue that the links with past history need to be loosened in order to permit present religious experience to play the full part that Ritschl himself desired. I argue further that Ritschl's failure to attend to the diversity of the Bible limits the potential of his ecumenical vision. In four sections I expound and critique Ritschl's theology from the perspective of the christocentric and communal foci of his use of the Bible. I then offer the revisions of Christocentricity and community that seem necessary in order for Ritschl's approach to be tenable today.

II

Ritschl's theology can be characterized as a christocentric New Testament theology, consciously constructed within the Pauline-Lutheran tradition. "Christocentricity" means that Ritschl explicitly and consistently presents the figure of Jesus Christ as the touchstone of all theological statements.[2] To call his a "New Testament theology" means that it uses the Bible normatively, placing greater emphasis upon the New Testament than on the Old, while fully respecting the importance of the whole biblical canon. As a theologian writing within the Pauline-Lutheran tradition, Ritschl affirms the importance of recognizing that theological reflection occurs within a particular historical community and within a specific religious tradition.

Christocentricity.   Ritschl attached great theological importance to historical knowledge about the person of Jesus of Nazareth. In his Christology, Ritschl seeks to link every theological statement about the person of Jesus with known data about Jesus of Nazareth. Thus, Ritschl states that "every form of influence exerted by Christ must find its criterion in the historical figure presented by His life."[3] The experience of redemption—of being made right with God through the person of Christ—can only be expressed in theological terms consistent with what we know of God in the life of Jesus of Nazareth. It would, for example, be theologically ille-

---

2. I use the word *touchstone* with caution, for it anticipates the results of my conversation with Ritschl. It could be argued that Ritschl's construal of Christocentricity requires a much stronger and more exclusive term than I offer here, e.g., "foundation" or "sole source." But it is the exploration of the tension between Ritschl's theory (which supports the use of "foundation") and practice (which tends more toward the "touchstone" metaphor) that enables this present enquiry to proceed at all. This essay, the expository section in particular, leans heavily on my earlier detailed study *Albrecht Ritschl and the Problem of the Historical Jesus* (hereafter *ARPHJ*) (San Francisco: Mellen Research Univ. Press, 1992).

3. *JR* 3:406 (*"in der geschichtlichen Gestalt seines Lebens"*) (see also 431, 432, and 468).

gitimate, according to Ritschl, to call Jesus "Lord" if it were not possible to be sure on historical grounds that Jesus displayed such "Lordship" in his earthly life.[4]

In presenting and seeking to adhere to this historical criterion, Ritschl is striving for objectivity in Christology. An objective norm, he hopes, will prevent sheer speculation or an overemphasis upon individual subjective experience, and it will help adjudicate between conflicting theologies. Further, in rooting christological statements firmly in the life of the earthly Jesus, Ritschl is pointing to the concrete, practical character of the theological undertaking (see further section IV below).

There is, however, a second aspect to Ritschl's Christocentricity, for he not only places great emphasis on historical knowledge for his understanding of the person of Jesus, but also locates his understanding of Jesus at the heart of his whole theology. Thus, it is striking that his theology, though couched in Pauline language and consciously constructed within the Pauline-Lutheran tradition, has the kingdom of God at its heart. In other words, Ritschl puts the key concept from Jesus' own teaching at the center of his own theology and explores that concept at decisive points in his own constructive theology.[5]

This second aspect of Ritschl's Christocentricity finds expression as an emphasis upon Christian particularity as distinct from other religious traditions. We have no other concrete knowledge of God as the one who redeems, except as the God who is the Father of Jesus Christ.[6] Ritschl believes he can best clarify the particularity (even uniqueness) of the revelation of God through the Christian tradition by means of a consistent, christocentric emphasis.[7]

For Ritschl, then, "Christocentricity," in practice, has four key elements: the distinctiveness of Christianity, the primacy of Christology in theology, an emphasis upon the kingdom of God, and a normative role for the work of the historian in the task of christological construction.[8]

4. Ibid: "Unless the conception of his present Lordship receives its content from the definite characteristics of his historical activity, then it is either a meaningless formula or the occasion for all kinds of extravagance."

5. E.g., after four introductory methodological paragraphs, *RV 2* continues with a section entitled "The Proclamation of the Kingdom of God." Similarly, the first of the four main sections of *ICR* is headed "The Doctrine of the Kingdom of God."

6. The complete Christian name for God is "The God and Father of our Lord Jesus Christ," *ICR,* §11; cf. also §1 and §12f. and *JR 3,* §27.

7. At this point "touchstone" (see n. 2) may be deemed inadequate on strictly expository grounds: see, e.g., *JR 3:6* and 202. On this question see S. Fisher's exploration of revelatory positivism in Barth, which includes reference to Herrmann's Ritschlian background [*Revelatory Positivism?* (New York and Oxford: Oxford Univ. Press, 1988)]. I am contending that Ritschl's "revelatory positivism" is not as "historically positivist" as frequently assumed.

8. The first definition of "Christocentrism" provided in F. L. Cross, *The Oxford Dictionary of the Christian Church* (London, New York, and Toronto: Oxford Univ. Press, 1957), 278, is thus too narrow. Though it is correct to note the opposition Ritschl displays to natural theology, even Ritschl does not claim that "God has never revealed Himself to man except in the Incarnate Christ." The issue, rather, is to clarify the particularity and the normativity of God's self-revelation in Christ.

Despite what has been said, Ritschl does not fall foul of a charge that can be brought against many of those engaged in the "quest for the historical Jesus." He does not, ultimately, render his whole theology dependent upon the findings of historical research. Though such research is, as we shall see, of great importance in Ritschl's theological method, the fact that Ritschl qualifies his seeming dependence on history places him at odds with the mainstream quest, at least as documented by Albert Schweitzer. The qualification Ritschl adds to his own historical interest in Jesus clarifies for his readers his understanding of the relationship of that interest to the task of christological construction and prevents the "normative" role played by the historian becoming a "determinative" role. It also introduces a second emphasis alongside Christocentricity in Ritschl's theology, namely, the importance of a religious community within which Jesus is to be interpreted.

Community.   Ritschl states this corporate emphasis clearly: "We can discover the full compass of His [Jesus'] historical actuality solely from the faith of the Christian community."[9] Christology is thus not simply a matter of stacking up historical data about Jesus of Nazareth, even if the historian's work does in some way function as a norm against which theological assertions are checked. Rather, Christology is about interpreting Jesus from the standpoint of the redeemed community. Only on the basis of an experience of redemption from within a particular historically rooted community is it possible to interpret Jesus with any measure of theological accuracy. For Ritschl this means being part of the Christian community.

"Community" is, however, a notoriously ambiguous term. Though often used in theological discourse, it is rarely closely defined. In seeking to clarify Ritschl's meaning of "community," one should note that the German *Gemeinde* lies behind the ambiguous English word. *Gemeinde* can itself mean "congregation" (a gathered community) or "parish" (all people in a particular geographical area). In practice, Ritschl's use relates to the former meaning. He is referring to those who specifically consider themselves members of the redeemed community, the church.

However, Ritschl speaks much of "Christ's community" and of the tension between the church and the kingdom of God. At the very least, therefore, we should be cautious about attributing to Ritschl a narrowly ecclesiastical interpretation of *Gemeinde*.[10]

9. *JR* 3:3. Cf. also *TM,* 210 (as quoted at the head of this essay). Though Schweitzer effectively paid lip service to Ritschl in *The Quest of the Historical Jesus,* this is more because Ritschl is not deemed eschatological enough in his reading of Jesus. Schweitzer is, however, correct to leave Ritschl largely out of his account, for Schweitzer in general pays little attention to those who quite explicitly showed *theological* interest in the figure of Jesus without assuming that historical enquiry alone would lead them to him.

10. See, e.g., *ICR* §§5 and 6, and *JR* 3, §35. Ritschl admittedly leaves unclear quite *how* the concepts of Christ's community (the church as Christ's followers at worship; the kingdom as Christ's followers engaged in ethical action) interrelate. But *that* they interrelate is not in doubt. Anyone, however, who can state that "activity of the most important

Furthermore, Ritschl's understanding of the communal nature of Christology (and theology) goes beyond merely the specific, concrete present community within which a believer finds him- or herself. Ritschl's attention to the corporate character of theology focuses not solely on the present, but also on the tradition of Christian communities throughout history. This dimension of Ritschl's emphasis on community is being addressed by his conscious attempt to be a theologian in the Pauline-Lutheran tradition. In this sense, Ritschl's theology takes on a confessional character. Ritschl is, however, not simply repeating either Paul or Luther uncritically. For Ritschl, belonging to a concrete *Gemeinde* entails also identifying with the historical tradition in which that *Gemeinde* stands. In other words, when interpreting Jesus from the perspective of faith, a person must be aware of being influenced by—being, indeed, to a considerable extent dependent on—the tradition of that historically rooted community within which one stands.

Biblical Theology.   We turn, thirdly, to the biblical character of Ritschl's theology. Ritschl sought to be consistently biblical. As the methodological preface to the second volume of *Justification and Reconciliation* makes clear, the Bible is the norm for Christian theology. How it does so must be explained. Ritschl does not offer as full a methodological explanation as his readers would wish. Close attention to the introductions in his three volumes of *Justification and Reconciliation* and to his actual use of the Bible, however, enables us to place his thinking in his own time and to suggest what a position continuous with and similar to his might look like in the present.

Ritschl saw clearly that to construct a biblical theology one does not simply quarry material from the Bible and re-present it in uninterpreted fashion. Nor can one easily read off a single train of thought from the biblical material and revise it for the present. The Bible contains, after all, different theologies.[11] One needs justification for a particular approach to the biblical material, a filter through which to read and understand its content. In his Christocentricity and his community emphasis, Ritschl finds two interpretive keys with which to read Christian Scripture.

Ritschl's christocentric interpretation of Scripture echoes Luther's approach and reworks it in a more historically conscious age.[12] Having identified Christ as the one to whom Scripture points, Ritschl sees fit to use the Jesus presented as Christ in the New Testament as a criterion for theological continuity.[13] Though Ritschl is striving to locate a theme of

kind for the service of the Church may be of no value whatever for the Kingdom of God" (*JR 3*:289) is keen to make clear that the church is not an end in itself. See also *ICR*, §9.

11. I have sought to show in *ARPHJ* III.4 that Ritschl, following Baur, permits some theological diversity in the New Testament, but not christological diversity.

12. As noted in Lotz, 43.

13. In an important footnote in the introduction of *RV 2,* 14ff., Ritschl qualifies his customary (and unsustainable) argument for the canonicity of the books of the New Testa-

continuity (a "center" or "theological core") throughout the Bible, he is also acknowledging in practice that a circle of interpretation exists when a later interpreter comes to its texts with a religious purpose. For Ritschl has identified Christ as the one to whom Scripture points on the basis of the movement back and forth between present experience and biblical text. Identifying the centrality of "Christ" as an idea in the Bible is not yet to do theology in the present. New theology is genuinely new and, as Christian theology, is rooted in an experience of Christ within a Christian community. But it relates back to the old in that it has inherited ideas from the past—in this case, the witness to Jesus as the Christ—in order to make any sense at all of that present experience of Christ. It relates to the past by checking itself against the primary witness.

In practice Ritschl attaches greater weight to the New Testament than to the Old. Though he sees both Testaments as bound together and marked off from other literature, Ritschl's theology is less a theology of both canons than a New Testament theology employing the Old Testament as its exclusive background.[14]

Where does one place Ritschl's use of the Bible vis-à-vis that of his contemporaries? Some clarity can be gained by comparing him with Martin Kähler and Bernhard Weiss. Like Kähler, Ritschl sees his biblical work (for example, *JR* 2) as very much united with the systematic (even apologetic) intent behind much of his theology (for example, *JR* 3). Ritschl is, after all, a dogmatician. He accepts, with Kähler, that the dogmatician's task is evaluating the biblical material. Studying the Bible theologically *is* already dogmatics, for the Bible provides the basic material to be reworked in the present. But the biblical material is not *our* theology, for it belongs to a past age.[15]

However, unlike Weiss, for whom biblical theology is primarily a historical discipline, Ritschl distinguishes between biblical and systematic undertakings but does not want to push them too far apart. After all, it was only accidental that volumes 2 (biblical material) and 3 (constructive, systematic treatment) of *Justification and Reconciliation* appeared separately.[16] Ritschl acknowledges that he is doing history when he reads the Bible, and thereby disclosing religious ideas from the past, but he sees also that engagement with the Bible means engagement with the subject matter of theology. Biblical theology does more than enable a reader to catalogue past ideas: it encourages the reader to ask the ques-

ment—namely, their understanding of the Old Testament—with a further criterion: their essential agreement in Christology. Christological unity is thus a presupposition of their common understanding of the Old Testament.

14. See, e.g., the extract from Ritschl's 1881–82 dogmatics lectures in Schäfer, 193. Cf. also *ARPHJ* II.1.4.

15. This is the sense that should be given to Ritschl's statement (*RV* 2:23) that the New Testament "presents a set of religious trains of thought." For a recent treatment of Kähler on the Bible, see J. C. O'Neill, *The Bible's Authority* (Edinburgh: T & T Clark, 1991), 167–78.

16. See the Foreword (*Vorrede*) to the first edition of *RV* 2.

tion of God in the present. It must do this to be true to the Bible's content.

Ritschl's desire to interpret the Bible for the present relates once more to his keenness to stress the experience and authority of Christian communities in the present.[17] Ritschl envisages a historically rooted but constantly changing living tradition of biblical interpretation. This understanding relates directly to his insistence that Christ is only to be interpreted on the basis of participation within a redeemed community. Consequently also, the Bible is only to be christocentrically interpreted. His attention to historical change is here qualifying the rather static criterion being employed within his Christology. Precisely because he wishes to stress historical particularity over universality,[18] his attention is drawn to the concrete, corporate contexts within which Jesus of Nazareth was and is proclaimed as Christ. A dogmatic interest in biblical interpretation can never make do with a mere restatement of biblical ideas. The task of dogmatic evaluation has to take present corporate religious experience very seriously indeed.

Biblical theology, then, for Ritschl, is Christian theology that takes the Bible as its norm, in the sense that it begins from a perspective of the present experience of Christ within a believing community—a community that stands in continuity with the diverse historical Christian communities that first witnessed to Jesus as Christ. The Bible is thus christocentrically interpreted from the standpoint both of the interpreters (those who experience Christ in the present) and of the text (which points to Christ throughout).[19]

III

We turn next to a critique of Ritschl's position. While the aim of this article is to highlight ways in which Ritschl's approach to theological method may be reappropriated, his position clearly cannot be left unchallenged. Three of its weaknesses and three of its strengths will be presented and explored briefly. On the basis of this critique it will then be possible to state how a modified version of his position may be tenable today.

Ritschl features prominently in John Macquarrie's chapter entitled "Positivist Christology" in *Jesus Christ in Modern Thought,* a chapter title that, Macquarrie states, he decided to use "only after careful consid-

---

17. See especially *ICR,* §3.
18. As stated throughout *TM,* e.g., especially 165, 183, 191, and 193.
19. John Macquarrie referred to Ritschl in a chapter entitled "Existentialist Christology" [in *Christological Perspectives,* ed. R. F. Berkey and S. A. Edwards (New York, 1982)], thus reflecting his uncertainty as to how to categorize Ritschl (see n. 20). Macquarrie is, however, quite right to highlight this aspect of Ritschl's thought. Any Christology is self-involving and therefore open to the charge of subjectivity. The issue is whether merely self-expression is at stake, or whether the Christology is undertaken as communal self-expression in the light of an experience of Christ. Ritschl's undertaking in theology can legitimately be called (Christian) "social existentialism."

eration." By positivism, Macquarrie means "a type of philosophy which deliberately restricts its field of inquiry to the realm of the positive, understood as constituted by observable and testable matters of fact, concerning which we can arrive at fairly reliable conclusions." "So," he continues, "the tendency would be to restrict theology in general and christology in particular to questions of history and ethics."[20] To a certain degree Macquarrie may be reading back from Ritschlianism into Ritschl at this point, but he has nevertheless identified a key weakness of Ritschl's position: his overdependence on history.[21]

Ritschl fails to distinguish clearly history (understood as the course and interrelationship of events) from history writing or historical research (understood as the recording and interpreting of events and enquiry into the records and interpretations thus produced.) This failure further weakens his position. But even in its most basic form—expressed as overdependence on history—this first weakness creates difficulties for Ritschl's construal of Christocentricity. By moving from the decisive, revelatory significance of the historical figure, Jesus of Nazareth, via the assumption that the Gospels contain reliable historical information about him, to the assumption that the Gospels can provide an objective (historical) check for present christological statements, Ritschl is making a number of illegitimate leaps. It will not do, in short, to confuse history with historical record, nor the Gospels with mere historical record. It cannot be assumed that history writing contains or reflects no subjective emphasis.[22] Therefore our understanding of Christocentricity, if it is to be at all a helpful concept in the present, must differ from Ritschl's.

We have noted already how, in practice, Ritschl has laid the foundations for a broader understanding of history, and thus also of Christocentricity. He has done so by recognizing the importance of the historicity of the communities upon which the figure of Jesus exerted an impact. It is along these lines that the reconstrual of Christocentricity as a legitimate and helpful theological approach to the interpretation of the Bible in the present will be made. As it stands, Ritschl's understanding of Christocentricity, though tenable insofar as it highlights that Christology controls theology, is inadequate, due to the rigid historical criterion at its heart.

A second weakness relates directly to the first. Ritschl's overly simple understanding of history and his overdependence on history cause him to overlook *the real, substantive theological differences* that distinguish

20. J. Macquarrie, *Jesus Christ in Modern Thought* (London and Philadelphia: SCM Press/Trinity Press International, 1990), 251.

21. It is striking that O'Neill, *The Bible's Authority,* 234, repeats the History-of-Religions accusation against Ritschl without any qualification (i.e., that Ritschl simply was not historical enough). Even now Ritschl is frequently read either through a Barthian or a Troeltschian critique and is rarely allowed to speak for himself.

22. Ritschl, following Baur, accepts that the Gospels have specific theological "tendencies." But the sureness with which Ritschl deems it possible to identify objective historical data is questionable.

one New Testament author's understanding of the person of Jesus Christ from another's (especially the differences among the evangelists). Ritschl did acknowledge, with Baur, some theological differences among the New Testament authors, but complete unity among them in matters of Christology seems necessary for his own theological position.[23] Since Ritschl, redaction criticism has drawn attention to the diversity of Christologies in the New Testament, a diversity that cannot be sidestepped. Ritschl's failure to explore the potential of his own thoughts—that theological differences do exist in the New Testament—limits the usefulness of his position.

Again, Ritschl's stress on the particularity of communities of the redeemed throughout history allows his position to be revised: on the basis of Ritschl's own premise, christological diversity reflects the way in which Jesus is called Christ in different historical settings. Within the New Testament, therefore, different communities express that theological conviction in diverse, historically contextualized ways. Hence, there is a Matthean Christ, a Johannine Christ, and a Pauline Christ. But it would be quite wrong to suppose that Ritschl has perceived this himself.

Clearly, Ritschl's methodological insistence on the primacy (and implied objectivity) of history has caused him to be restricted in this way. For in stressing the historical importance of Jesus—as objective revelation—Ritschl is in turn prevented from exploring sufficiently the way in which the New Testament authors, via a theological interpretation, appropriate the historical significance of Jesus in new historical settings. Ritschl is, in short, prevented from seeing fully how Christian revelation always operates with respect to at least two poles in history (Jesus' and any present setting), and prevented from respecting adequately the imaginative act of interpretation required to link the two poles within the overarching Christian story.

A recognition of Ritschl's failure adequately to address the existence of theological (including christological) diversity in the New Testament has two consequences: (1) it challenges the certainty with which Ritschl appeals to the historical criterion located at the heart of his Christology (and thus his construal of Christocentricity); (2) it questions the extent to which Ritschl truly permitted his stress on historical particularity over universality to hold sway in his theology.[24]

To clarify a third weakness, it is necessary to spell out how Ritschl uses the philosophy of Kant in his theology. Ritschl's indebtedness to Kant is well known.[25] Less well known is his indebtedness more directly

23. Cf. notes 11 and 13; and for what immediately follows, see, e.g., W. R. Barnett, "Historical Relativism and Christology in the Thought of Wilhelm Dilthey and Albrecht Ritschl" (Ph.D. diss., Chicago, 1976). In essence it is the History-of-Religions School's approach to Ritschl. But Barnett is more sympathetic.

24. There is, in short, an implicit metaphysic [as recognized and uncovered by R. P. Busse, "The Implicit Metaphysical Scheme of Albrecht Ritschl" (Th.D. diss., Lutheran School of Theology at Chicago, 1984)].

25. E.g., Macquarrie, *Jesus Christ in Modern Thought*, 253.

to Lotze and his attention to Lotze's qualification of Kant's position.[26] In brief, Ritschl affirms Kant's basic philosophical viewpoint that humans cannot know "things in themselves." On this basis, abstract speculation must indeed give way to practical commitment. Metaphysics must give way to ethics. In Christology, speculation about the nature of Jesus Christ (for example, using the Chalcedonian definition) must take second place to a consideration of the practical impact of the person of Jesus Christ in human experience.

However, because Ritschl received Kant in part through Lotze, the rather simplified picture just cited must be qualified significantly. Ritschl's late philosophical work, *Theology and Metaphysics,* shows that he does not banish metaphysics entirely from his work as a theologian and had never sought to do so.[27] Ritschl, unlike Kant, did not claim that we are unable to make deductions from what we perceive and experience (the phenomenal) about what really is (the noumenal). He stated, with Lotze, that it is possible to infer back from the phenomenal to the noumenal (though without any guarantee of total accuracy). Like Kant, he does not dispute the existence of the noumenal realm (how could he?), and his Lotzean qualification permits a process of venturing back behind the phenomenal realm. But Ritschl's overarching Kantian framework remains intact to the extent that the phenomenal remains prior and more immediate.

In Christology, therefore, we must begin with the Jesus of history when trying to understand him as the revealer of God. This approach does not mean that the Christ of faith is only an interpretation or that there is nothing behind, beyond, or within the Jesus of history. According to Ritschl, we cannot clarify what is behind or beyond Jesus of Nazareth, called Christ, before we have become clear about him in relation to our present experience of Christ. Ritschl's is truly a Christology from below,[28] in that speculation about his nature from the perspective of God is deemed illegitimate. Discovering who Jesus is from the point of view of Jesus' and our historical particularity is the correct approach.

However, even accepting that such a Christology from below is a legitimate exercise, Ritschl's epistemology needs closer attention. Its limitations contribute the third main weakness in his theological position, which can now be formulated: Ritschl *has a weak ontology at the heart of his Christology.* By "ontology" here I mean an account of "what re-

26. Paul Wrzecionko, *Die philosophischen Wurzeln der Theologie Albrecht Ritschls* (Berlin: Alfred Töpelmann, 1964), remains the best study.
27. Even if the text—as J. Draper ("The Place of the Bible in the Theology of Albrecht Ritschl" [Ph.D. diss., Durham, England, 1984], 7f.), following Wrzecionko, points out—also reveals that Ritschl is no great philosopher!
28. Pannenberg has noted this of Ritschl [*Jesus—God and Man* (London: SCM Press, 1968), 36f.]. When Ritschl explicitly follows Luther (e.g., in *TM,* 152f. and *JR* 3:399), the argument "from below" is, of course, quite different from what has recently been meant by "Christology from below."

ally is" in a transcendent, nonmaterial sense about the person of Jesus. Because Jesus, like any human being, is not simply the sum either of bodily parts or sense experiences, some account of who he is in relation to God is required. More than this, however, if Jesus called Christ may in any sense be said to be present with believers now, then an explanation of the ground of such experience as spiritual reality is essential, lest it be claimed that the Christian phenomenon be explicable solely in terms of the impact of a (past) historical figure.[29]

In failing to recognize the impact of his overdependence on history, Ritschl fails to venture far beyond the phenomenal realm. In both theory and practice, he insufficiently permits the more speculative, metaphysical aspect of the theological task (the "speaking from God," to use Bultmann's phrase) to play much of a role. His apologetic tract *Theology and Metaphysics* (1881; 2d ed. 1887) displays a tendency toward the antimetaphysical, while also revealing that Ritschl is fully aware that theology cannot possibly dispense with metaphysics altogether.

Ritschl's Christology does not, in fact, collapse into mere functionalism. His stress on a present, corporate experience of Christ[30] itself indicates that ontology is not absent from the method and content of his thought. But as far as the two particular concepts under scrutiny in this article are concerned, this weakness in ontology means that Ritschl is prone to construe the theological task with insufficient attention to the depth and particularity of believers' experience of Jesus as Christ in both past and present. This tendency is ironical, given his emphasis upon present, communal experience. But it is striking that Ritschl appears nowhere to explore *the way in which* the figure of Jesus is actually able to function as the *fortwirkende Kraft* (continuing power or abiding force) for the Christian community in any age, in any sense other than a memory.[31] He clearly expects that continuity in Christian life depends on more than a mere mental image. An ontology is implicit in this expectation, but Ritschl fails to spell out what he means.[32]

29. Ritschl's epistemological shortcomings have long been noted in Ritschl studies, especially in older critical work, e.g., by A. E. Garvie and James Orr. The short definition of ontology here is not meant to resolve the complex philosophical question whether Christianity—and specifically Christology—must always lean on Plato's thought in formulating an adequate ontology. It is, however, meant to indicate that a response must be found to forms of postmodernism that would consign all ontological deliberation to the garbage can. As a "modern" (i.e., post-Kantian) theologian, Ritschl is rightly cautious about claiming too much in the realm of metaphysics. As a Christian theologian, he cannot be satisfied with the view that "phenomena," or even "signs," are all we have. For a bold defense of ontology in the face of the postmodernist challenge, see, e.g., Huston Smith, "Postmodernism's Impact on the Study of Religion," *Journal of the American Academy of Religion* 58 (1990): 653–70.

30. And the fact that Ritschl's christocentric theology depends on readings of the corporate experiences of Christ reflected in Mark's and John's Gospels particularly (see *ARPHJ*).

31. *JR* 3:387 (German text *RV* 2, 2d ed., 360). This is, to my knowledge, the nearest Ritschl comes to clarifying *how* Christ relates to believers in the present.

32. I am convinced that there would be value in gaining a clear understanding of the meanings of the word *Bild* (picture/image) as used in German Protestant Christology in the

In other words: Ritschl's Christocentricity, in being focused solely on the historical person of Jesus of Nazareth, does not appear to include a sufficient account of the historical and existential impact of the person of Jesus on those who followed and follow him. The particularity of the communities which believers belong(ed) to and form(ed) and within which Jesus is actually experienced as Christ is given insufficient weight. Ritschl's existentialism, though it rescued him from mere positivism, is left underdeveloped.[33]

Three weaknesses have now been spelled out. These are, I contend, the main weaknesses of Ritschl's position that bear on the concepts of Christocentricity and community. In his overdependence on history, his failure to attend to pluralism, and his weakness in ontology, Ritschl places too much emphasis upon historical data about Jesus of Nazareth in relation to the particular (but ill-defined) "first community" of followers. As a result of the first two weaknesses, Ritschl fails to allow historical particularity to play its full part. The specific, concrete character of the many diverse Christian communities recording and expressing the impact of the figure of Jesus the Christ upon them (in past and present) is left insufficiently explored. In turn, and as a consequence of the third weakness, the way in which Christ as the ground of all experience of God is encountered in new, diverse historical contexts is inadequately expounded and explained.

There are, however, a number of strengths in Ritschl's theological position. To these we now turn.

IV

Three strengths that have a bearing on our central question—what understanding of biblical theology is possible today?—will now be considered.

1. *Ritschl's emphasis upon the corporate nature of faith experience, biblical interpretation, and theological construction.* Ritschl's stress upon the importance of interpreting Jesus as the Christ from the perspective of the redeemed community has already been mentioned. It was noted how this emphasis qualifies the (historical) objectivity sought through the christocentric focus of his theology. More specifically, Ritschl's understanding of Christocentricity is in practice broadened to

period 1850–1920. See my "Defining Christianity after Ritschl: History, Theology and the 'Picture of Jesus' in Late Nineteenth Century Protestant Thought" [*Papers of the American Academy of Religion Nineteenth Century Theology Working Group*, ed. S. Briggs and R. P. Busse (Berkeley, 1989), 71–85] for a preliminary sketch. Gadamer's discussion of the ontological value of the picture [*Truth and Method*, 2d ed. (London: Sheed and Ward, 1979)] should be noted here.

33. But his existentialism is, therefore, important nevertheless (cf. n. 19 above). His actual dependence on the theology of particular evangelists (cf. n. 30) also enables him in the end to evade the simple charge of positivism. His *practice,* if not his theory, shows him operating with a canon within the canon and indicates a way forward for a Christian theology construed biblically.

include the impact of the person of Jesus Christ upon any given present community of the redeemed. Ritschl is striving for objectivity (via his stress on the earthly Jesus), thus seeking to ensure that Christian tradition is not merely a matter of passing on in-house language relating to private experience. The Christian tradition is available in principle to any discerning enquirer. What is said about Jesus in faith is consistent with what is known historically; it is not a preposterous fabrication. At the same time, Ritschl wishes to take seriously actual lived religious experience and to do this without overindividualizing the attention given to religious experience.[34] His experiential emphasis, therefore, focuses on the redeemed community, for here Christ is discovered and Christ's identity is explored.

As we have seen, though he extends this observation neither far enough (that is, back in the New Testament) nor deep enough (that is, by asking what ontologically binds together any common experience of Jesus as Christ through history and across diverse cultures), Ritschl does want to take current, corporate Christian experience seriously. For Ritschl, theology is, in the first instance, reflection on the experience of Jesus Christ gained within the believing community. This reflection takes place with reference to that present experience, referring to the Bible and historical research, with Jesus Christ at the heart of both the immediate experience and the reflective task undertaken.[35]

When considering this strength in relation to our prime concern— what does Ritschl have to teach us about biblical theology in the present?—we can see that the Bible functions as a check for a theology begun on other grounds, namely the experience of Christ in a corporate setting. To talk of biblical theology means, therefore, to talk of a Christian theology measured against biblical material, which functions as a record of earliest Christian experience.

2. *Ritschl's recognition of the need to stand in a particular tradition in order to undertake any interpretation at all.* Related to the importance of a corporate experience and reflective community is Ritschl's stress on a continuity through history provided by a corporate, reflective community. Through his focus upon his own participation within the Pauline-Lutheran tradition of Christianity, Ritschl demonstrates the need to identify historical roots and continuity. This continuity, as Hefner has shown, is not simply a matter of thoughts and ideas, but a way of living. Christian faith is for Ritschl both a theory for life and a praxis for living.[36]

---

34. The root of his charge against Pietism. Ritschl's stance toward Pietism is worth further enquiry. Why someone who seemed to be so hostile to the movement should spend so much time and so many words (three volumes of over 1,600 pages) writing about it deserves adequate explanation. At this stage I can only conclude that his stance displays a clear case of *Haßliebe.*

35. In this Ritschl acknowledges his debt to Schleiermacher (e.g., *JR* 1:443f., 445f., and *TM,* 199f.).

36. Hefner.

Because he does not want to stress universals, however, Ritschl must find a norm for choosing between diverse, and perhaps conflicting, construals of Christianity. Through the historically continuous (and, it is also assumed, theologically accurate) Pauline-Lutheran tradition Ritschl himself finds such a norm. "Getting Christianity right" in the present becomes a matter of conforming to the way in which this tradition has understood Christianity. Behind this theological judgment, Ritschl believes, is a historico-theological conclusion: that Pauline Christianity represents the legitimate development of primitive Christianity.[37]

Ritschl has been criticized for trying to construe Christian continuity in this way. H. Richard Niebuhr has been especially critical of Ritschl's approach, noting its apparent absorption of Christ into culture. Locating Christian continuity so closely with cultural continuity does not appear to leave room for Christian faith to be critical of that culture (we might add: critical of ecclesiastical culture in particular).[38] Rupp is less censorious, recognizing in Ritschl's theology "impressive resources for critical engagement with culture."[39] Ritschl's concern to locate the discovery of religious truth firmly in the particulars of history and human culture is not, then, a sellout to whatever form of Christianity one chooses or whatever form happens to be the order of the day. Ritschl is simply respecting the fact that Christianity—as any religion—has no option but to operate within a specific culture.

The decisive point to note here is that the resources in Ritschl's theology that permit a critique of culture—Christian culture included—are precisely those that militate against the particularity he so keenly wants to stress. For example, Jesus as Christ offers a critique of all our time-bound, historically rooted attempts to understand him; the kingdom of God—as a supramundane concept—judges all our efforts to embody it, the church especially.

Ritschl thus highlights in practice the tension between the particular and the universal with which all Christian theology struggles. His insistence on the priority of the particular should, however, be deemed a strength, even if his failure to attend adequately to universals (a matter that a concern for ontology instantly raises) has created problems. This emphasis on continuity through the particularities of history serves as a reminder that religion is not primarily about ideas, but about living.[40]

---

37. Though Petrine Christianity is not devalued in the way that F. C. Baur's thesis had suggested. The two versions of Ritschl's account are found in the two editions of *EK* (1850 and 1857).

38. Niebuhr, 91–101.

39. Rupp, 48.

40. In the light of the way that understandings of the doctrine of the incarnation have developed (especially recently), it could now be suggested that a stress on incarnation would have enhanced Ritschl's position at this point. Ritschl seems unable to explore incarnation independently of the Chalcedonian definition.

Turning once more to our immediate task (what might "biblical theology" mean?), it becomes clear that to stand in a hermeneutical tradition is not to be bound by that tradition. Rather, to stand in a hermeneutical tradition means that one's present construal of Christian faith cannot be self-authenticating. A theology is not formulated by simply restating biblical (especially New Testament) ideas, nor by expressing any current corporate faith. Theology attempts to express the significance of an experience of God (understood in Christian terms as the present experience of God in Christ) through a specific, identifiable tradition and culture of faith, with reference back to the Bible. All three elements—experience, tradition, Scripture—are essential. Though logical priority remains on the historically particular in the present—where God in Christ is concretely experienced in a particular believing community— both the biblical reference and the channel for biblical interpretation are equally important. The reference back to the Bible is undertaken diachronically through a specific theological and cultural channel. This theological and cultural channel—the "hermeneutical tradition"—offers a way of assessing and, as necessary, adjusting fresh expressions of experiences of Christ. Ritschl is advocating the channel of the Reformed (especially Lutheran) tradition as the best means of construing theology and of understanding the Bible.[41]

3. *Ritschl's conviction that practice and commitment do matter in theology.* Being keen to stress the particular over the universal, Ritschl also wants to demonstrate the concrete significance of Christian faith in the way that people live. It is, in short, no surprise that Ritschl should be accused of reducing theology to ethics. But it is also no surprise that Ritschl's theology should have had discernible effects upon the Social Gospel movements and through to liberation theologies (as testified elsewhere in this volume).

Ritschl's orientation toward praxis is striking. Yet despite this orientation, Ritschl does not seem fully aware of the explosive potential of his theological approach. He could not, for example, have foreseen the way in which the attention he gave to the kingdom of God—the way he understood the concept, and the basis upon which his understanding rested—would prove so influential (positively through the Social Gospel,

41. In personal correspondence, Darrell Jodock has helpfully challenged my reading of Ritschl at this point. Accepting that the Pauline-Lutheran tradition is especially important for Ritschl does not mean that he simply assumes that Lutheran ecclesiastical culture should be the form in which the content of faith is best received or expressed. When turning from a consideration of the theological tradition within which Ritschl seeks to work to a broader understanding of a hermeneutical tradition, it is more accurate to point to Ritschl's dependence on the broader Reformation tradition, given how much he drew on other Reformers and how he supported the Union Church in his own day. The difficulty of a tension between a confessional base and a broader, ecumenical outlook is, however, a problem for any Christian even today. The fact remains that Ritschl was more Lutheran than Reformed in terms of his own church affiliation.

negatively through Johannes Weiss) upon the future of Protestant theology. Be that as it may, since Ritschl the kingdom of God has been at the forefront of discussions about the place of ethical activity in the Christian life.[42]

Considering once more our immediate concern—that of the significance of this strength of Ritschl's thought for an understanding of biblical theology—it becomes apparent that Ritschl's approach tends toward highlighting relevance and practical usefulness in biblical interpretation. Though these emphases cannot strictly be called criteria for biblical interpretation, as liberation theologies above all have shown and as any adequate account of the relationship between theology and ethics must always show, a theology that cannot be lived is worthless.

Lazy formulations of such emphases would continue the misreadings of Ritschl that have adversely influenced Ritschl study for so long. Ritschl's practical emphasis by no means results in a selection from the biblical material on the basis of sheer expediency, any more than it produces the sheer Christianization of current cultural forms.[43]

This strength does, however, relate to Ritschl's taking seriously both the audience of the biblical text in the present and his own audience as a theologian. In terms of reader-response criticism, Ritschl is taking the "real reader" of both the Bible and his own work into account. This is hardly surprising for one who was keen to stress the importance of the religious experience of the present Christian community. But here the stress on relevance and practical usefulness is pressed further: the real readers themselves have needs and questions that must be addressed through their contact with the Bible itself and the living tradition through which the Bible is interpreted and in which they, as real readers, stand.

Again to speak in current terms rather than in terms contemporary to Ritschl, we can see that the respect for contextualization in all theological construction is vital. Ritschl's desire to let the Bible "speak"—while not pretending it can do this easily across many centuries—and his desire to defend the relevance of Christian theology in his day take him into realms currently occupied by many forms of liberation and "minority discourse" theologies.[44]

Ritschl's position does not, however, leave unanswered the question of how—in response to the many conflicting demands of the present moment, and the differing contexts that create diverse theologies—decisions

---

42. E.g., *TM*, 194; *ICR*, §§46–77; and *JR* 3, §§62–68. See also Walter Wyman, Jr., "The Kingdom of God in Germany: From Ritschl to Troeltsch," in *Revisioning the Past: Prospects in Historical Theology,* ed. Mary Potter Engel and Walter E. Wyman, Jr. (Minneapolis: Fortress Press, 1992), 257–77.

43. The latter being, in essence, Barth's accusation.

44. The continuity between Ritschl's theology and liberation theologies (see n. 19) now becomes apparent.

might be made about legitimate continuity in Christian theology. His theology is not one of Liberal indifference. Its practical concern made Ritschl's theology relevant and persuasive in his time. A reconstrual of the norms he sought to build into his theology can again inform our current attempts to find a path through the many theological discourses of our own time.

To the reconstrual of Christocentricity and community as norms for a biblical theology in the present, then, we now turn.

V

In the light of the presentation and critique of Ritschl's use of Christocentricity and community as norms within his biblical theology, it is now necessary to assess whether Ritschl's approach can be adapted and adopted in the present. I contend that it can be appropriated in revised form.

Clearly, Christocentricity can no longer be construed in terms of a direct correspondence between historical data about Jesus of Nazareth and theological claims about Jesus as the Christ. Ritschl's criterion collapses on at least two grounds: (1) it assumes that the historical theologian can be confident enough in the results of her or his historical research to use such findings as an objective norm for theology; (2) it effectively makes theology dependent on the findings of historical research. Any understanding of Christocentricity for today must, therefore, relate less to historical-critical criteria strictly applied to the biblical material and much more to the practical impact of the figure of Jesus of Nazareth, witnessed to as Christ, in past and present. Historical concerns are far from disregarded, but they do not control the construal of Jesus as the Christ in the way that Ritschl seems to suggest. Because Ritschl in practice did not adhere strictly to his own implied method (that is, he attached great weight to present, corporate religious experience over and above what could, in fact, be checked out against an objective, historical norm), his approach itself offers clues for a way forward.

Christocentricity is best explored by a reconsideration of what, at root, Ritschl was trying to achieve through his radical (if overstated) historically rigid Christocentrism. Ritschl was seeking to insist that knowledge about God is based exclusively on the revelation of God, by God, and that that revelation is normed by the person of Jesus Christ. Ritschl himself extended this emphasis to mean a rejection of all forms of natural theology. He was keen to demonstrate that any genuine knowledge of God is not a result of metaphysical speculation but of personal encounter. Revelation was therefore paramount.

There is no reason in the present to move away from this emphasis upon the priority of revelation, even if it may be necessary to stress that such revelatory positivism need not be construed quite in Ritschl's manner or that of the early Barth.[45]

One marked shift is, however, called for, in that Christocentricity needs to undergo a change of focus so that what is *included* in the concept is more central than what is *excluded*. The concept needs to be rescued from its function in Ritschl's theology as a counter to natural theology and made a theological key by which the Bible (as "classic" past Christian tradition) and present theological formulations (current attempts to spell out who God is and what God is doing) are to be read and evaluated. "Christocentricity" thus denotes the centrality of a particular understanding of God: one who shares at the deepest level of human experience, suffers to the uttermost, is not overcome in death, promotes relationship, builds a kingdom founded on love and justice. At root a christocentric approach to both Bible and theology thus attempts to enter the circle of interpretation set up by the impact of the person of Jesus upon the ongoing understanding of God preserved within the Christian tradition, an impact that directed and now functions as a norm for that understanding of God. A Christocentrism formulated in this way better enables Christ to be the touchstone of faith.[46]

We can clarify such an understanding of Christocentricity in four ways. Christocentricity must be construed *experientially, ontologically, eschatologically,* and *across faiths.*

The *experiential* construal of Christocentricity means that the particularity of an encounter with the living Christ is to be located in the present and not simply in the life and times of Jesus of Nazareth.[47] The biblical records are part of the cycle of interpretation that verifies current encounters with Christ. Conversely, fresh encounters with Christ provide a new (and always corporate) christocentric focus for the understanding of the Bible.

That such present encounters with Christ—the ways in which we understand God being present with us by God's Spirit—are more than mental exercises reminds us of the necessity to explore the *ontological* character of Christocentricity. Here Ritschl's weakness is brought to mind and corrected. The way in which God in Christ is experienced in the present takes us beyond the realm of recollection or mere thought. Experiences of the living Christ rest on a ground that both informs the

45. Despite all Barth's protestations to be breaking totally with his teachers, there is continuity with Ritschl here, as Richmond has noted. See also S. Fisher, *Revelatory Positivism?*

46. See above, n. 2. The enquiry has thus shown that the issue between "foundation" and "touchstone" relates to the distinction between the historical ("back there") versus "the ongoing historically particular" ("here and now") that Ritschl never quite resolved.

47. This is neither an argument for an idealist, abstract Christ nor a way of reducing "Christ" to a formula, but a recognition that Christology by definition understands Jesus of Nazareth theologically and thus interprets his life as part of a larger theological whole.

aesthetic and moral dimensions of human life and provides intellectual stimulus to theologians.[48] Reference to moral and aesthetic dimensions does not of itself entail ontology. Postmodernism has shown this. But because Christology demands an account of the ground upon which present experiences of Christ rest, then a "relatively adequate" Christology (Tracy!)—and a present construal of Christocentricity—will be ontological.

The present Christ—as the God who has come—reminds us, too, of the God who is yet to come, in the sense that no one has wholly grasped God. Christocentricity also needs, therefore, to be construed *eschatologically* as a reminder that all interpretations of God, as known in and in relation to Christ, fall short. We have enough to go on. God has revealed more than enough of God's very self for us to grasp what salvation is about. But no Christology is wholly adequate. And none wholly plumbs the depths of a present encounter with Christ.

Finally, Christocentricity must be construed *across faiths*. This article is not the place for detailed enquiry into this highly complex question. Yet the point is worth making that just as the church is always subject to the judgment of God, whose will is to usher the kingdom into the world (where God reigns is always beyond where Christians might think God reigns), so also a Christian perception of where Christ in the present might be is always under the judgment of a God who in Christ might speak beyond Christianity. "Christocentricity" is thus not to be construed in a narrow ecclesiastical manner.[49]

As far as an understanding of biblical theology is concerned, this fourfold construal of Christocentricity means that the Bible is best understood—and Christian theology is therefore best undertaken in relation to the Bible—where persons are open to new understandings of where Christ is and what Christ is doing, even beyond Christianity.

In order to explore further how the movement back and forth between Jesus of Nazareth and his impact upon ongoing experience and understanding of God in Christ works out in practice, it is necessary to draw on the second key to interpreting the Bible theologically, that is, community.

God can only be christocentrically understood: that is a basic Christian contention which has logical priority even over a doctrine of the Trinity.[50] Such Christocentricity must be understood corporately. Only a

48. Following W. Herrmann, some sense of the distinction between the (ontological) "ground" and the "content" of faith vis-à-vis the person of Jesus Christ must be made.

49. The achievement of Kenneth Cragg's difficult but stimulating book, *The Christ and the Faiths* (London: SPCK, 1986), is that it tackles precisely this question. Cragg's concern to explore the way in which "Jesus as the Christ can be studied both as the crux of Christology and also as the touchstone of all faiths" (5) and his exploration of Judaism primarily through "Messiah and peoplehood" (chaps. 5 and 6) are especially interesting.

50. The recent collection of essays, *Christian Uniqueness Reconsidered*, ed. G. D'Costa (Maryknoll, N.Y. Orbis, 1990), is to be welcomed for its willingness to adopt a modified—

people who have entered into relationship with God can know what it means to hold to a christocentric doctrine of God. Ritschl saw this clearly. Unclarity resulted when he did not fully work out the distinction that had to be drawn between church and kingdom. If God in Christ is encountered only by those who stand within the redeemed community, and yet the kingdom of God and the church are not simply to be identified, then Ritschl must clarify what the "redeemed community" actually is. This he does not do.

Other essays in this book deal with Ritschl's understanding of community and its impact upon current theological thinking in greater depth than is possible here. I focus on one aspect of community that seems required as a result of our conversation with Ritschl.

Ritschl's orientation toward praxis, and his stress upon the kingdom of God as a "supernatural," "supramundane," and meta-ecclesial concept that includes that emphasis upon praxis, suggests that his understanding of the redeemed community certainly relates to those who do God's will through love of God and neighbor. He seems to imply that such love may constitute unwitting membership of Christ's community. Understandably, this implication has caused problems for Ritschl's theology, because his critics claim to have found here his Achilles heel. Ritschl is either reducing Christianity to ethics, or he is not making, in fact, a real distinction between church and kingdom. For if the kingdom consists of those who are aware of membership of Christ's community, what is that if not the church?

Another reading is, however, possible, a reading that links directly with the sketch of Christocentricity just offered and makes sense of Ritschl's exploration of the distinction between kingdom and church. What must fall by the wayside, if we are to follow this reading and maintain a radical Christocentricity, is Ritschl's rigid separation of Christianity from other faiths.[51] If we understand as Christ's community those who do the will of God by means of loving God and neighbor—with all that that entails—(as Ritschl appears to do),[52] and if we maintain the church/kingdom distinction, then Christocentricity might inform our quest for a concomitant understanding of community that can function adequately as a norm for biblical theology.

Christ is, in short, the one who creates the community of the kingdom of God. But we only know what the kingdom of God is because our understanding both of the kingdom and of Christ is guided by the impact of Jesus of Nazareth. Christocentrism has driven us toward

non-triumphalist—inclusivism vis-à-vis other faiths. Five chapters consider Christology from this perspective; four choose rather to begin from a trinitarian standpoint.

51. *JR* 3, §27. Ritschl is here developing a general understanding of religion yet is distinguishing Christianity from it.

52. E.g., *ICR*, §5.

Jesus of Nazareth, and only toward the church insofar as the church keeps alive in living memory Jesus as the Christ. Christocentrism drives us beyond the church to where Christ in the present creates new forms of community in which the kingdom of God is evident. This construal of community is consistent with Ritschl, while requiring of him a reduction in his religiocentrism. Ritschl needs, in short, to be less rather than more church-centered to enable his sharp perception of the importance of corporate Christocentrism to carry its full weight.

What do these insights mean for an understanding of biblical theology? Simply this: Christian theology is best done—and the Bible best understood—from a standpoint at which people corporately embody that for which Jesus of Nazareth stood. In this corporate context, where Christocentricity and community meet, there God as known in and through Jesus who is called Christ will inform the reading of the Bible being undertaken.

Such corporate contexts may, of course, be churches (that is, identifiable Christian communities). Some groups may, however, have inherited kingdom values embedded in a particular culture or have discovered them through hard experience. Such groups, which reflect the presence of Christ and yet are not identifiably Christian, might well be settings in which theology is or could be done. From a Christian point of view, however, the biblical focus would be decisive for the circle of interpretation to be set properly in motion.[53]

This understanding of corporate Christocentrism also addresses Ritschl's failure to acknowledge the christological pluralism in the New Testament. Acknowledgment of the particularity of different contexts reminds us that Christ has, of necessity, to be understood in different ways. In turn, the New Testament reveals itself to be a pluriform norm, supporting many—but not necessarily all—interpretations ventured of Jesus as the Christ.

VI

What understanding of biblical theology is possible today? To summarize: all Christian theology is, and must be, biblical, in the sense that it must inevitably find its key themes confirmed and supported in the Bible and, through a living tradition, be able to specify the conceptual link between a biblical idea and a current formulation. The Bible does not "control" present formulations in the sense of unduly limiting the explo-

---

53. Ritschl himself sees that worship needs ethical action in order to be complete (*ICR*, 266f., n. 18), and that action needs reflection (to be made aware of its motivation in God). One might, therefore, conclude with justification that the "point" of reading the Bible is to prompt theological reflection: to enable those who strive for peace and justice and all for which the kingdom of God stands to dare to ask the question of God in the midst of their human activity. Ritschl's emphasis on Christocentricity then reminds such readers that daring to pose the question of God *must* entail perceiving God as known in Jesus Christ.

ration of the key theological themes supported by it. It does, however, function normatively by providing for theological interpreters parameters within which the exploration of those key themes is possible.

The Bible's diversity permits broad parameters to operate, for no Christian theology can hope to relate to the whole of the Bible. Any theology must relate to part of it and be able to show that its "reading" addresses and takes account of the Bible's central subject matter: God as revealed.

Our discussion of Ritschl's own theology has led us to Christocentricity and community as two theological themes derived from the Bible which we must consistently use and understand afresh. In any corporate setting in which the question of God is posed or presupposed, there Christian faith offers a corporate christocentric rereading of its foundational texts, read through the present experience of Christians in community, where Christ is believed to be currently present.

This activity of doing theology through biblical interpretation in constant interaction with living corporate experience is never complete, nor is it an exclusive discipline. Christ is always bigger than Christians believe. In this sense, then, theology has a much more radical ecumenical agenda than Ritschl himself ever envisaged.

PART THREE

Christian Community and the Kingdom of God

5

Ritschl's Doctrine of Christian Community

RICH M. WALL, JR.

Was Ritschl the typical bourgeois of his era? In order to answer the question, one must examine the criticisms of the neoorthodox theologians, since they were the first to pose the question. Such an examination will comprise Part I of this essay. A second part will consider the objections of those who would defend Ritschl against the neoorthodox charge. In this connection, a brief discussion of the so-called "Ritschl Renaissance" is in order. At the end of Part II, I will advance the thesis that Ritschl's doctrine of Christian community is actually better suited to the task of recovering Ritschl's own practical intentions than is his doctrine of the kingdom of God. Part III is more historical in nature and will attempt to carry forth the suggestions of the second section— namely, to investigate the practical intentions imbedded within Ritschl's doctrine of Christian community. Part IV will then critically examine the political implications of those intentions, while Part V will assess Ritschl's significance for the contemporary study of theology. The final section will offer some brief concluding observations.

I

Over the century that now separates us from Ritschl's death, Albrecht Ritschl's theological legacy has certainly been variously interpreted by the many authors who have attempted to assess the significance of this late nineteenth-century figure. The general historical influence that Ritschl exercised upon his immediate contemporaries in pre–World War Germany is beyond doubt. Though one should not exaggerate either the importance or the extent of later "Ritschlianism," it may still be said that by the end of Ritschl's own life in 1889, one could look out over the German academic world and count at least one disciple of his for every university in the land, with the sole exception of the University of Heidelberg.

Among the later "Ritschlians" can be numbered such famous churchmen as Wilhelm Herrmann, Adolf von Harnack, Julius Kaftan, Theodor Häring (Ritschl's own successor at the University of Göttingen), Johannes Gottschick, Martin Rade, Ferdinand Kattenbusch, and Otto Kirn. Their assessment of Ritschl, though often critical, was nonetheless always appreciative. Perhaps the most laudatory, and also the most famous, of Ritschl's earliest pupils was Adolf von Harnack, who extolled his former mentor for the great energy, almost compulsive at times, with which he endeavored to comprehend the essence of the Christian religion in itself and in its historical and ecclesiastical development up to the modern era, even venturing the opinion that one should rank him with the theological greats, from Origen and Augustine to Schleiermacher.[1] Harnack's appreciation of Ritschl went beyond the merely historical, however, and embraced his entire interpretation of the Christian religion:

> Ritschl's uniqueness, following Luther, consisted solely in this: that he looked upon religion, and above all the Christian religion, as a powerful reality in and for itself, distinguishing it from every philosophy; further, that he strongly emphasized its historical-positive nature and thereby repudiated speculations over the so-called "natural religion and theology"; that he also held together faith and ethics in closest union; and, finally, that he employed the specific characterization of the Christian religion in the chief confessional traditions as the most important key for a more profound understanding of Christianity. This originality of his theological thinking dominated both the major works and all the individual essays which he composed during the height of his powers.[2]

Given this rather sanguine interpretation of Ritschl's accomplishments by one of this century's most highly regarded church historians, it seems incredible that Karl Barth, himself one of Adolf von Harnack's most promising students and, in the eyes of many today, this generation's greatest theologian, should declare only ten years later that Ritschl has the significance of an episode in more recent theology, and not, indeed not, that of an epoch.[3] What could possibly account for this radical shift in mood and interpretation? To be sure, Barth did not care for the easy optimism and self-sufficiency with which Ritschl dismissed many of the burning historical questions relating to the Scriptures and the Christian

---

1. Adolf von Harnack, "Albrecht Ritschl: Rede zum hundertsten Geburtstag am 30. April 1922 in Bonn gehalten," *Erforschtes und Erlebtes.* In *Reden und Aufsätze,* new ed. (Gieszen: Alfred Töpelmann, 1923), 4:335.
2. Harnack, "Albrecht Ritschl: Rede zum hundertsten Geburtstag," 335–36.
3. From a 1932 lecture on Ritschl delivered at the University of Bonn, and later compiled with other lectures in Barth, 654–61. The quoted passage may be found on p. 654.

tradition. But this can hardly explain the severity of Barth's attack, since many of Ritschl's own disciples voiced this same concern over the latter's "biblicism" and "historicism."[4] On the contrary, Barth's rather negative assessment of Ritschl's theological legacy appears to have been motivated by more practical concerns, as he himself admits in a 1957 lecture on Protestant theology in the nineteenth century:

> For me personally a day in the beginning of August in that year [1914] has impressed itself as the *dies ater*. It is the day on which 93 German intellectuals published a profession of support for the war policy of Kaiser Wilhelm II. Included among the signers I was shocked to have to see the names of pretty much all my teachers-theologians whom I had until then loyally honored. Having been estranged from their ethos, I observed that I would also no longer be able to follow their ethics and dogmatics, their exegesis and historical interpretation. For me in any case the theology of the nineteenth century had no future any more.[5]

For these very practical, indeed political, reasons Barth launched his historical attack upon Ritschl as the very epitome of the national-liberal German bourgeois of the age of Bismarck.[6] He explains further:

> With Ritschl reconciliation, to put it baldly, means the realized ideal of human life. It is the intended result of justification. All Ritschl's thinking springs from this result. . . . The quintessence of the task imposed upon man, which at the same time is his highest good and his own final aim, is the kingdom of God, in which the love of one's neighbour is activated. But the kingdom of God can only be lived for within the communities which have been naturally determined, particularly in the regular working activity of one's moral profession, and not outside them, so that loyalty to one's profession is at once the true fulfilment of the model of Christ.[7]

Many other "neoorthodox" and "dialectical" theologians joined in Barth's criticism of Ritschl. But perhaps the most noteworthy on the American scene was H. Richard Niebuhr, who styled Ritschl as the most "representative" of the "Christ-of-Culture" type, the second of five such

4. Wilhelm Herrmann, another of Barth's teachers, certainly did not share Harnack's laudatory assessment of Ritschl, especially when it came to ranking Ritschl with the great Friedrich Schleiermacher. According to Herrmann, "Ritschl did not seem cognizant of the fact that he had not attained the greatness of Schleiermacher. We are grateful to him for what he has given us. But we would be doing him an injustice if we were to fail to acknowledge the limitations by which he lagged far behind the humanity and free-spiritedness of the great Schleiermacher." From "Albrecht Ritschl, seine Grösse und seine Schranke," in *Festgabe von Fachgenossen und Freunden A. von Harnack zum siebzigsten Geburtstag dargebracht,* ed. Karl Holl (Tübingen, 1921), 406.

5. This lecture was delivered to the Goethe Society in Hannover in January of 1957. It is reprinted in Karl Barth, *Die protestantische Theologie im 19. Jahrhundert* (Hamburg: Siebenstern Taschenbuch, 1975), 2:572–90. The quoted passage is from pp. 574–75.

6. Barth, 656.

7. Ibid., 657–58.

types which he developed in *Christ and Culture*. What Niebuhr meant by the "Christ-of-Culture" type was an accommodation of the Christ who is confessed to the culture in which one must live. He believed Ritschl to be its premier example inasmuch as his theology, while containing certain dualities, never really contemplated any serious division between Christ and culture, forgiveness of sin and ethical striving for perfection, Christian community and ethical society, Christian calling and Christian vocation. According to Niebuhr, however, it was largely by means of the idea of the kingdom of God that Ritschl achieved the complete reconciliation of Christianity and culture.[8] For the kingdom of God, as portrayed in Ritschl's writings, represented nothing less than the synthesis of the great values esteemed by democratic culture: the freedom and intrinsic worth of individuals, social cooperation, and universal peace.[9]

One of the great ironies of history has been that the fate of German Liberalism has depended upon the successes of neoorthodoxy, for even now many within the neoorthodox camp, or just outside it, find it difficult to appreciate the positive dimensions of Liberal theology. They are continually haunted by a host of questions. For example, why should one bother to study Ritschl, inasmuch as his conceptualizations are hopelessly bourgeois? Indeed, why bother to study nineteenth-century theology at all? What could one possibly learn from this period that would be of any benefit today, in a world rife with gross injustice, class warfare, and environmental disintegration? Perhaps such questions *should* haunt us. But the intense depreciation of the past that these questions suggest can become, and has in fact become, counterproductive to the task of constructively reappropriating the Christian tradition (and, yes, even the Liberal tradition) for theology today.

With the waning interest in neoorthodoxy over the last thirty years, however, there has arisen the genuinely novel prospect of evaluating Ritschl from a more objective standpoint. One begins to wonder, for example, whether Barth's assessment of Ritschl was not excessively motivated and mediated by his contact with such later "Ritschlians" as Adolf von Harnack and Wilhelm Herrmann, rather than with Ritschl himself. Of course, one must admit that, if taken individually, many expressions in Ritschl's own works would appear to justify the neoorthodox critique, and I do not mean to detract from these. One thinks, for example, of Ritschl's rather lofty estimation of the German national state as the necessary precondition for the realization of the kingdom of God in his *Instruction in the Christian Religion* §61:

> The state is acknowledged as God's ordering, and obedience to judicial authority is prescribed as a religious duty. This is because the community of laws, being a necessary means for securing ethical freedom, is also the in-

8. Niebuhr, 98.
9. Ibid., 99.

dispensable condition for the Christian, if he is to fulfill the imperative of the kingdom of God in all the spheres of ethical interaction.[10]

Or, with regard to one's civic vocation, Ritschl's remarks in *The Christian Doctrine of Justification and Reconciliation,* vol. 3, §68:

> Moral activity in our calling [vocation] is the form in which our life-work as a totality is produced as our contribution to the kingdom of God, and in which, at the same time, the ideal of spiritual personality as a whole in its own order is reached.[11]

One gathers the impression that Ritschl was simply incapable of envisioning any other societal form by which the kingdom of God could be realized than that which already existed in Prussian Germany, and that this failure undercut his otherwise quite radical historical ethic of the kingdom of God. (The elements of this radical historical ethic are dealt with in greater detail elsewhere in this book.)

Quite the opposite is the case, however, with Harnack and Herrmann, both of whom appear to have definitely confronted the major social movements of their day (including socialism) and rejected them in favor of an individualized ethic of the human heart—something that was more in keeping with Schleiermacher than with Ritschl![12] Herrmann's *Ethics* and Harnack's *What Is Christianity?* epitomize this trend toward individualization and privatization. But it was in his address to the fifth annual meeting of the Protestant Social Assembly (ESK) of 1894 that Harnack openly proclaimed his opposition to the socialists of Prussian Germany:

> The Gospel is the glad tidings of benefits that pass not away. In it are the powers of eternal life; it is concerned with repentance and faith, with regeneration and a new life; its end is redemption, not social improvement. Therefore it aims at raising the individual to a standpoint far above the conflicts between earthly success and earthly distress, between riches and poverty, lordship and service. This has been its meaning to earnest Christians of all ages, and those who are unable to appreciate this idea, fail to appreciate the Gospel itself. . . .
>
> It has nothing to do with such practical questions of social-economics as the nationalisation of private property and enterprise, land-tenure re-

---

10. *ICR* in *TE*, 246.

11. *JR 3,* §68, 668.

12. Schleiermacher has often been called the "Father of Modern Theology" for a number of reasons, one among them being his emphasis upon religion as based primarily in a "religious feeling" rather than in a thinking or a doing. This position was expressed most succinctly in his early essay *On Religion: Speeches to Its Cultured Despisers* (New York: Harper & Row, 1958), but was also reiterated in the introduction to his major work, *The Christian Faith* (Edinburgh: T & T Clark, 1976). For a more generalized comparison between Ritschl and the later Ritschlians, however, see Rupp, esp. pp. 45 and 48.

forms, restriction of the legal hours of work, price-regulations, taxation, and insurance; for in order to settle these matters, such technical knowledge is required as is altogether outside the province of the church, and if it were to meddle with them at all it would be led into a secularisation of the worst description.[13]

Herrmann was no better when, in his address to the fourteenth annual meeting of the same Assembly, he sought to press behind the radical words of Jesus to his "mental outlook" in order to justify the growing nationalism and militarism of a Germany under the dominion of Kaiser Wilhelm II:

> If then the words of Jesus be understood as due to His mental outlook, they will not obscure the fact that the pursuit of power and possessions, as protected by law, is a moral obligation. . . . If we have once understood the mind that Jesus wishes to produce in us, we cannot fail to see that we must become as free and independent as He.
>
> As a result of that frame of mind whereby we are united to Him, we desire the existence of a national state, with a character and with duties with which Jesus was not yet acquainted; we will not let ourselves be led astray, even if in this form of human nature various features are as sharply opposed to the mode of life and standpoint of Jesus as is the dauntless use of arms.[14]

No wonder Barth reacted with such disdain toward the Liberal theology of his day! But how far removed all this was from Ritschl's own way of thinking! For Ritschl emphasized the essential unity between the love of God and the love of neighbor—between worship in the church and ethical activity in one's civic vocation, one's work in the kingdom of God and the furtherance of brotherhood among all peoples (and not just Germans!).[15] According to Ritschl, one reality could not be had without the other; on the contrary, both realities continually stand in reciprocal relation one to the other. And it is precisely on account of this concern that many scholars today have attempted to rescue Ritschl from the relative obscurity to which he has been consigned

13. Adolf von Harnack, "The Evangelical Social Mission in the Light of the History of the Church," in Harnack and Herrmann, *Essays on the Social Gospel,* ed. Maurice A. Canney (New York: Putnam's, 1907), 9 and 83.

14. Wilhelm Herrmann, "The Moral Teachings of Jesus," in Harnack and Herrmann, *Essays on the Social Gospel,* 211, 217. For an excellent comparison of the ethics of Wilhelm Herrmann and Albrecht Ritschl, see Hermann Timm's essay, *Theorie und Praxis in der Theologie Albrecht Ritschls und Wilhelm Herrmann* (Gütersloh: Gerd Mohn, 1967).

15. On this last point, see *ICR,* §6: The broadening of the concept of neighbor to include human beings as human beings, i.e., as ethical persons, opposes the kingdom of God to the narrower ethical communities (§8) which are limited by the natural endowment [*Ausstattung*] of human beings and by the natural restrictions on their common activities" (*TE,* 223, 266).

by Barth and others, and to recover the radical elements that are implicit (if not actually explicit) in Ritschl's own theology.

II

Most representatives of the "Ritschl Renaissance" have focused their energies on reassessing Ritschl's doctrine of the kingdom of God, which they presume expresses most clearly the practical aim of his theology. According to Rolf Schäfer, for instance, the beauty and radicalism of Ritschl's original ethic consisted in its ability to comprehend at one and the same time the religious (or dogmatic) dimension of human existence and the ethical duty of love toward one's neighbor in the world, and to accomplish this by reference to God's will (as revealed in Jesus Christ) to establish a kingdom upon the earth. This ethic also had the advantage, according to Schäfer, of being able "to explain why Christian activity should not remain bound to the sphere of the individual but rather should, from beginning to end, take place within the confines of a community."[16]

Many others have joined Schäfer in his attempt to rescue Ritschl's original ethic of the kingdom from the morass of moralism and individualism to which it has been subjected for so many years. Norman Metzler and Philip Hefner have, for example, compared Ritschl with the "eschatological school" of Germany, among whom are numbered Wolfhart Pannenberg, Carl Braaten, and Jürgen Moltmann.[17] Hefner, in particular, has pointed out some rather specific challenges that, he believes, Ritschl's ethic brings to bear upon the "eschatological school."[18] Most notably, he believes that Ritschl's emphasis upon vocational activity in the world, humanity's integration and harmonization with nature, and the formation of the self through concrete activities of love, all lend a measure of concreteness to one's vision of God's coming kingdom.

Notwithstanding the many accomplishments of these men and of this line of reasoning, I still question the usefulness of going back exclusively to Ritschl's doctrine of the *kingdom* in order to assess his theological and ethical significance for the contemporary era. I would argue, first of all, that Ritschl's emphasis upon the doctrine of the kingdom of God as a framework for his dogmatic system was a relatively late development.

---

16. Rolf Schäfer, "Johannes Gottschick und Theodor Häring—zwei Sozialethiker der Ritschlschen Schule," in *Theologen und Theologie an der Universität Tübingen,* ed. Martin Brecht (Tübingen: Mohr Siebeck, 1977), 383. See also Rolf Schäfer, "Das Reich Gottes bei Albrecht Ritschl und Johannes Weiß," *Zeitschrift für Theologie und Kirche* 61 (1964): 68–88.

17. Cf. Norman Metzler, "The Ethics of the Kingdom" (Ph.D. diss., Evangelical-Theological Faculty of the University of Munich, 1971), 438. For a summary of Ritschl's significance for current theologies of the kingdom, see *TE,* 45–47.

18. Philip Hefner, "The Concreteness of God's Kingdom: A Problem for the Christian Life," *Journal of Religion* 51 (July 1971): 189–93.

Originally, the kingdom of God was treated as only one of two parts of the Christian *Gemeinde,* or community. As such, the kingdom described the moral and ethical activity of that community in the world; whereas the church (or *Kirche,* in German) described the religious component of the same. Nevertheless, both components were considered to be dimensions or subsets of the one larger reality—the Christian community—that was active in these two ways. By the time the third edition of the *Instruction in the Christian Religion* (1886) had been published, however, the kingdom of God had supplanted the Christian *Gemeinde,* or community, inasmuch as it was placed at the beginning and end of the piece so as to frame the work as a whole. The *Gemeinde,* though still an important part of the theological system, now became a subordinate element to the kingdom of God rather than the reverse, as had been the case in Ritschl's earliest writings. One therefore senses a definite shift of emphasis in Ritschl's writings away from a dogmatics centered in the *Gemeinde* toward one centered in the kingdom of God.

But why are Ritschl's earlier ideas to be preferred? Why not assume instead that he saw some good reason to shift his emphasis from the *Gemeinde* to the kingdom and would himself recommend acceptance of his later position? In answer, I would argue that a shift of emphasis in dogmatics almost always entails a corresponding shift of emphasis in ethics. The central question is not simply one of theological clarity or relative doctrinal emphasis, but of practical—indeed, political—consequence. There may, indeed, have been many good reasons why Ritschl chose to focus upon the kingdom in his later work. Perhaps he was concerned about relating each individual moral will to the larger will of God in a more comprehensive manner. Perhaps he wished to have the kingdom of God serve as something of a "bridge" between the religious and ethical dimensions of the Christian life. Whatever the reasons for this shift of emphasis to the kingdom, it did not come without some cost. By emphasizing the centrality of the Christian community in his earliest writings, Ritschl had been able to unite the secular reform of society with the religious disposition in a dynamic and institutional way, and this was expressed in his concern for church-sponsored educational reform of the society.[19] However, with the shift of emphasis to

19. See, for example, "Über die Begriffe: sichtbare und unsichtbare Kirche," *Theologische Studien und Kritiker* (1859), 224: "Just as the Evangelical believes in the one church, so the church remains the final object of his practical striving. The means for this enterprise, however, consists in participation in those agencies of the church by which the latter realizes and represents itself as a moral community. In this sense, Melanchthon and Calvin labeled the church 'visible.' And by means of the marks of the confessional tradition and cultic morality, the church is capable of being judged empirically." Or again, "Die protestantische Lehre von der Kirche," *Monatschrift für die evangelische Kirche der Rheinprovinz und Westphalens* 9 (1851): 130: "Not only does the church as an institution, but also the church as a moral community, depend upon the communion of saints for its foundation and goal. But that which is love at the center of the living fellowship must now become law at the periphery—i.e., it must become morally educative."

the kingdom, one senses a growing restiveness in Ritschl's work over the question of moral perfection, which appears to accompany the emphasis upon faithfulness in one's vocation and comes to be attached more and more to the notion of the divine kingdom itself. For example, Ritschl candidly states in his 1874 lecture, *On Christian Perfection:*

> An individual's moral life-work is perfected only insofar as he directs his work in a particular vocation toward the common good of the people and proves it by a sense of self-worth [*berechtigtem Selbstgefühl*] which accompanies the successful completion of that life-work. For it is common knowledge that whoever does not take up a vocation not only fails to accomplish anything of public benefit, but also suffers injury to his moral character.[20]

One can thus trace a movement away from a concern for church-sponsored educational reform of society, which dominated the earliest writings on the *Gemeinde,* toward a growing preoccupation with one's own vocational faithfulness and moral perfection in the later writings on the kingdom of God. In light of this, one must question whether one can simply reappropriate Ritschl's doctrine of the kingdom today without also reappropriating those other, more objectionable elements of bourgeois vocationalism and moral perfectionism (assuming, of course, that one does not do violence to Ritschl's actual thought). Indeed, the close connection between the kingdom and a bourgeois ethic of "faithfulness in one's vocation" seems to have actually been *endemic* to Ritschl's later theology.

Finally, I would argue that Ritschl's later theology of the kingdom was never directly related to, nor derived from, Ritschl's own political and ecclesiastical praxis. It would certainly be difficult to prove this, in any case, since most of his writings on the kingdom of God were not polemical in nature and therefore afford little insight into the practical intent of Ritschl's conceptualizations (contrary to Schäfer's opinion). Such is not, however, the case with Ritschl's earliest articles on the *Gemeinde,*[21] for a diligent study of the earliest of the articles, written be-

---

20. From Cajus Fabricius, *Albrecht Ritschl: Die christliche Vollkommenheit* (Leipzig: Hinrichs'sche Buchhandlung, 924), 12–13.

21. The following is a partial list of Ritschl's articles on the Christian community, written between 1850 and 1869:

1850	*EK* (rev. 1857).
1851	PLK.
1852	"Herr Dr. Hengstenberg und die Union, *GA* (1893) 1:52–67.
1854	*Über das Verhältniß des Bekenntnisses zur Kirche. Ein Votum gegen die neulutherischen Doctrinen* (Bonn, 1854). (Also in *GA* [1896] 2:1–24.)
1854	"Über die kirchliche Parteilage." Published as Beitrag II in *Leben* 1:432f.
1856	"Über Confession und Union" (unpublished).
1858	"Der Gegensatz der morgenländischen und abendländischen Kirche und die Unionshoffnungen Gagarins und Harthausens," *Protestantische Monatsblätter für innere Zeitgeschichte* (1858), 338–58.
1859	*SUK.* (Also in *GA* 1:68–99.)

tween 1851 and 1869, uncovers a polemic that constantly informed Ritschl's own constructive system. At every turn the reader is struck by Ritschl's sharp criticism of the ecclesiastical excesses of his day. On one front, he upbraids Enlightenment theology for its religious subjectivism and anticlericalism. On another front, he censures Catholicism for its objectivist confusion of religion and clericalism. And on yet another front, he condemns Lutheran Confessionalism for its particularist insistence upon divisive creeds in an age of growing nationalism and unification.

As much as Ritschl would have enjoyed that "quiet time for the work of the mind, so necessary for the successful enterprise of systematic theology,"[22] he nevertheless succumbed to the pressures of his day. Ritschl forged his theological system out of the fires of conflict with the forces of opposition—whether they be Rationalist, Catholic, or Confessionalist. Because this perspective affords us the clearest window into the practical—indeed, political—nature of Ritschl's theology, we must use it to investigate his doctrine of Christian community and, by extension, also his ethics.

III

Ritschl's doctrine of Christian community may, first of all, be regarded as a polemical *defense of ecclesiastical religion,* over against those representatives of Enlightened thought who disdained institutionalized religion of almost every sort.[23] These "Rationalists" of the nineteenth century (among them Paul de Lagarde, a contemporary of Ritschl's on the faculty at Göttingen) maintained the inherent superiority of natural reason and the religion of the individual conscience over and above ecclesiastical traditionalism. Moreover, they blamed the Protestant Reformation for the general degradation of modern German society. In Paul de Lagarde's opinion, Protestantism had perpetuated German disunity. "By sanctioning the princes' rebellion and by thus introducing cae-

1861   "Die Gründe der politischen Gestaltung der christlichen Kirche in den er-
            sten drei Jahrhunderten," *Vorträge für das gebildete Publikum,* Erste
            Sammlung, Elberfeld (1861), 187–205.

1862   "Evangelium und Katholicität," *Zu Albrecht Ritschls hundertstem
            Geburtstag,* published on March 25 in *Die christliche Welt* 36 (1922):
            201–10.

1869   "Die Begründung des Kirchenrechtes im evangelischen Begriff von der
            Kirche," *Zeitschrift für Kirchenrecht* (1869), 220–79. (Also in *GA*
            1:100–46.)

22. Albrecht Ritschl, "Die Entstehung der lutherischen Kirche," *Zeitschrift für Kirchengeschichte* (1876): 1:51–110. Reprinted in *GA,* 170–217, and in unpublished translation by Philip Hefner as "The Emergence of the Lutheran Church," 27–28 (photocopied).

23. Cf. Lotz, 166. However, the focus here is upon Ritschl's Reformation studies generally.

saropapism," it had surrendered Germany to barbarism.[24] And according to Jacob Burckhardt,

> the accomplishments of a thousand years, the vessel of a religion, the correlate of a thoroughly formed popular culture had been stolen from [the people] and thoroughly destroyed. And in Germany this had not even happened in tragic battle, but with a sudden appeal to general undisciplined action beside which the positive new "faith" meant little.[25]

In both men's opinion, only the destruction of Christianity as a state-sponsored religion would bring about the moral and cultural unification of the German states.

In order to counter this "cultured" criticism of Protestant Christianity, Ritschl stressed the moral and ethical importance of the Protestant church, as a religious-political organization, for the reform of German society. In his address of 1883, entitled "Festival Address on the Four-Hundredth Anniversary of the Birth of Martin Luther, November 10, 1883," Ritschl remarked, "one will discover in Luther's efforts on behalf of the renovation of the Christian religion and Church the key to his indirect influence on the formation of the states and the general intellectual life."[26]

Ritschl's earlier articles on the doctrine of Christian community anticipated the claims of the "Festival Address" in that they also constantly appealed to *the necessity of visible church structures for the moral reorganization of all peoples in the kingdom of God.*[27] According to these earlier articles, "the church is not an imagined ideal as in Plato's Republic, but actually exists, and does so by virtue of the divine power of the gospel and sacraments, by which the church's presence is also outwardly knowable."[28] Because it mediates the historical revelation of God in Jesus Christ, "the institutional church serves as the requisite for salvation or communion with Christ."[29] Salvation, therefore, is not primarily a matter of the individual conscience, but rather depends upon the concrete agencies of the church.

Likewise, the moral organization of society also depends upon the agencies of the institutional church. According to Ritschl, "those factors of divine virtue [that is, the gospel and the sacraments] which establish and constitute the communion of saints do so only in order that

---

24. As quoted by Fritz Stern in *The Politics of Cultural Despair: A Study in the Rise of the Germanic Ideology* (Berkeley and Los Angeles: Univ. of California Press, 1963), 70–72. (In Lotz, 163–64.)

25. Burckhardt, *On History and Historians* (New York: Harper & Row, 1965), 117, as quoted in Lotz, 162.

26. David Lotz's English translation of this speech appears in Lotz, 188. The German original, "Festrede am vierten Seculartage der Geburt Martin Luthers, 10. November, 1883," was first published in *DAR*, 5–29.

27. *SUK*, 217–18 and 221–22; see also PLK, 128–29, and *ICR*, §13 and §85 (*TE*, 226 and 258–59).

28. *SUK*, 206. Cf. also "The Emergence of the Lutheran Church," 18.

29. PLK, 127.

they might also embrace and then permeate the moral association of the family, or for that matter, the moral association of the people [*sittliche Volksgemeinschaft*]."[30] Social reform does not depend upon the rational reorganization of political structures as such, but rather follows from the religious motive peculiar to the Christian church.[31] A general knowledge of universal ethical precepts does not, of itself, suffice to bring about that kind of activity which is appropriate to those precepts. For the individual moral will remains unproductive as long as it is enervated by a continuing sense of guilt and estrangement from God.[32] Only with the reception of divine forgiveness, as proffered in the sacraments and in the proclamation of the gospel, is the individual moral will then liberated to pursue the universal ethical end of the kingdom of God. In the words of the *Instruction,* "the mutual union of man through action springing from love . . . is realized by men only in their union with the community of their lord Jesus Christ" (§13).

In conscious opposition, therefore, to those "extreme radicals" who sought to "define the church simply as an arrangement of the state by which its citizens are blinded and corrupted,"[33] Ritschl emphasized the importance of the institutional church for the moral organization of nations in the kingdom of God. He attempted to show that the Rationalist devaluation of institutional religion was at best impractical, since the reorganization of human society along moral lines could not depend upon some imagined Ideal of the human spirit, and at worst illusory, since the individual moral will required liberation from the feeling of guilt and estrangement from God before it could effectively serve the ultimate ethical end in the kingdom of God. For this reason, Ritschl emphasized the importance of the institutional church as a legal-political community for the moral reformation of society. In this sense, then, the church—as a visible, institutional organization within the larger society—"remains the final object of one's practical striving" in the establishment of the kingdom of God upon the earth.[34] And the Union Church of Prussia served as the premier model in this regard.

30. *SUK,* 218.

31. In *ICR,* §10, Ritschl states quite emphatically, "A knowledge of universal ethical precepts, as such, is never sufficient to call forth and organize the activity that is appropriate to those precepts. This activity follows only when a special, indeed a religious, motive or ground of obligation is linked with knowledge of the universal precept" (*TE,* 224). Again, in §19 of the same work, Ritschl summarizes, "The imperative of the moral association of all men as men could become effective as a practical principle only insofar as it grew out of the religious motive of the specifically Christian community (par. 10)." (*TE,* 228). Clearly, the burden of *ICR* is to place ethical activity in the kingdom of God upon the sure foundation of the religious sense of community (*religiöse Gemeinsinn*).

32. *JR 3,* §35. Cf. also Lotz, 39, n. 34.

33. *SUK,* 222.

34. *SUK,* 221. This does not mean that Ritschl viewed the church and the kingdom of God as coterminous realities (cf. *ICR,* §9). It does mean, however, that the church's proclamation serves as a fundamental, empirical presupposition for ethical activity in the kingdom of God.

Such statements have, of course, occasioned the charge that Ritschl reduced Protestant Christianity to a type of "neo-Kantian moralism" by making the church into a sort of state within the state.[35] Indeed, because Ritschl laid such stress upon the church as an institutional community, he brought upon himself the charge of "Romanism" in his own day. But such criticisms, whether past or present, are too one-sided and polemically motivated to suffice for an adequate description of Ritschl's doctrine of Christian community. For they not only fail to consider the polemic against the Rationalists that *necessitated* Ritschl's emphasis upon the church as institution, but they also ignore the corresponding critique that Ritschl launched *against* Roman Catholicism.

The German Catholics of the late nineteenth century looked upon the church primarily and essentially as an institution—a type of "state within a state."[36] Such was the theological heritage of the Roman church from Augustine to that time. Submission to the external, legal forms of the church sufficed to ensure one of inclusion in Christ's own body. Individual faith was not considered a determinative factor in this regard, since it did not admit of empirical observation, nor could it be trusted as an accurate measure of the divine saving grace vouchsafed in the sacraments of the institutional church. In the words of Cardinal Bellarmine, a contemporary of Ritschl's:

> No inner disposition is necessary in order for someone to be a member of the true church, but rather simply the external confession of faith and the participation in the sacraments. For the church is a human community on the same order as the French monarchy and the Benedictine Republic.[37]

From this perspective, the church became analogous to the state, forcing external consensus even when such betrayed the individual conscience.

This sort of ecclesiology served German Catholic interests in the Palatinate (or Pfalz) quite well, since it provided the means by which

35. Evidence that might support this conclusion can be found in *SUK*, 208: "The church, however, also has political marks . . . and in this respect, it has an existence as a legal association comparable to that of the state." Ritschl, however, later modified this opinion in *ICR*, §85: "According to the Protestant view, all the attributes of a state are excluded from the concept of the church" (*TE*, 259).

36. Ritschl used the phrase "state within a state" in order to condemn the Roman Catholic overidentification of the Christian community with the legal, institutional power of the Vatican State. The phrase was not intended to imply any subordination of the Roman church to the German territories. On the contrary, Ritschl always believed that the role of church and state should remain strictly separate, on the Lutheran model of the two kingdoms (though Ritschl does not refer explicitly to this latter doctrine inasmuch as it would conflict with his own understanding of the kingdom of God). According to Ritschl, the church should never take upon itself the power of the state in order to enforce beliefs or ecclesiastical practices. However, the Roman church had, in fact, assumed those very functions which were reserved strictly for the German territories (in particular the Prussian state) under God's providential order. Thus, it had become a sort of "state within the state"—a theological impossibility, according to Ritschl's way of thinking. (See *ICR*, §85, and "Evangelium und Katholicität," *Die christliche Welt* 36 [1922]: 205.)

37. As cited by Ritschl in "Evangelium und Katholicität," 205.

Catholics could establish themselves as a minority opposition movement against growing Prussian (and therefore Unionist) interests.[38] The hierarchy could enforce consensus among its own members, thereby ensuring a united political front against Prussian aspirations in the region. Conflict was inevitable, however, as German Evangelicals (for reasons of employment) moved into the western regions and as Roman Catholics began to foist their particular religious system not only upon their own members, but also upon these new immigrants, claiming that external obedience to the local hierarchy constituted the prerequisite for membership in the only "true" (that is, "catholic") church.

Such a view of the church can hardly be said to characterize Ritschl's doctrine of Christian community, since he eschewed religious compulsion of every sort. To be sure, Ritschl did stress the importance of ecclesiastical structures for nurturing individual faith and fostering the moral reorganization of society and to that extent did give Catholicism the credit it was due. For him, however, the importance of the institution rested upon moral and ethical, not religious, considerations. In more than one place, Ritschl acknowledged "the necessity of political forms for the church as a *moral requirement* and as an unavoidable means for the actual existence of the communion of saints,"[39] but that was as far as it went. The church's organizational structure was only morally necessary as a means to an end; it did not constitute the church's essence as a "communion of saints."

Ritschl's defense against the Catholic excesses of the Palatinate may be regarded, therefore, as an attempt to rescue *the Christian church, as a specifically religious institution,* from its rather unfortunate association with other, more purely political institutions. According to Ritschl, participation in the outward or legal forms of the church does not constitute the church's essence, since "political obedience to the hierarchy, and to the whole membership of the church connected with it, can take place without any conversion, without any religious conviction whatsoever."[40] Rather, God alone, by the power of his Word, constitutes the church as a "communion of saints." In this connection, Ritschl agreed with Franz Delitzsch, the noted Lutheran Confessionalist of the nineteenth century: "The church does not owe its existence and unity to its own fickle behavior, but rather to the immutable acts of God."[41] Thus, the identity of

38. See John E. Groh, *Nineteenth Century German Protestantism: The Church as Model for Social Change* (Washington, D.C.: University Press of America, 1982), 191–96. Following Prussian annexation of the western regions under the terms of the Congress of Vienna (1815), it became apparent that Prussian unification meant the eventual subjugation of the Roman hierarchy to the claims of the state. Catholic opposition was inevitable and soon climaxed in demonstrations at Cologne in 1837–39, and in the formation of the Catholic Central Party, a conservative opposition party, by Joseph Goerre in 1844.

39. *SUK,* 204 (italics in original).

40. *SUK,* 200.

41. F. Delitzsch, *Vier Bücher von der Kirche,* 121, cited in Ritschl's *Über das Verhältniß des Bekenntnisses zur Kirche, GA* (1896) 2:20. (Hereafter, "Verhalt.")

the church as the universal society of true believers is constituted by God's synthetic judgment, which is perceptible to faith alone (and therefore "invisible" apart from that faith).

In conscious opposition to the German Catholics of the western and southern provinces, who insisted upon obedience to the legal-political forms of the church in order to secure for themselves a type of state within the state, Ritschl emphasized the religious foundation of the church which is based upon the preaching of the gospel. In his address to the Gustavus Adolphus Society on January 1, 1862, entitled "Catholicity and the Gospel,"[42] Ritschl made his opposition to Romanism exceedingly clear: In claiming "catholicity" for itself, the Roman church had actually succeeded in doing nothing more than promoting its own particularistic doctrines and institutions at the expense of German church unification.[43] Ritschl sought to combat Catholicism on its own terms by insisting that true "catholicity" could be vouchsafed to the church only in its religious dimension—that is, as a product of faith in the gospel of God's forgiving grace, and not as a result of external adherence to the church's legal-political constitution. Ritschl notes in this connection:

> Wherever the gospel is preached and acknowledged, and wherever the community of believers exists, there love and sympathy and intercession overrun all boundaries and extend to everyone who stands upon the same foundation of the gospel and to everyone who strives toward the same goal of the divine kingdom, no matter what the complexion of their confession may be and no matter how their liturgy may differ from our own.[44]

Ritschl reiterated this position on a number of other occasions, claiming that it was the gospel and the gospel alone which, as "the constant and effective act of God, . . . effects faith and establishes the communion of saints in the world—which is in fact the church."[45] True catholicity, and therefore the true nature of the church as "communion of saints," finds its foundation in the synthetic judgment of God and the faith of the religious community, and not in external compliance with the church's legal-political forms. Because the Union Church espoused just this view of "catholicity," it alone mirrored true "catholicism," since it alone included all churches within its fold, even the Roman Catholic! Thus Ritschl sought to defeat German Catholics on their own terms.

Of course, this emphasis upon the religious foundation of the church, independent of every legal-political structure of the same, led to charges from the Confessionalist side that Ritschl had reduced Christianity to a

---

42. Published on the occasion of Albrecht Ritschl's one hundredth birthday as "Evangelium und Katholicität" in *Die christliche Welt* 36 (1922): 201–10. (Hereafter, "Ev. u. Kath.")
43. See Ritschl, "Ev. u. Kath.," 204–5.
44. Ibid., 209.
45. "Verhalt," *GA* 2:14.

form of "Idealism" that ignored the natural structures of the real world. In this sense, the Confessionalist criticism of Ritschl paralleled that of Roman Catholicism.

The Lutheran Confessionalist concern centered upon the need for concrete ecclesiastical confessions to measure accurately the teaching of those within the church.[46] In their opinion, religious conviction, without the aid of binding confessional documents, failed to provide the means necessary to adjudicate differences among churches and among individual Christians within the church. Consequently, they believed that Rationalist efforts to achieve ecclesiastical union apart from the specific confessions of the church would remain ultimately frustrated, since the very means for discussion and reconciliation were excluded from the outset. In the words of one Lutheran Confessionalist named Kahnis, "The Lutheran Confession is the rule of faith and doctrine—the point of unity for the congregation, as well as the point of distinction from all other communities."[47] Perhaps even more blunt are the words of Otto von Naugard: "The essence of the church *is* its confession."[48]

Naturally, this theology not only served the Confessionalists' need to maintain their own particular identity in a nation of competing ecclesiastical institutions, but also served the practical political interests of the Lutherans in the western and southern provinces. Much like their Catholic counterparts, the Confessionalists' insistence upon external compliance to particularistic creeds became a means of asserting the independence of the western and southern provinces from Prussian control. Although political opposition among southern Lutherans did not reach its climax until the Prussian war with Austria in 1866, it was nevertheless a certainty that "Confessionalists adapted rather well to the particularism of the territories, mirroring the Awakening in this regard, and providing little support for liberals, who wanted German unification to serve as a prelude to liberalized state constitutions."[49]

Ritschl himself was not unaware of the parallelism that existed between Lutheran Confessionalism and Roman Catholicism. (Indeed, on one occasion Ritschl called Confessionalism "the Catholic church's terrible twin" [*eine schlechte Doublette der katholischen Kirche*].) Neither was he ignorant of the practical consequences that their respective understandings of the church entailed.[50] Consequently, Ritschl employed much the same argument against Confessionalism as he did against Catholicism; he appealed to the religious foundation of the church, un-

46. See "Verhalt," *GA* 2:18.
47. Kahnis, *Die moderne Unionsdoctrin* (Leipzig, 1853), as cited by Ritschl in "Verhalt," *GA* 2:1.
48. Von Naugard, *Die kirchliche Gemeindeordnung, ein Vortrag* (Stettin, 1851), 5, as cited by Ritschl in "Verhalt," *GA* 2:1–2 (italics in original).
49. Groh, 191. Cf. also 173–91 generally.
50. "Verhalt," *GA* 2:13. See also "The Emergence of the Lutheran Church," 29.

derstood as a "communion of saints," over against the moral and ethical necessity of the church, understood as a legal-political association.[51]

However, Ritschl did acknowledge some important differences between the two movements, and this acknowledgment conditioned the specific method used by Ritschl in combating confessional particularism. Unlike its Roman Catholic counterpart, Confessionalist ecclesiology did not eventuate in a state within a state, but rather in an understanding of the church as a type of school.[52] The Confessionalists did not seek to enforce external compliance to the church's hierarchy or legal constitution so much as external compliance to the church's objective doctrines. However, like its Roman Catholic counterpart, Confessionalist ecclesiology did manage to equate conformity to external forms with membership in the one true church of Christ. The practical result for Protestantism, therefore, was the splintering of the church into a host of competing confessional churches and independent sects.[53]

Given these differences, Ritschl believed that most of the "New Lutherans" (for example, Hofmann, Hengstenberg, Neander, Münchmeyer) had deluded themselves into thinking that a confederative church union, based upon competing confessional claims, could in any sense be achieved, especially on the model of the failed Frankfurt Parliament of 1848.[54] The very claim to divine truth inherent in Confessionalism necessarily meant excluding other confessional bodies from the Union.

In conscious opposition to that sort of creedalism which manifested itself in ecclesiastical divisions as well as in territorial particularism, Ritschl attempted to show that unity was, in fact, possible only in the light of forgiving grace in Christ—that grace which is attested by the Augsburg Confession itself. In his article of 1854, entitled "On the Relation of the Confession to the Church," Ritschl notes:

> as surely as the Reformed and Union churches are founded upon the same gospel as the Lutheran church, and as surely as they all confess the gracious will of God which is freely vouchsafed to them in Christ to be the foundation of their salvation, so are they all one church.[55]

---

51. "Verhalt," *GA* 2:13: "It is a Roman Catholic perspective . . . that norms the concept of the church by the legal authority of its marks and leaves the issue open whether members of the church enjoy an inner religious, or an external legal relationship with those marks." See also "Verhalt," *GA* 2:2–5, 11–15; and *SUK*, 220ff. Also, for a general treatment of Ritschl's polemic against Orthodoxy, see Lotz, 170–86, and *TE*, 31–32.

52. *SUK*, 217–18; *ICR*, §§86, 87; and "The Emergence of the Lutheran Church," 41.

53. See PLK, 129–30.

54. Hengstenberg, for example, felt that the Prussian Union had forced unity upon the individual churches at the expense of specific convictions each church held regarding its own confessions. He advocated, instead, a loose association (or confederation) of churches that would acknowledge the independence of each constituent member within the larger assembly. See Ritschl, "Herr Dr. Hengstenberg und die Union," in *GA* 1:52–67. Cf. also "Verhalt," *GA* 2:2–3.

55. "Verhalt," *GA* 2:15.

For Ritschl, therefore, the Lutheran creed itself demanded the affirmation of God's saving grace over and above every particularistic dispute over doctrine. And it was the original Reformation understanding of that creed that maintained that "only when believers unabashedly acknowledge the divine foundation of their salvation—that is, only when their *doctrina evangelii* [with emphasis upon the *evangelii*] is pure—does their confession function as a true mark of their life to unbelievers."[56] Because the Union Church acknowledged the true, Reformation understanding of the creed, Ritschl believed that one could not abandon the Union cause, since it was "the very epitome of the Reformation church concept itself."[57] Thus, Ritschl sought to establish the Union Church on the same foundation as that to which the Lutherans appealed in their defense of separate Confessionalist churches.

IV

The preceding discussion has shown that Ritschl did not develop his doctrine of the Christian community from the confines of the university lecture hall, but rather out of a constant polemic with three key ecclesiastical contenders: the Confessionalists, the Catholics, and the Rationalists. At each juncture Ritschl not only demonstrated the inherent theological weaknesses of his opponents, but also related those weaknesses to the actual social and political practices of his day. In this regard, Ritschl's practical interest in the Prussian Union Church played a decisive, if not also critical, role.

One may, therefore, be tempted to conclude that Ritschl's doctrine of Christian community simply served the universalist pretensions of the Prussian Union Church; his emphasis upon the Word of God and the corresponding faith of the religious community seems to have provided the theological means necessary for co-opting all competing religious communities into one universal church of God. A clear example of this ecclesiastical co-optation can be found in Ritschl's article on "The Protestant Doctrine of the Church," written in 1851. In this article Ritschl observes:

> The fact that two diverse churches were established upon these two theological systems [the Lutheran and the Calvinist] was a mistake; and the fact, moreover, that those two churches were split into a whole series of territorial churches without any common or legal means of recourse was a second mistake. And both mistakes have taken their toll in the decline of Protestant Christianity. Given this situation, therefore, Protestantism cannot remain indifferent toward its legal structure nor toward its lack of structural unity. Rather, what was incapable of proof from a dogmatic standpoint shows itself to be both a necessity and a duty from an *ethical*

56. "Verhalt," *GA* 2:14.
57. "Verhalt," *GA* 2:19.

standpoint—namely, that one should *strive to make the confessional communion an institutional communion as well.*[58]

Other remarks of a more indirect nature serve to confirm the thesis that Ritschl viewed the establishment and advancement of the Union cause as nothing less than a moral duty, inasmuch as he believed that external ecclesiastical cooperation constituted the necessary means for the conversion of the people, and therefore also for the moral transformation of society at large.[59]

Moreover, in this context, a second question arises as to whether Ritschl did not also simply mirror the Prussian political platform of his day within the context of the Union Church. In other words, did Ritschl not simply assume that unifying the German states would automatically entail unifying the territorial churches of Germany, or that the political platform could easily be transplanted to the field of ecclesiastical polity? This question draws its strength from the most practical of Ritschl's statements regarding the church.[60] Indeed, in a report to the Prussian minister of culture and religion, von Mühler, regarding the recent actions taken by the Hannoverian Provincial Synod in October of 1869, Ritschl made one of the most candid observations of his career, linking his interest in the Prussian Union Church to his own pan-Germanism:

> I would declare unto Your Excellency my historical observation that Lutheranism since 1850 in Hannover, Royal Saxony, and Mecklenburg has been used in the middle states as a means of political resistance to Prussia's pan-Germanic policies; that Vilmar's similar inclinations were also determined by an attempt to bring the electorate of Hesse into the anti-Prussianist movement; that the struggle of Harleß against the Union and against the well-known "pan-Germanic" policies of the same movement are certainly not unrelated; and that the Lutheranism of the clergy in Prussia itself has been bound up, both jointly and severally, with the policies of the *Kreuzzeitung* Party, which are directed against Prussia's pan-Germanic cause. . . . These local champions of Lutheranism falsely imagine themselves to be champions of an autonomous and universal church policy, whereas in fact their own Lutheran ecclesiasticism is above all a symptom of political particularism. And their pretended autonomy will result only in harming the Lutheran church itself—that is, as long as this attitude is present within Protestant Christendom.[61]

58. PLK, 130 (italics in original).
59. See notes 70 and 71 below.
60. One such statement can be found in §88 of *ICR*: "The provincial government of the church in Germany is now a condition for the union of the different protestant provincial churches within themselves and with each other and ought not be judged and depreciated by the example of the conditions in America or Scotland. According to protestant doctrine, there is no exclusively ideal form of church government, and the course of protestant history in Germany justifies the assertion that the maintenance of the unity of the provincial churches has protected the protestant church against being split into sects and conquered again by Romanism [and Bonapartism?]" (*TE*, 262).
61. *Leben* 1:73–74. Cf. also previous note.

However convincing this statement, and others, might appear to be in vouchsafing the hypothesis that Ritschl simply mirrored the Prussian political agenda on the ecclesiastical level, such an explanation of Ritschl's overall conception of the church seems a bit too facile. This rather predictable line of interpretation follows (almost slavishly) the perspective set forth by Otto Ritschl in the now famous biography of his father's life and work.[62] The picture drawn in that work consists of two basic suppositions: (1) that Albrecht Ritschl retreated absolutely from the "political sphere" (as it is narrowly defined by Otto) following the disappointments surrounding the failed Revolution of 1848, and (2) that Ritschl's later theological and ecclesiastical statements of the 1850s are therefore to be considered in isolation from the political concerns of the fifties, as if they had been formulated solely with a view to the academy. These two suppositions have together provoked another, more recent, supposition: (3) that Ritschl's later endorsement of Bismarckian "reform from above" should be taken as indirect confirmation of the thesis that Ritschl's interest in the church during the 1850s in fact served (however latently) to bolster the pretensions of the Prussian aristocracy over against the Germanic territories.

The preceding sections of this paper have endeavored to show the inadequacy of the second of these three suppositions. Ritschl's interest in developing a doctrine of Christian community was certainly not limited to the academy, but rather exhibited a threefold polemic directed against the major "political" movements of the church of his day. The third supposition is a bit more difficult to refute and falls outside the formal scope of this paper. Nevertheless, attention should be drawn to the fact that Ritschl's endorsement of Bismarck's political agenda was always tenuous at best. Ritschl embraced Bismarckian politics only after the war with Austria in 1866, and only after several conscious attempts on the part of Bismarck to co-opt the entire Liberal party.[63] Ritschl and many others in the older Liberal tradition submitted to Prussian hegemonic control only because they concluded that it was the one realistic option left to them. Therefore, the conclusion is not justified that Ritschl's support of Prussian policies in the 1860s is in any way directly related to his "withdrawal from politics" in the 1840s or his specific ecclesiastical concerns of the 1850s. Nor is one justified in reading the earlier articles on the Christian community in the light of later statements from the 1860s regarding Prussian pan-Germanism.[64] The relationship between each of these three aspects (or periods) in Ritschl's life and thought is far more complex than this supposition would admit.

62. *Leben.*
63. See Groh, chap. 8, pp. 333–88, generally.
64. One should note that all of the statements that were adduced to support the view that Ritschl's adherence to the Prussian Unionist cause only mirrored his Prussian pan-Germanism were written *after* 1866!

These observations lead to a more formal refutation of the first supposition mentioned above, namely, that Ritschl's response to the circumstances surrounding the failure of the Revolution of 1848 somehow constituted a "retreat from the political" and a corresponding entrance into matters more formally "academic" or "ecclesiastical." In considering the nature of Ritschl's political involvement in the 1840s, one must first of all admit that Ritschl's "political concern" did indeed reflect the general expectations of the liberal bourgeoisie of his day. Like most of them, Ritschl assumed that constitutional reform would open the way for the middle class to participate more fully in the governmental process, and that this would then create the conditions necessary for national unification. He also assumed that such political reform would exercise a salient influence upon church structures, thereby insuring the success of the Unionist movement. Ritschl therefore considered the liberalization of the political process to be a *necessary precondition* for ecclesiastical unification.

However, one must immediately hasten to add that Ritschl's interest in politics appears to have been *largely ecclesiastic from the very beginning*. Indeed, Ritschl seems to have been unconcerned with the strictly political issues that had preoccupied the first few sessions of the Frankfurt Assembly and cites at length only the debate over the question of church order that occurred during the Monday session of the Paulskirche assembly:

> The Ultramontane and radicals for different reasons want complete independence of the church from the state. Old Liberalism wants as close a dependence as possible, with deference to the police, inasmuch as the powers of the church are incomprehensible and incommensurable as far as it is concerned. . . . It remains to be seen, however, whether a third conception will find the correct path by which the inner autonomy of the church can be joined with the moral tie of the church to the state, while at the same time being able to avoid the sort of political encroachments typical of the Catholic church.[65]

This interest in the church's reforming role within the larger society should certainly not be viewed as a fleeting concern that Ritschl entertained only momentarily during the course of the Frankfurt debates. On the contrary, it functioned as a practical locus around which all other interests of a (more narrowly) political nature were organized, as his reports from the Frankfurt Parliament indicate.

Rather than assuming a "withdrawal" from the political sphere and a turn to matters "more narrowly ecclesiastical" in scope, one should probably speak of a line of continuity that extends from Ritschl's earlier political involvement in the Frankfurt Assembly to his later struggle for ecclesiastical reform. Precisely because Ritschl considered the liberalization of the political process to be the necessary *precondition* for ecclesi-

---

65. In a letter to his father, dated Aug. 25, 1848, in *Leben* 1:144.

astical unification (*as a means to an end*), he was able to maintain his broader "political" interest in the reforming possibilities of a Prussian Union Church, despite the fact that his expectations for a liberalized state constitution had become frustrated and his political involvement with the Frankfurt Assembly had come to an abrupt end. One should not allow Ritschl's isolated statement regarding a "withdrawal" from "politics," uttered as it was in a moment of deep despair following the forced adjournment of the Frankfurt Parliament,[66] to prevent one from recognizing the essential continuity of thought and "political" involvement (in the broader sense) that stretched from 1848 to 1869. On the contrary, one should accept Ritschl's own account of the Frankfurt Assembly and seek to understand the degree to which his later doctrine of the Christian community represents a consistent response to the problem posed by the Revolution of 1848: "It remains to be seen, however, whether a third conception will find the correct path by which the inner autonomy of the church can be joined with the moral tie of the church to the state, while at the same time being able to avoid the sort of political encroachments typical of the Catholic church."[67]

Ritschl's earliest articles on the doctrine of Christian community, written between 1851 and 1869, appear to exemplify just this sort of measured theological response to the church issue, as this was embodied at the Frankfurt Assembly and then later formulated by Ritschl himself. On the one hand, these early articles seek to base the inner autonomy of the church upon the faith of those believers who live within the larger society.[68] Social reform is considered to be impossible apart from the elimination of estrangement from God and the concomitant communication of the universal end of the kingdom of God that comes with the forgiveness of sin.[69] On the other hand, these articles also demonstrate a concern for establishing the church's moral and political ties to the state. The morally educative role of the church is the practical means by which it is to become the premier reforming agent within society.[70] The ques-

66. In a letter from A. Ritschl to his father, written on Feb. 11, 1849: "I am withdrawing completely from politics and hope only that the Constitutional Convention (which the Philistines shun as reactionary, Prussian, Protestant, and professorial) would break up. Then the common rank and file (who always know more about everything anyway) will see for themselves how to organize the Conservative Party" (*Leben* 1:148).
67. In a letter to his father, dated August 25, 1848, in *Leben* 1:144.
68. Ritschl's polemic against the Rationalists should be noted in this regard: "Today there are to be sure men who are of such an extreme radicalism that they seek to define the church simply as the creation of the state, whereby its citizens are blinded and corrupted. These individuals do not sufficiently appreciate the moral and cultural significance of the church, not to mention its specifically religious foundation and purpose. But even if we ignore this perversion of moral judgement, there is still lacking any specific belief by which the church, in this sense, can be appraised" (*SUK*, 222; cf. also PLK, 128–29, and *SUK*, 200.)
69. See note 32 above.
70. Cf. Ritschl's remark in PLK, 128–29: "Not only does the church as an institution, but also the church as a community of moral activity, depend upon the communion of saints for its foundation and goal. But that which was love toward the center of the active fellowship must now become law toward the periphery—i.e., it must become morally ed-

tion whether this educative role is individualistically or socially conceived is not addressed in these articles. What is of importance for this essay, however, is the role played by the legal dimension of the church as the necessary precondition for the existence of the communion of saints or the kingdom of God in the world.[71]

V

Ritschl's own agenda, which grew out of his political and ecclesiastical activity at the Frankfurt Parliament in 1848 and remained normative throughout his entire theological career, continues to be important for us today: How are we to balance the inner autonomy of the Christian community with its moral and ethical tie to the state? Over the course of history many answers have been given to this question, and they have usually fallen into one of two categories, which Ernst Troeltsch (following Ritschl) labeled "church" and "sect":[72] either the Christian community seeks to become an all-encompassing, all-controlling power ("church") within the society, Christianizing entire peoples and civilizations, and compromising itself when it seems more productive to do so; or the Christian community seeks to live by the radical ethic of Jesus, renouncing the world and its claims upon the community, and withdrawing into the relative obscurity and ineffectiveness of its own little world ("sect"). And yet one wonders, with Ritschl, whether there is not a third way between these two extremes.

Troeltsch was ultimately unable to map out a course between what he considered to be the two dead forms of Christianity, except to explore in preliminary ways a "third type" based upon spirit-mysticism.[73] But neither was Troeltsch able to predict the polarization of our society along the lines of "church" and "sect," and thus the revitalization of his own categories. For our society has been literally torn between religious Left and Right, political Left and Right, activism and passivism—and the Christian community has participated in this splitting. Significantly, Jürgen Moltmann has adopted Troeltsch's typologies in order to explain the dilemma in Christianity today. However, he does not attempt to solve the contemporary dilemma by developing a "third type," but rather affirms a strategy that embraces both dimensions of the church in a creative and dynamic process. According to Moltmann,

> the world-wide church needs the example of the groups committed to consistent discipleship, which demonstrate the liberty of Christ more unhesitatingly than church leaders and more radically than the masses. Every

---

ucative. In this sense, Reformation theology was correct in its demand that education be considered a mark of the true church."

71. See, for example, *PLK,* 129, and *SUK,* 220ff.

72. Ernst Troeltsch, *The Social Teaching of the Christian Churches* (Chicago: Univ. of Chicago Press, 1981), 2:993.

73. Ibid., 1006ff.

power of alteration which is immanent in a given system needs orientation towards an alternative which transcends that system. So as long as large-scale church organizations exist, we have to reckon with alternative forms of the Christian life. They and their criticism must be recognized by the established churches. They must not be pushed into the underground as irregular fringe groups. They are of quite vital importance for the mainstream churches, and must be accepted as "pacemakers".[74]

At the same time, however, he believes that

every alternative that transcends the given system—an alternative based on renunciation of the world and on resistance—remains ineffective if it is not related to the forces of alteration immanent in the system itself. Regulated discipleship groups and spontaneous movements for Christian action are putting themselves in a social ghetto of their own accord if they do not want to have a reforming effect on church and society. Without the large-scale churches these groups have no basis in the rank and file. Unless it affects the church which is open to the world, the practice of denying the world loses its relationship to the world altogether.[75]

Corresponding to this strategy is a concept of the church as "a committed congregation" or "the church as an event":

"The church as an event", as fellowship and action, needs the church as an institution, because of its historical continuity and the extra-territorial solidarity of its groups. On the other hand "the church as an institution" needs "the church as an event" because of its practical vitality. Of course this is merely a notional and typical allocation of characteristics. . . . Like other social institutions, the church is a living process.[76]

As an instance of "the committed congregation," Moltmann points to Latin American "grass-roots" communities and to community work in American and English slums.[77] Unfortunately, however, Moltmann is not quite clear how these communities relate to the state. And so the question surfaces once again: How can the inner autonomy of the church be joined with its moral tie to the state?

Here I believe Ritschl can contribute something to political and liberation theologies, since his conception of the *christliche Gemeinde* (or Christian community) encompasses both of these dimensions (its inner autonomy and its moral tie to the state) in a single concept, without conflating them. The autonomy of the community is located in its religious dimension; the moral tie, in its ethical dimension. The autonomous community is termed *church,* since it visibly gathers around the preaching of the Gospel and the administration of the sacraments. The moral tie of

74. Moltmann, 325–26.
75. Ibid., 326.
76. Ibid., 333.
77. Ibid., 328–32.

the community with the state is termed *the kingdom of God,* since it is
present wherever Christians exercise love for their neighbor. The Christian community encompasses both and is directed toward both. And yet
the relation between the two is not one of identity but one of mutual re-
ciprocity—a dynamic relation based on different activities. As Ritschl
explains in the *Instruction:*

> The community of believers must fulfill its mission in these two relations
> in such a way that the two lines of their activity shall stand in reciprocal
> relation to one another, but it is a mistake so to identify the two as to use
> the same name interchangeably for them both. For the actions by which
> the community becomes a church are not those by which it unites itself to
> the kingdom of God, and vice versa. (§9, n. 18)

Exactly how these dimensions can be confused will not become clear
until we have cited concrete examples. We have already seen how Ritschl
employed the distinction between the ethical and religious dimensions
against the Rationalists, Confessionalists, and Roman Catholics. However, in order to employ the same distinction today, we must list other
opponents.

One thinks, first of all, of the classical Marxist critique of religion,[78]
which, like the Rationalist argument Ritschl confronted, considers
Christianity to have exercised a generally negative influence upon society. It indicts religion for allowing appeals to the next life to lull the
working masses into complacency rather than working for change in this
life. And so, some Marxists say, people would be better off if they
avoided religion altogether, or at least worked outside of it, in order to
transform societal structures. Against this devaluation of religion and
church, Ritschl would probably respond today much as he did to the Rationalists of his own day: These Marxists underestimate the usefulness—
indeed, the necessity—of visible church structures for the new order they
seek. They look upon the Christian community as simply an ideology or
a religious feeling and not as a visible, institutional power within the
world. They must therefore begin to see the ethical dimension of the
Gemeinde in the visible church of God.

One thinks, secondly, of the pronouncement on ecclesiology delivered
by the Liberation Theology Group at the 1987 Annual Meeting of the
American Academy of Religion in Boston—namely, that the "church" is
present "wherever there is the struggle for liberation and justice in the
world."[79] Here we meet a tendency diametrically opposed to that of the
classical Marxists: Whereas the Marxists reject the church in favor of activity in the world, the liberationists at the American Academy of Reli-

---

78. I distinguish the classical Marxists here from the neo-Marxists, particularly of the
Frankfurt School, who would criticize the classical statements in much the same way as I
have done here and would grant far more importance to institutional religion in reforming
the society than would the classical Marxists.

79. *AAR/SBL Abstracts 1987* (Atlanta, Ga.: Scholars Press, 1987).

gion redefine the church *in terms of* that activity. Ironically, this latter position parallels that of the Roman Catholic Ultramontanists in Ritschl's own day, who equated the church with a type of "state within a state." Ritschl's defense against the liberationists at the American Academy of Religion would therefore probably sound very much like his response to the Ultramontanists: The church is, in its very essence, a religious reality, wholly constituted by God and perceptible to faith alone. As such, it is distinct from ethical activity in the world, and therefore also from all merely moral or political institutions. The liberationists at the American Academy of Religion, therefore, err in making the church dependent upon certain social activities, and they have thus confused the church with the kingdom of God. As a consequence, they either transmute the church of Christ into a political organization, or they lose sight of whatever reason they had to remain within the institutional church, since the institutional structures are so "saddled with imperfections," as they (and Ritschl!) put it.

The previous examples should serve to illustrate the utility of Ritschl's distinction between the religious and the ethical dimensions of the Christian community. However, the connections between the two dimensions may still be in doubt. What is of significance in Ritschl's theology of Christian community, however, are precisely these connections. On the one hand, the community as church and as kingdom of God comprise the self-same subject in history. On the other hand, the two aspects of the community—the one religious and the other ethical—mutually condition one another throughout history. It would probably be best, therefore, to speak of a historical circle, wherein Christ moves the community to religious awareness, then to ethical activity, and then back again to a fuller and richer faith.

The circle has four components or movements:

1. The intention of Christ to include all humanity in a kingdom of God necessarily entails the idea of a "moral fellowship."[80]
2. Because this fellowship or community comes into being only by reason of a religious estimate of God's intention in Christ, it can exist only in relation to the faith of the community's individual members.[81]
3. Conversely, as the individual members relate themselves to God's final end (which is to include all of humanity in a moral community), they will strive to realize that moral community in the world.[82]
4. Finally, as others are incorporated within the moral fellowship,

---

80. *JR 3*, §34.
81. *JR* 3:138–39, 562.
82. *ICR,* §§10 and 13.

they are once again related religiously to the final end of God by faith and moral education.[83]

The circle is now complete. The purpose of Christ to include all of humanity in a moral commonwealth conditions the whole and drives it forward through history; and religious faith forms not only the basis for, but also the necessary form by which, the community attains that end.[84]

Thus, we see that Ritschl's conception of the Christian community is not static, but dynamic, and in this way much like Moltmann's notion of the "committed congregation." The institutional and ethical aspects condition one another mutually in a historically creative way; and all the while, the community remains critically independent of the larger society and yet also a vital source of change from within it. Indeed, one may compare this conception with that of *ecclesiogenesis* in Latin American liberation ecclesiology, as long as one is careful to note the considerable differences in terms of theological starting point and ethical praxis.[85]

---

83. *JR* 3:111.

84. Ritschl's teleology was diametrically opposed to Richard Rothe's. Instead of the state eventually assuming all the duties of the Christian faith and rendering the institutional church superfluous, Ritschl believed that the church would gradually assimilate all peoples and nations unto itself and thus bring an even greater "kingdom of God" upon the earth—the kingdom of international peace or, as he put it, the "commonwealth of nations." This opinion is evidenced most clearly in *JR* 3:22: "We must therefore recognise the fact that the individual enters upon the common human task of Christianity, never merely as an individual, but always under the conditions, whether favourable or unfavourable, of his peculiar national education. The truth here brought out is completed by the further observation that, in order to fulfil its destined end, Christianity must win over the nations as wholes. That is, it can only really accomplish its universal human purpose when it brings under its influence all the social conditions under which the spiritual life of individuals exists. A Christianity which should remain anti-national in the minority of a people would destroy the necessary foundation on which the spiritual existence of its adherents rests, and thus itself sink into a fruitless particularism. . . . If the nations [therefore] fulfil their destined end, namely, their development into one whole supernatural humanity, through their reception into the religious community of Christianity, then this whole is also the object of the decisive operation of God which determines its peculiar origin and existence" (*JR* 3:134–35, 138). Although Ritschl's ecclesiology clearly evidences a propensity toward ecclesiastical triumphalism (which also characterized the Roman church of the Middle Ages!), it also includes many positive points. These may be found, as has often been stated, in Ritschl's earliest articles on the Christian community, since those articles are more concerned with balancing the independence of the church with its moral tie to the state.

85. See, for example, Leonardo Boff, *Ecclesiogenesis: The Base Communities Reinvent the Church* (Maryknoll, N.Y.: Orbis, 1986), and Boff, *Church: Charism and Power* (New York: Crossroad, 1985). Latin American liberation theology always begins with concrete liberating praxis. Religious faith then (and only secondarily) reflects back upon this praxis in the worship experience of the Christian community. The circle that Ritschl draws is therefore inverted in liberation theology. It no longer proceeds from faith, to ethical activity, and back again to faith; on the contrary, it proceeds from liberative praxis, to faith, and back again to praxis. This distinction may sound trivial at first glance, but it is absolutely crucial, since it provides a revolutionary critique of the bourgeois assumptions of the liberal model—namely, that ethical activity must proceed from the internal working of divine forgiveness upon the individual moral disposition (character building through one's vocational faithfulness!). The outcome for social ethics is therefore far more revolutionary.

VI

I feel compelled to conclude with a plea for understanding. If a new assessment of Ritschl's theology is to be at one and the same time both fair and critical, one must avoid adopting certain presuppositions wholesale, as we have seen in the introductory section of this essay. Rather, one must judge Ritschl's doctrine of Christian community within the context of the constraints of his own day. One should not so much try to seek out those elements in the Ritschlian system which have "a more enduring significance" as endeavor to recover the practical intentions inherent within his own doctrine of Christian community.

Nevertheless, we must be critical of those intentions as well. We must judge the adequacy of Ritschl's theological statements not only with respect to his own era but also to the contemporary era, which no longer regards German nationalism to be the desirable goal or the terrible threat it once was. We cannot and should not, therefore, be expected to accept Ritschl's naive and *ständisch* approach to the complex social and political problems of his day, rooted as it was in the bourgeois, nationalistic assumptions of late nineteenth-century Germany. For example, Ritschl consistently maintained that an individual could fulfill the universal moral law of love, but only within the narrow confines of one's vocation. As he often stated, "The universal can be realized only in the particular." By admitting this, however, he gave more credence to the development of virtue and the perfection of moral character than would be acceptable today. What makes his view even more untenable is the fact that he interprets all these virtues conservatively, and that he seems to have presupposed a static nineteenth-century conception of vocation that would leave the basic social structures of the world untouched.

An even more basic difficulty for Ritschl's social ethic, however, lies in his dogmatics in particular, in the idea of "homogeneity" between the divine and human end, or between the kingdom as "highest good" and the kingdom as "communal task." Because Ritschl does not entertain the possibility of a *conflictive* relationship between God and the human agent, he also leaves no room at all for a conflictive relationship between the individual and the state. Hence, no real change is effected among the structures of society, from the religious side at least; rather, one is called to "self-control, conscientiousness, discretion, and kindliness" within one's ethical vocation—a vocation that is largely determined by the state. Practically, then, religion becomes the pawn of the state, to be used as the latter sees fit—that is, as a means to some political end. This is precisely the sort of social ethic Karl Barth opposed in his earliest years as a pastor at Safenwil, and rightly so.

However, we also live in an age in which extremists on both the Right and the Left seem to have lost touch with the specifically religious foundation for sociopolitical action—an age that all too readily confuses the church either with the status quo or with "the struggle for liberation and justice in the world"—an age that seeks once again to reduce the Christian religion to the dimensions of the ethical and the moral, whether on the Right or the Left. In this new age, it now appears tragic that Ritschl's original vision of ecclesiastically instituted reform of the social order has become obscured by later Ritschlians, and perhaps also by the later Ritschl himself, in favor of a more insistent appeal to the kingdom of God as emergent within society. This tragedy has been compounded in recent years, as modern-day prophets of a secularized Christianity herald past mistakes as new advances and once again accommodate themselves to the larger culture at hand—whether this be in the form of an ideology that espouses "America as God's New Kingdom" or one that champions "God's Coming Revolution" in the world. It would, therefore, seem wise to follow Ritschl's advice and critique the later developments by the original insight. The need to recover a sensibility for the religious and relate this meaningfully to contemporary social issues is more urgent than ever before. Perhaps we would not be too remiss if we were to appropriate Ritschl's own statement for our day: "The Conservatives and the Marxists, for totally different reasons, want complete separation of church and state. The Far Right wants as close a dependence as possible, with deference to the police. . . . It remains to be seen, however, whether a third conception will find the correct path by which the inner autonomy of the church can be joined with the moral tie of the church to the state." Perhaps the search for this third conception will itself reveal that our own age is not so far removed from that of Albrecht Ritschl, and that we are proximate in spirit if not entirely one in social location.

6

The Centrality and Bipolar Focus of Kingdom

Ritschl's Theological Import for the Twentieth Century

HANS SCHWARZ

From my seminary days I remember being taught that Albrecht Ritschl was a Kantian who emphasized an exclusively this-worldly dimension of God's kingdom, which was to be realized in human vocation. Therefore Ritschl's theology was outmoded, a typical product of nineteenth-century cultural Protestantism. Yet that portrayal is a caricature. As this article will show, Ritschl's notion of the kingdom had a decidedly twofold or bipolar focus: a this-worldly one in which we engage through various dimensions of our earthly vocation and a future-directed aspect becoming fully inaugurated through God's own doing. Ritschl brought together in amazing clarity two important aspects of the New Testament, the Gospels' emphasis on the kingdom of God and the Pauline insight on justification. For this reason it is not surprising that Ritschl's foundational insights are still very much alive in German theology and, for that matter, in any theology that adorns itself correctly with the adjective "Christian." But Ritschl was also a product of his own age, the nineteenth century, which advocated an idealized kingdom. The eschatological urgency of the concept had not yet been discovered. Therefore twentieth-century theologians, whether overtly or implicitly building upon Ritschl's bipolar focus on the kingdom, have amended this concept with a more dynamic outlook.

Humanity's faith in progress, prevailing through much of the nineteenth century, was paralleled by theology's notion of the kingdom of God. The latter served both as a stimulus for human advancement and as its corrective, so that progress would not deteriorate into utopianism. By pointing to humanity's striving for moral completion, Immanuel Kant had contributed to the idea of the kingdom of God. In it Hegel saw the complete realization of the notion of freedom, guaranteed by the state. Schleiermacher discovered faithfulness to one's profession as the arena in which the kingdom would be realized. Richard Rothe saw state and church merged into the ideal kingdom, the absolute theocracy. And finally, there came Albrecht Ritschl with his interpretation of the kingdom of God.

THE CENTRALITY OF THE KINGDOM
AND ITS BIPOLAR FOCUS

Ritschl touches on the kingdom of God in many of his writings, including an address on the occasion of the four hundredth anniversary of Martin Luther's birth. The Christian religion, Ritschl observes, explains trust in God by means of the idea that the uniting of humanity into God's kingdom is the end toward which the world is moving. Therefore the world order and its course are subjected by God to that end, so that those who love God and are loved by God will serve all things, even the negative ones, to their ultimate good.[1] In announcing volumes 2 and 3 of his magnum opus, *The Christian Doctrine of Justification and Reconciliation* (1874) (*Die christliche Lehre von der Rechtfertigung und Versöhnung*), he again praises Luther for his insistence on justification and communion with God. In faith toward God's special guidance, in patience and humility, the Christian overcomes the experience of all evil that stems from the world. Through faithful exercise of one's special calling and the experience of freedom, a person contributes to the final goal of this world: humanity as a moral community.[2]

Ritschl refuses to merge the kingdom of God with the church, as had been done since Augustine, and also refuses to abandon the kingdom concept, since its absence would only lead to individual moralism.[3] He accepts the rediscovery of the idea of the kingdom by Kant and accepts Schleiermacher's linking of the concept with the Christian faith, but in contrast to them he sees the kingdom as *the* principle of Christian ethics. When love is enacted, the shared supernatural bond of humans as spiritual beings does not find its area of activity outside, but within the special communities of marriage, family, citizenship, and nationhood. Possible egotism is eliminated through the communal aspect of the kingdom, and the natural gifts contained in these communities are enhanced.

The theocentric thrust of Ritschl's notion of the kingdom of God becomes evident in *The Christian Doctrine of Justification and Reconciliation* when he makes this concept part of his doctrine of God:

The Kingdom of God is the *summum bonum* which God realises in men; and at the same time it is their common task, for it is only through the ren-

---

1. Albrecht Ritschl, "Festrede am vierten Seculartage der Geburt Martin Luthers (10. November 1883)," in *DAR*, 11.
2. Albrecht Ritschl in *Göttingische gelehrte Anzeigen*, part 36 (September 9, 1874), 1134.
3. Cf. ibid., 1134f., for the following material.

dering of obedience on man's part that God's sovereignty possesses continuous existence. These two meanings are interdependent.[4]

The social dimension of the kingdom becomes even more obvious in the
following statement:

> Justice is the communal activity of those who belong to the kingdom of
> God. It is the obedience through which the dominion of God exercised
> through Christ becomes effective. The public good of being obedient to
> God's will is the plant which emerges out of the seed through the encour-
> aging power of the proclamation of the kingdom of God. And both the
> general and the particular moral order, which are equivalent to peace, are
> the fruit to which the individual who acts justly contributes in various ca-
> pacities, and from this contribution either a few or many will benefit, and
> from it the moral community will either receive its regular lease on life or
> gain a vigorous new impulse.[5]

The concept of the kingdom figures most prominently in Ritschl's *Instruction in the Christian Religion* [*Unterricht in der christlichen Religion*] in which he presents a summary of his own theology. Through the
title Ritschl intentionally calls to mind Calvin's *Institutes,* which he
wants to leave behind, as well as Melanchthon's *Loci* and Peter Lom-
bard's *Sentences.* Initially intended for the instruction of religion in
higher education, the *Unterricht* had its strongest impact as a summary
of Christian theology for theology students. The first of its four parts,
which comprises nearly one-third of the text, focuses on the doctrine of
the kingdom of God.

Ritschl declares: "The kingdom of God is the divinely ordained highest good of the community founded through God's revelation in Christ;
but it is the highest good only in the sense that it forms at the same time
the ethical ideal for whose attainment the members of the community
bind themselves to each other through a definite type of reciprocal action."[6] He sees the Christian notion of the kingship of God derived from
Israelite religion. But, since it is no longer connected with political and
liturgical conditions, it surpasses Old Testament thought. In the divine
self-revelation as love, God demonstrates that through the creation and
the governance of the world God aims at the final goal of the union of
humanity in the kingdom. This also shows, according to Ritschl, that before the creation of the world God already willed the founding of the
community of the kingdom.[7]

Ritschl is aware that there is no rectilinear progress toward the kingdom. Yet the Christian will not become disheartened by the seemingly

---

4. *JR* 3:30 (*RV 3,* 2d ed., 29).
5. *RV* 2, 2d ed., 292f. This is my own translation.
6. *ICR* in *TE,* §5, 222. [*Unterricht in der christlichen Religion,* ed. G. Ruhbach (Gütersloh: Gerd Mohn, 1966), 15.]
7. *ICR,* §14, 226 [20f.]

aimless entanglements of the present or the suffering of the just at the hands of the unjust, because these experiences help to exercise the moral solidarity of humanity as prefigured in the kingdom.[8] Ritschl also knows that the moral task of establishing a common rule has been recognized outside Christianity, but such a practical principle can only become effective if it stems from a special impetus. Here we see the enduring significance of Jesus for the Christian community, because through his calling he was exclusively designated to lead humanity toward the kingdom, and in no way did he deviate from this aim.[9] Jesus showed a unique solidarity with God by realizing the final aim of the kingdom in his own personal life. All our actions should also focus on the final goal of the kingdom of God so that they are done for the common good.

Ritschl realizes that as a product of the Christian community the kingdom of God is still in the process of becoming and encounters at every point the opposing currents of evil.[10]

> As a member of the Christian community one is called to the kingdom of God as man's highest good and his highest common duty, because it is the final purpose of God himself. At the same time, however, by the very recognition of this destiny there comes an increase of the feeling of guilt and separation from God which arises from our own sin and our solidarity with the sin common to all men.[11]

Therefore the forgiveness of sins and reconciliation with God together are the shared assumptions of the Christian community, as it realizes the kingdom. Reconciliation with God has nothing to do with our not having tried hard enough to do the good or our having some kind of inherent weakness, but is connected with the actual, uniquely Christian experience of God.[12] Christian perfection, which corresponds to the personal example of Christ, produces a moral life and forms a moral and religious character. One consequence is that all our actions in our particular moral calling are focused on the ultimate goal of the kingdom. Another is that within our respective settings we show ourselves to be children of God and exercise dominion over the world.[13]

It would be tempting to label Ritschl's understanding of the kingdom of God as purely moral.[14] Yet, for several reasons this would be wrong:

1. The kingdom of God is both the eternal aim of God for the world and the moral task of humanity that serves to accomplish this

8. *ICR*, §18, 228 [23].
9. *ICR*, §21ff. 229f. [25].
10. *ICR*, §27, 232 [35].
11. *ICR*, §34, 236 [39].
12. *ICR*, §34, 239 [42].
13. *ICR*, §57, 245 [50].
14. Contrary to Christian Walther, *Typen des Reich-Gottes Verständnisses. Studien zur Eschatologie und Ethik im 19. Jahrhundert* (Munich: Christian Kaiser, 1961), 155.

aim. This means that the kingdom has a bipolar focus, consisting first of the divine initiative and then of our human response.

2. Through the incarnation the kingdom breaks into time and is realized in Jesus' activity. Jesus therefore becomes the example of a morally perfect humanity, and by providing justification he enables us to pursue the kingdom.

3. Jesus founded a religious community, the church, which serves as a means to further the kingdom. The community aims at bringing the kingdom ever more perfectly into this world.

Because of human sinfulness the completion of the kingdom also has a future dimension. Though Ritschl does not admit that we tread water, so to speak, there is no timetable for the inauguration of the kingdom. While the kingdom does not simply exist in faith, Ritschl also does not equate human faithfulness with success in bringing about the kingdom. When in the future the natural conditions of our spiritual life in the present world order are eliminated or changed, then the kingdom will also emerge as a supernatural and supraworldly goal.[15] Since Ritschl did not indulge in mysticism and speculation, and since the stringent causal determinism of his own age was widely accepted, he was very cautious with assertions related to the eschatological dimension. Yet, contrary to the claims of a subsequent generation, he did not eliminate this facet from his concept of the kingdom.

A MODEST ASSESSMENT

As James Richmond writes, Ritschl, "perhaps more than anyone in the Christian tradition, wrestled with the problem of significantly relating the Kingdom of God and human action to the fabric of Christianity."[16] Indeed, Ritschl's interest was not so much in a worldview as in a view of life. The individual Christian was no longer seen as a spectator of the course of the world, but as a responsible member of the community, both of the ecclesial community and of natural configurations in family, state, and vocation.[17] Through faith in Jesus Christ as Lord and Savior, people are freed from themselves and available for service in God's world.

Ritschl rejects the romantic equation of the kingdom of God with culture in favor of a Kantian notion of the moral kingdom of reason.[18] The realm of reason is an ideal, as everything unconditioned remains ideal, but it is also the goal of an infinite approximation. At the same time the

---

15. *ICR,* §76, 254.
16. Richmond, 271.
17. Cf. the insightful comments by Horst Stephan, "Albrecht Ritschl und die Gegenwart," *Zeitschrift für Theologie und Kirche* 16 (1935): 29f.
18. Cf. Paul Tillich, "Albrecht Ritschl zu seinem hundertsten Geburtstag" (1922), in *Gesammelte Werke,* vol. 12 (Stuttgart: Evangelisches Verlagswerk, 1971), 157.

kingdom of God is a reality, not only as a beginning, but as a real break-ing-in "in the midst of you." The unconditional does not only lie at the end of history, so that history conditions it, but is also above history, so that it breaks into history. Therefore, in each historical period the king-dom of God and the kingdom of the world exist simultaneously. Thus the kingdom of God is more than the kingdom of reason; it is the pres-ence of God and therefore grace. It is also more than a supernaturally guided rational kingdom of ethical domination of the world. Since the religious embraces the moral, it is unfair to accuse Ritschl of reducing the religious to the ethical.[19] The kingdom of God is the final aim of both God and reconciled humanity.

From recognizing the kingdom as God's goal for humanity and as Jesus' own aim, Christians are summoned to moral action within their vocation in the world. In Ritschl's understanding of humanity's vocation for the kingdom, and his understanding of the kingdom as such, the demands of Christ and of cultural values are not in conflict but in har-mony. This harmony led H. Richard Niebuhr to observe that we en-counter here a "Christ of culture" and not a Christ who transforms culture.[20] As a result, the affirmation of the world gains the upper hand, while the radical critique of the world is shortchanged.

Ritschl showed much restraint concerning actual practice, whereas for his students this kind of restraint disappeared. They put theology in the midst of life and attempted to bring to the important issues of their times the newly rediscovered gospel, as distilled from the Bible and focused by Reformation insights. The journal *The Christian World* (*Die christliche Welt*), is one of the most impressive witnesses for the courage with which the followers of Ritschl tackled many hot and controversial issues. We should also not overlook the *Protestant Social Assembly* (*Evangelisch-Soziale Kongress*) to which Adolf von Harnack, a Ritschlian in his own right, decisively contributed. The Assembly was a gathering of lawyers, historians, economists, and the-ologians who wanted to win the alienated workers back to church and state. Similarly, Walter Rauschenbusch and the Social Gospel movement—or even the Swiss Socialists—showed an indebtedness to Ritschl. Why was the master much more hesitant than the followers to embark on a more radical and constructively critical course? Was it just that he was "constitutionally middle-class" and accepted the then given political socioeconomic system as the best possible under the prevailing circumstances?[21]

Perhaps Ritschl's conservative stance also had something to do with his interpretation of the sources for his notion of the kingdom. We re-member that Ritschl found the idea of the kingdom of God historically

---

19. Welch 2:19, in his assessment of Ritschl.
20. Cf. Niebuhr, 94ff.
21. So Welch, 24.

grounded in the person of Jesus. As God's final goal, the kingdom is the end Jesus came to announce and for which he founded the community of his followers. The business of Christ's vocation, as Ritschl expressed it, was to establish the universal ethical fellowship of humanity. Yet exactly at this point immediate criticism surfaced through Ritschl's son-in-law Johannes Weiss.

When Weiss published *The Preaching of Jesus concerning the Kingdom of God* (1892, Engl. trans. 1971), he affirmed, in clear opposition to Ritschl:

> The Kingdom of God, in Jesus' view, is never an ethical ideal, but is *nothing other than the highest religious Good,* a Good which God grants on certain conditions. This does not imply a Pharisaic conception of reward but naturally only a person who is entirely detached from αἰὼν οὗτος can really possess and enjoy this Good in the Kingdom of God. Otherwise he lacks completely the proper spiritual disposition; hence, participation in this Kingdom corresponds only to that which is spiritually possible. This interpretation of the Kingdom of God as an innerworldly ethical ideal is a vestige of the Kantian idea and does not hold up before a more precise historical examination.[22]

For Weiss the kingdom is totally otherworldly and its realization is up to God alone, not human action. People can only create the conditions for the kingdom demanded by God. Weiss also denies that Jesus thought of a this-worldly development of the kingdom. When Jesus talked about the kingdom that has already commenced, then, he was expressing a prophetic, future-directed view. Generally, however, the realization of the kingdom was thought to be still outstanding. Therefore, Jesus showed no inclination to perceive in the newly shaped piety of his followers any preliminary realization of the kingdom.

According to Weiss there can be no distinction between a preliminary inception and a final completion of the kingdom. "The disciples were to pray for the coming of the Kingdom, but men could do nothing to establish it."[23] Weiss therefore concludes

> that the dogmatic religious-ethical application of this idea in more recent theology, an application which has completely stripped away the original eschatological-apocalyptic meaning of the idea, is unjustified. Indeed, one proceeds in an only apparently biblical manner if one uses the term in a sense different from that of Jesus.[24]

Johannes Weiss does not want to preclude systematic theology from using the idea of the kingdom. To the contrary, he is convinced that it is

22. Weiss, 132f. (*Die Predigt vom Reiche Gottes,* 1st ed., as reprinted in: Johannes Weiss, *Die Predigt vom Reiche Gottes,* 3d ed., ed. Ferdinand Hahn, introd. Rudolf Bultmann [Göttingen: Vandenhoeck & Ruprecht, 1964], 244.)
23. Weiss, 129 [241].
24. Ibid., 114 [236].

a valid concept for awakening a vigorous religious life, but theologians should admit that they are using the concept differently from Jesus. We no longer share the eschatological sentiment of early Christianity, Weiss contends. We no longer pray that this world may pass away and God's grace may break in, but we live in joyful confidence that our own world may evermore become the arena of God's intended humanity. Though we are convinced that this world will continue, we hope that as the community of Jesus Christ we will someday be assembled in the heavenly kingdom.

Though Johannes Weiss identifies the eschatological fervor missing from Ritschl's system, his own view fails to foster this fervor, since theologically he advocates (with Ritschl) the belief in human amelioration, and since historically he points to Jesus' eschatological message of a completely otherworldly kingdom. It is not surprising that neither avenue was tenable once the aftermath of World War I was fully recognized. When the euphoric feeling of the nineteenth century abated, Ritschl's system could not but look archaic. Its biblical basis was at least tenuous, and its view of humanity as virtuous was far from being accurate. Even Ernst Troeltsch showed more promise, since he was more in tune with the large issues of modernity confronting the Christian faith.[25] Yet the giants of neo-Reformation theology, Karl Barth, Rudolf Bultmann, and Paul Tillich, though disavowing any rootedness in the preceding theological tradition, still betray the lasting influence of Ritschl and his notion of the kingdom.

THE KINGDOM OF GOD IN NEO-REFORMATION THEOLOGY

Rudolf Bultmann calls the kingdom of God "the dominant concept of Jesus' message."[26] In his book *Jesus,* he interprets the kingdom of God to mean the eschatological salvation for all humanity, which brings to an end all this-worldly activities. He rejects the notion that the kingdom could be the highest good, so to speak, the crowning conclusion of our goods. The kingdom of God as the eschatological otherworldly salvation stands in strong contrast to our relative this-worldly goods. The kingdom is not a highest good as understood by ethics;[27] it is not a good that can be approached through our willing and acting or realized through human conduct; the kingdom of God is a supernatural and otherworldly entity constituted solely through God's acting. It is of no interest to us as a state of being, but concerns us only as a miraculous event, which means for us the decisive either/or of our decision for or against God's

25. Cf. Stephan, "Albrecht Ritschl und die Gegenwart," 34f.

26. Rudolf Bultmann, *Theology of the New Testament,* trans. Kendrik Grobel (New York: Charles Scribner's Sons, 1951), 4.

27. Rudolf Bultmann, *Jesus and the Word,* trans. L. P. Smith and E. H. Lantero (New York: Charles Scribner's Sons, 1958), 35.

good. This decision is our free action and implies radical obedience toward God. The kingdom of God is radically in the future,[28] not something for which one can prepare so that at a certain point this future can be attained. The kingdom of God is a power that wholly determines the present, though it is totally future. One cannot describe the kingdom of God, because in so doing one would project one's ideals and desires into it and would rob it of its actual otherworldly character as God's rule.

Several points in Bultmann's interpretation are noteworthy. While he emphasizes with Ritschl the centrality of the kingdom, he rejects with Weiss its ethical dimension. Like Weiss he emphasizes the eschatological content of the idea of the kingdom. Yet, contrary to Weiss, he recognizes that the kingdom, though a future goal, reaches into the present in determining our human activities. After rejecting what he calls a dualistic anthropology, Bultmann is rather optimistic about our part in the kingdom. Similar to Ritschl, he contends that once humanity has recognized this as the right decision, it can decide in favor of the kingdom and follow God's will. However, since Bultmann is apprehensive regarding an ethical dimension to the kingdom (though pointing to the need for a decision and aligning oneself with God's will), his concept of the kingdom remains rather static. The kingdom looms ahead and enlightens our lives, but it does not take on more precise contours, nor does it draw near.

Karl Barth usually has little good to say about Albrecht Ritschl. Even in his *Protestant Theology in the Nineteenth Century* (1952, Engl. trans. 1959), he attempts to diminish Ritschl's significance from inaugurating an epoch to being merely an episode. When a theologian so vigorously disclaims any indebtedness, however, our suspicions should become even more acutely aroused. James Richmond is certainly correct in stating that the Ritschlian roots of certain Barthian leading ideas seem to be proved "beyond all reasonable doubt."[29] We could mention here the aversion to natural theology, mysticism, and pietism, the insistence on God's Word as it comes to us through the biblical documents, and the inclusion of ethics within the corpus of systematic theology.

Since Barth did not finish his *Church Dogmatics,* both eschatology and the kingdom of God receive only passing treatment. Helmut Gollwitzer conjectures that in the eschatological part of his *Church Dogmatics* Karl Barth would have gone back to his earlier interpretation of Romans.[30] Barth would have insisted that the kingdom of God involves the hope of a cosmic fulfillment, including not only the reconciliation of humanity and nature, but also a new harmony among humans; the kingdom includes not just the vertical dimension (of eternal life for the indi-

---

28. Cf. ibid., 51.
29. Richmond, 285.
30. For the following material cf. Helmut Gollwitzer, *Reich Gottes und Sozialismus bei Karl Barth. Theologische Existenz Heute,* No. 169 (Munich: Chr. Kaiser, 1972), 35.

vidual in communion with God), but also a horizontal component. Though Barth, especially in his early period, had emphasized the otherworldliness of the kingdom, he never restricted eschatology to the divine grace that happens to the individual in the Word of proclamation. In this respect Karl Barth was not a disciple of Rudolf Bultmann.

Barth, in reflecting on his early period, concedes that at that time he had to say: "A Christianity that is not wholly and utterly and irreducibly eschatology has absolutely nothing to do with Christ. . . . Redemption is that which cannot be seen, the inaccessible, the impossible, which confronts us as hope."[31] Similarly, he had interpreted the tension between the "then" when we first believed and the "now" of our present existence as a continual tension, having no connection with the tension of two points in time and nothing to do with church history. This emphasis on otherworldliness in defiance of a so-called cultural Protestantism made Barth, as he concedes in his *Church Dogmatics,* miss the distinctive point of Romans 13:11ff., "the teleology which it [this passage] ascribes to time as it moves towards a real end."

Barth objects to the theory that had been developed in opposition to the Ritschlian school "that the whole momentum of the New Testament message and of the New Testament faith lay in the hope of Jesus' return and the setting up of the kingdom of God on earth—a hope that had not been fulfilled and was therefore erroneous." Barth now sees the kingdom of God much more as Ritschl did, as something that also reaches into this world. Almost in a complete reversal Karl Barth can now say, when meditating on the Sermon on the Mount:

> As an announcement of the kingdom of God, the Sermon on the Mount makes the following declaration. Here on this earth and in time, and therefore in the immediate context of all human kingdoms both small and great, and in the sphere of Satan who rules and torments fallen man, God has irrevocably and indissolubly set up the kingdom of His grace, the throne of His glory, the kingdom which as such is superior to all other powers, to which, in spite of their resistance, they belong, and which they cannot help but serve.[32]

The kingdom of heaven is seen not just as a future possibility; the overwhelming and decisive emphasis "is not on the future but on the present." Barth would not concede that humanity can help establish the kingdom; it is the kingdom of the eternal God himself and therefore is a gift. Human life is marked by hope to the extent "that it can be lived as new life only as we hear the Word of Jesus, to the extent that man has

31. For the quotations that follow see Karl Barth, *Church Dogmatics,* vol. 2/1, trans. T. H. L. Parker et al. (Edinburgh: T & T Clark, 1957), 634ff., and cf. Karl Barth, *The Epistle to the Romans,* trans. from the 6th ed. by E. C. Hoskyns (London: Oxford Univ. Press, 1933), 331f., 432, 498, where he emphasizes the exclusively otherworldly and nontemporal dimension of the kingdom.

32. For the following quotations see Karl Barth, *Church Dogmatics* 2/2:688ff.

continually to look beyond himself in order, in that moment, to be able to live in this moment the life of the new man. But it must also be realised and said that in this moment it is objectively present as new life." With Jesus the kingdom and the new humanity that goes with it have appeared. "Because this has happened, the covenant is completed, its history is closed, and the time still left has become a mere running out of time to its appointed end." Here the kingdom of God is pulled into time in such a way that in faithful anticipation we have to await the end of time.

It is not surprising that in "The Christian Community and the Civil Community" (1946) Barth claims that the true state must have its original image and example in the true church.[33] The state exists already in the kingdom, whether the state knows it or not. The church, therefore, must be a witness to the kingdom, reminding everyone of it. This does not mean that the state gradually becomes the kingdom of God. "The Kingdom of God is the Kingdom where God is without shadow, without problems and contradictions, where He is All in All: it is the rule of God in the redeemed world."[34] Here Barth comes very close to Ritschl's own understanding of the kingdom. Yet, in contrast to Ritschl's individualized notion of vocation, Karl Barth emphasizes the ecclesiological aspect of the community. While this emphasis is convenient for pronouncements of a corporate nature—such as the *Barmen Declaration* (1934), which was decisively shaped by Barth—an individual ethics of the kingdom has not come into focus. Barth is more interested in molding the (political) community than the individual Christian.

We should also not overlook Karl Barth's deep indebtedness to the Religious Socialists and their interpretation of the kingdom of God. He can even identify the kingdom of God with true socialism, both as the goal of God's history with humanity and the present movement here on earth.[35] As Barth still asserts in his *Church Dogmatics*, pure doctrine cannot be separated from praxis. Yet the decisive word must be seen in "the proclamation of His kingdom as it has already come and comes" and not "in the proclamation of social progress or socialism."[36] We notice here a bipolar focus that, though intent on "God's revolution," is much in the line of Ritschl. Barth's view, however, contains an added urgency that may stem from the fervor of the Religious Socialists.

Paul Tillich devotes the fifth part of his *Systematic Theology* to the topic "History and the Kingdom of God." The symbol "kingdom of

33. Karl Barth, "The Christian Community and the Civil Community," in his *Community, State and Church: Three Essays*, intro. Will Herberg (Garden City, N.Y.: Doubleday, 1960), 188.

34. Ibid., 167.

35. Cf. Gollwitzer, *Reich Gottes*, 7.

36. Karl Barth, *Church Dogmatics*, vol. 3/4, trans. A. T. MacKay et al. (Edinburgh: T & T Clark, 1961), 545. Gollwitzer's interpretation, *Reich Gottes*, 23, makes Barth sound much more radical than he actually is.

God" has a double character, manifested in an inner-historical sense in the presence of the divine Spirit and in a transhistorical aspect in eternal life.[37] This twofold connotation makes this symbol very important and at the same time extremely difficult. Tillich admits that, strangely, it has lost most of its persuasive power in the churches, though Jesus' first message was the proclamation of the nearness of the kingdom and Christendom continued to pray in the Lord's Prayer for the coming of the kingdom. Though the symbol "kingdom of God" contains the possibility for expressing immanent and transcendent elements, usually one of the two predominates.

Tillich sees in history a preparation for the central manifestation of the kingdom of God. He points both to pre-Christian developments and to the proleptic element contained in the present. The history of the reception of the central manifestation of the kingdom is the history of the church. Yet the church also anticipates what will occur in the future. The representation of the kingdom of God in the churches is as ambiguous as the realization of communion in the Spirit within the churches; it is at the same time revealing and concealing. There are victories of the kingdom of God in history, victories against the disintegrating consequences of the ambiguity of power.

In history the fragmentary actualization of the kingdom of God stands in tension with the still expected kingdom. If one absolutizes the fragmentary fulfillment of the goal of history, demonic distortions occur. On the other hand, if the realization of the kingdom within history is not discerned at all, then utopianism and disappointment follow each other and prepare the ground for cynicism. Therefore it is important for the churches as representatives of the kingdom of God in history to uphold the tension between the presence of the kingdom and its expectation. "The fragmentary victories of the Kingdom of God in history point by their very character to the non-fragmentary side of the Kingdom of God 'above' history. But even 'above' history, the Kingdom of God is related to history; it is the 'end' of history."[38] Though human life on earth and earth itself will cease to exist, the goal of history goes far beyond this end. It is the end of time, meaning the consummation of history.

Since Tillich does not cite sources in his *Systematic Theology*, it is difficult to ascertain whether Ritschl's impact can still be seen. Though his emphasis on the kingdom motif can also stem from Religious Socialism, it is certainly exceptional that he would devote such a large portion of his *Systematic Theology* to the kingdom. It is also significant that the eschatological urgency of the kingdom, pointed out by Johannes Weiss and continued by Rudolf Bultmann, is completely missing in Paul Tillich. Similar to Ritschl's outlook, the overriding category is the histor-

---

37. Cf. for the following material Paul Tillich, *Systematic Theology,* vol. 3 (Chicago: Univ. of Chicago Press, 1963), 357–94.
38. Ibid., 394.

ical process. The central manifestation and the preliminary realizations of the kingdom occur in history. Yet, contrary to Ritschl, prime significance is accorded the kingdom's ecclesiological aspect. To be sure, Tillich concedes that in history the kingdom of God is usually advanced by groups of people or individuals who live latently in the church, so that through their preparatory activities the visible church can become the vessel for the movement of history toward this goal. But this prophetic role of individuals or groups can hardly be equated with the concept of vocation prominent in Ritschl's understanding of the kingdom and its promulgation.

THE ESCHATOLOGICAL ASPECT OF THE KINGDOM IN CURRENT THEOLOGY

Wolfhart Pannenberg is three generations removed from Ritschl. Over this distance a direct line of influence is even more difficult to demonstrate. Following a hint made by Philip Hefner, however, James Richmond claims that the "Ritschl-Weiss historical nexus" in its "real implications [is] just now being fully unfolded by the current 'eschatological' school of theology, which includes Pannenberg, Carl Braaten, and Jürgen Moltmann."[39] Yet, to determine the place of the kingdom in Pannenberg's theology is a difficult task, since his *Systematic Theology* is not yet finished. The portions that have so far been published do not give much insight into the significance of the kingdom for his theology as a whole.

In the first volume of his *Systematic Theology*, Pannenberg discusses extensively Ritschl's rejection of "natural theology" in favor of a theology of revelation and observes that this trend was picked up in the twentieth century, especially by Karl Barth.[40] Yet Pannenberg labels Ritschl's concept of natural theology "confused" (*verworren*). In volume 2 Pannenberg is more appreciative of Ritschl, especially of his insistence on a Christology from below.[41] Yet he follows Weiss's criticism of Ritschl, claiming that it cannot be rightly said that Jesus founded or inaugurated the kingdom of God, especially not in connection with his alleged founding of the Christian community.[42] By dating the foundation of the Christian church to the earthly activity of Jesus, and by identifying the church with the kingdom of God proclaimed by Jesus, Ritschl saw the activity of the resurrected and exalted One too much as a rectilinear continuation of the earthly activity of Jesus between his baptism and crucifixion. Pannenberg then sides with Ritschl when he asserts, against Schleierma-

39. Richmond, 272.
40. Cf. Wolfhart Pannenberg, *Systematische Theologie*, vol. 1 (Göttingen: Vandenhoeck & Ruprecht, 1988), 1:112ff.
41. So Wolfhart Pannenberg, *Systematische Theologie*, vol. 2 (Göttingen: Vandenhoeck & Ruprecht, 1991), 2:318f.
42. For the following see ibid., 350.

cher, that the central point of Jesus' proclamation is the insistence on the nearness of the kingdom. He further agrees with him that there is a connection between the notion of the kingdom and the Old Testament expectation of God's rule. To assess in a more extensive way how Pannenberg develops his own understanding of the kingdom, we must await volume 3. Yet, from volumes 1 and 2 and from his earlier publications, it is already clear that Pannenberg develops major points of his own theology in critical dialogue with Ritschl.

Pannenberg admits that the future of the kingdom of God, which has become concrete in Jesus of Nazareth as the future of the existing world, characterizes his *Jesus—God and Man* (1964, Engl. trans. 1968) and his slender volume *Theology and the Kingdom of God* (1969, Germ. trans. 1971);[43] the same idea can also be noted in his much earlier "Dogmatic Theses on Revelation." Pannenberg considers the announcement of the coming kingdom of God to be at the center of Jesus' message. To be sure, Pannenberg observes, within the last few decades dogmatic reflection has given less attention to the kingdom, perhaps in reaction to the predominant nineteenth-century idea of the kingdom being contingent on human activity. However, he finds something good in this nineteenth-century emphasis: Where humans do the will of God, there, according to Jesus' message, the will of God and God himself come to rule. Pannenberg thus finds quite understandable the nineteenth-century view that obedience to God's will helps establish the kingdom. What stands between the nineteenth century and us is Johannes Weiss, with his emphasis on the eschatological interpretation of the kingdom, the significance of which, according to Pannenberg, theology has still not adequately grasped.

Pannenberg insists that theology must reclaim the fundamental eschatological dimension of Jesus' message.[44] But, unlike Weiss, he contends that the kingdom cannot only be seen in antithesis to everything presently existing, to the this-worldly reality. In contrast to the hope in the future current among his contemporary Jews, Jesus emphasized the present effectiveness of the coming kingdom. The kingdom does not allow us, however, to talk only about its present impact without considering the futurity of God and his kingdom. The presence of the kingdom must be understood as a foreshadowing of its future, qualifying all present experience in the light of the certainty of the immediately impending coming of the kingdom. Pannenberg concludes that, although it is alien to our thinking that the future determines the present, it certainly represents New Testament and Jewish thought.

---

43. Wolfhart Pannenberg, in his preface to *Theologie und Reich Gottes* (Gütersloh: Gerd Mohn, 1971), 7 (not contained in the English original of *Theology and the Kingdom of God*).

44. For the following cf. Pannenberg, 51–55.

It is interesting how Pannenberg regards the church. In order to be true to Jesus' message, he asserts, every Christian church must understand itself as a community related to the kingdom of God as proclaimed by Jesus.[45] Yet the kingdom is not confined to, or identical with, the church, for it also touches the future of the world and all of humanity. Pannenberg affirms that "communion with Christ is identical with one's dedication to the Kingdom of God as the future of the world," and that "Christ's rule is nothing else than the preparing of the way for the Kingdom of God. Where Christ rules, the Kingdom of God is already dawning."[46]

But Pannenberg is very emphatic that the kingdom will not be established by humans. The kingdom is not the result of some human plan, but belongs to God. It cannot be identified with the church or any part of the church. Yet whoever acts in the service of the kingdom, that is, to further the good of society, acts also for the good of the church.[47] Thus the church must always be concerned about the kingdom of God among people, since the coming kingdom is no otherworldly phenomenon, but "the future fulfillment of humanity."[48] Hope for the future kingdom recognizes that the kingdom remains incomplete. Yet this hope does not remain complacent. Through the power of its certainty in the future, the power of love and hope transforms the present. Hope-active-in-love acknowledges the preliminary status of its activities and remains open for the future of God's kingdom.

Pannenberg's interpretation of the kingdom shows a creative combination of Ritschl's emphasis on the present within the structures of family, state, and world community—the latter, though, not yet recognized by Ritschl—and the eschatological hope as pointed out by Weiss. Yet, in contrast to Weiss, this interpretation of the kingdom does not lead to an interim ethic that, since the kingdom will never come, regards the kingdom and itself to be obsolete now. Quite the contrary: all our ethics must be interim, since the kingdom is not yet fulfilled, although its future has gained undeniable credibility through the coming of Jesus. While Johannes Weiss had pointed to the eschatological dimension of the kingdom and at the same time discredited it as lacking present relevance, Pannenberg rightly recognizes its relevance. The eschatological dimension shows us the dynamic structure of the kingdom and encourages human involvement in behalf of the kingdom, made manifest in its preliminary foreshadowing.

In contrast to Pannenberg, Jürgen Moltmann hardly mentions Ritschl. In the three major works of his early period (1965–75), *Theology of Hope, The Crucified God,* and *The Church in the Power of the Spirit,*

---

45. Cf. Pannenberg, 73.
46. Pannenberg, 76f.
47. Cf. Pannenberg, 84.
48. Pannenberg, 85.

Ritschl is only mentioned twice, and then only in passing. In his later writings, such as *The Future of Creation* (1977, Engl. trans. 1979) and *The Passion for Life* (1977, Engl. trans. 1978), the picture remains unchanged. The reason is obvious. Moltmann focuses on the present, and his dialogue with the past is conducted only selectively. Pannenberg, however, with his attempt to establish a universal, historical view (*Universalgeschichte*), is in conversation with the whole of the Christian tradition, which, for the nineteenth century, means especially Hegel, Schleiermacher, and Ritschl.

Moltmann does not explicitly converse with Ritschl, even when discussing topics for which attention to him would prove beneficial. For instance, Moltmann picks up the theme of the kingdom of God in his *The Church in the Power of the Spirit* (1975, Engl. trans. 1977), but not once is Ritschl even mentioned. Moltmann is much less hesitant than Pannenberg in making the connection between the church and the kingdom, saying: "The church in the power of the Spirit is not yet the kingdom of God, but it is its anticipation in history."[49] Christianity is not yet the new creation, but is the working of the Spirit of the new creation. Therefore the churches understand their own existence and their task in history in a messianic sense, anticipating what is hoped for and at the same time representing it. Moltmann does not divide history and eschatology, assigning the former to this world and the latter to the next, but claims that the eschatological kingdom of God enters into history in the present (though still disputed and hidden) rule of God. The eschatological kingdom is the power that determines the present.[50] In this respect the future has already begun.

In a more recent major publication, *The Trinity and the Kingdom* (1980, Engl. trans. 1981), with which he opens an intended five-volume set of *Contributions to a Systematic Theology*, there is again no mention of Albrecht Ritschl. In a major section on the kingdom his dialogue partner is Joachim of Fiore. Moltmann asks there how God's Trinity is properly related to the kingdom and arrives at the conclusion that we must rediscover the truth of Joachim's trinitarian view of history.[51] The history of the kingdom must be understood in a trinitarian sense, though not in terms of historic succession. We must realize that with the kingdoms of the Father, the Son, and the Spirit, we denote already present layers and transitions within the history of the kingdom.[52] Since the three persons of the Trinity have everything in common except their distinct personhood, they cannot be defined in relation to one another in terms of power and properties, but must be seen in terms of community and interpersonal sig-

49. Moltmann, 196.
50. For the following material cf. Moltmann, 190–96.
51. Cf. Jürgen Moltmann, *Trinität und Reich Gottes. Zur Gotteslehre* (Munich: Chr. Kaiser, 1980), 221.
52. Cf. ibid., 226.

nificance.[53] According to Moltmann, therefore, a trinitarian concept of the kingdom would lead us away from political and clerical monotheism and toward the kingdom of freedom and mutuality. Had Moltmann paid closer attention to Ritschl, he would have escaped much of his trinitarian speculations. He could have instead grounded his kingdom ethic in a Christology from below, which, through its bipolar focus, mitigates against oppressive domination by both clerics and absolutistic monarchs. Moltmann could still have maintained, just as did Ritschl, that the kingdom is not just an otherworldly concept, but in some sense is to be inaugurated already in the present. It is unfortunate that Moltmann does not explicitly converse with Ritschl, since their intentions, though not the process of realizing them, are closely akin to one another.

The key concept for Moltmann is *anticipation,* an idea he already developed in his *Theology of Hope* (5th ed. 1965, Engl. trans. 1967). If applied to the relationship between history and eschatology, anticipation is a defense against both fervent enthusiasm and tragic resignation. According to Moltmann, the kingdom of God becomes present in history through the rule of God. It is manifested through Word and faith, through obedience and fellowship in the opportunities that are grasped, and in free cooperation for the life of the world. The obedience to the will of God that transforms the world is inseparable from the prayer for the coming of the kingdom. Thus for Moltmann the emphasis on the inauguration of the kingdom lies in the present. Here an affinity to Ritschl is clearly noticeable; yet, in contrast to Ritschl, he emphasizes the ambiguity and hiddenness of the rule of God, disallowing any progressive manifestation of the kingdom. Going even beyond Ritschl, he shows, in a similar way to Pannenberg, that the eschatological dimension of the kingdom allows and calls for its present anticipation.

In conclusion we note that the two leading German theologians, Wolfhart Pannenberg and Jürgen Moltmann, are deeply convinced of the centrality of the kingdom. Yet the bipolar focus on the present and the future, which meant for Ritschl mainly the this-worldly and the otherworldly, has been freed from its static "both/and" and transformed into a dynamic tension. The present anticipation is only possible because of the future fulfillment, and the future fulfillment is only credible because in the Christ event the future has already become present. This reciprocal relationship between the two foci of the kingdom, which for neo-Reformation theology was still a vertical arrangement, has now become a dynamic goal-orientation. This also goes beyond the static and disillusioned eschatological concept of the kingdom introduced by Johannes Weiss. It emphasizes Ritschl's truthfulness to the Christian vocation by summoning Christians, individually and corporately, to the present as

---

53. Cf. ibid., 215.

the arena of their responsibility, without relinquishing the future fulfillment of the God-wrought hope. In a scripturally warranted expansion
and modification, Ritschl's program is still very much alive in today's
theology.

Yet, is this also true for today's church? When we survey the topics
treated in such widely circulated periodicals as *Evangelische Kommen-
tare* (*Protestant Commentaries*) or *Lutherische Monatshefte* (*Lutheran
Monthly*), we notice that their agenda is quite different from that of *Die
christliche Welt* (*The Christian World*), the once popular periodical influenced by followers of Ritschl. To mention just one example: These
journals no longer call attention to what is happening to Christians in
different parts of the world, as did *Die christliche Welt,* but they report
about political tendencies in countries in which various Christian
churches are present. Abandoned is the notion that there is a city of God
(to use an Augustinian term) living in a hostile world populated by citizens of this world. The church is now seen as a watchdog, calling attention to the injustices occurring in the world.

This current mood is expressive of the conviction that this world is to
be Christianized, moving toward standards more acceptable to the
Christian vision. Since, however, the majority of people have no clearly
defined allegiance to the church or to Christian standards of conduct,
the ethical summons issued by the church does not differ much from
commonly promulgated human rights.

In part, this different thrust reflects a changed situation. In Ritschl's
time the church in Germany was a state church, symbolized by a close
union between throne and altar. Today, state and church are more separate, and the German *Volkskirche* (people's church) carefully guards its
independence from the state. Yet the people have not changed that
much. Then as now, a large contingent is simply unchurched. The main
thrust in Ritschl's time, therefore, was to win back the alienated working
class along with the intellectuals.

Today, however, the church has largely abandoned the goal of win-
ning back its nominal members or the growing number of people who
have left the church permanently. Yet it still feels a mandate of responsibility for all people. The church attempts, therefore, to use its influence
through the media and legislation to steer the people toward what it has
discerned to be the common good. The result quite often is that the
church is perceived as a lobbying group that hardly differs from other
more political powers. This behavior would not be problematic if the
church were, indeed, intent to win the people back to itself instead of
merely nudging them toward the common good. Its present behavior indicates that the church has abandoned its stance as the city of God and
compromised its vision of the kingdom. Small wonder, as surveys show,
that in ethical, political, and religious outlook members of the church

hardly differ from other citizens. The kingdom, therefore, is in danger of being totally relegated to the other world, having abandoned its firm anchor in this world.

Whether this otherworldly vision still influences and shapes the hopes and aspirations of the this-worldly community, as theology would like, is doubtful. Theology must return to its own source of inspiration, translating its own vision of the kingdom—which, as indicated, is very much scripturally warranted—into today's ecclesial practice. The two foci of the kingdom, with its dynamic goal-orientation, cannot be relegated to the status of a purely theological construct, or in the long run the church will preempt its own reason for existence. What has been said here about the German situation could easily be applied to the American scene. There, too, the distinctions between the life and outlook of church members and other members of society become increasingly blurred as the churches relinquish more and more of their role as stewards and representatives of the vision of the kingdom. Therefore Ritschl's program, which (with modification) is also a program of Christian living and aspiration, should be pulled off the library shelves and put into practice.

7

Building the Kingdom

The Legacy of Ritschl's Thought for the Americas

_____ WILLIAM R. BARNETT

In what many regard as a postmodern, postliberal, post-Christian, even postreligious age, observers can hardly be blamed for thinking that nineteenth- and early twentieth-century Liberal Christian theology[1] is irrelevant to contemporary concerns. Albrecht Ritschl's thought is a primary example of that earlier liberalism; its relevance to twentieth-century theology in the Americas has, to say the least, been obscure. To be sure, by the turn of the twentieth century, several North American university and seminary professors knew Ritschl's theology or that of the "Ritschlians." But by the 1920s and 1930s, the neoorthodox on-slaught (led by Karl Barth) against German Liberal theology, and against Ritschlianism in particular, destroyed Liberalism for many American Protestants. Certainly by the time of Reinhold Niebuhr's *Moral Man and Immoral Society* in 1932, a naïve, optimistic version of the Liberal social gospel became impossible for many.[2]

And yet, for at least two reasons, that is not the end of the story. First, despite the twentieth century's horrific examples of human depravity, Walter Rauschenbusch's version of the social gospel remained a theological resource for North American Protestantism (including the black civil rights movement). (Rauschenbusch's version was most nearly, but not un-critically, reflective of Ritschl's understanding of the Kingdom of God.)

1. The term *Liberal theology* refers to that theology since the seventeenth century which reached a positive accommodation with modern modes of thought, especially modern methods of historiography and the natural sciences. During the late nineteenth century in the United States, some Liberal theologians employed the emergent social sciences in an attempt to achieve social change; their movement was known as the "social gospel."

2. Reinhold Niebuhr, *Moral Man and Immoral Society* (New York: Charles Scribner's Sons, 1932). Niebuhr never mentions or criticizes Ritschl or Ritschlianism directly in this work; his criticism is directed more generally at Liberal theology and culture.

And second, many representatives of black theology, including Martin Luther King, Jr., have continually dealt with themes found in Ritschl's understanding of the kingdom of God.

This discussion will describe the general outlines of Ritschl's theology of the kingdom of God, indicate how Walter Rauschenbusch adapted it to the North American scene, and show how it influenced the thought of Martin Luther King, Jr. Subsequently, I shall show that a this-worldly, social interpretation of the kingdom of God in black theology today is consonant with Ritschl's understanding of the kingdom as the universal goal of humankind. I shall also discuss problems posed by African American experience for affirming such a Ritschlian view of the kingdom. Because Ritschl took so seriously the necessity of a modern reinterpretation of the Christian gospel, attention to these complex thematic relationships can sharpen our critical awareness of the strengths of Liberal theology for the present.

RITSCHL'S UNDERSTANDING OF THE KINGDOM OF GOD

More appreciative attention to Ritschl's theology in recent years has made the general outline of his notion of the kingdom of God widely known. Here I will not offer a summary of Ritschl's understanding of the kingdom or of the critical literature, but will only identify those themes relevant to American liberationist theologies.

Drawing critically upon the thought of Friedrich Schleiermacher and Immanuel Kant, Ritschl proposes a this-worldly, historical understanding of God's activity. Assuming that Christian doctrine is secondary reflection upon life experience, Ritschl thoroughly reinterprets the biblical and theological tradition and provides an understanding of the kingdom of God that emphasizes the present reality of God's activity in the world. The kingdom of God is not the ephemeral realm of an afterlife; neither is it identified with the whole of history in general. It is, rather, a social force for good opposed to socially organized evil (what Kant called the kingdom of sin).

More positively for Ritschl, the kingdom of God is the *summum bonum*, the divinely intended final end or goal of humankind in history. Crediting Schleiermacher even more than Kant for having observed the social character of the kingdom of God, Ritschl emphasizes that the "ethical activity of the individual cannot be isolated from the cooperation or from the appropriation of others."[3] The kingdom of God is the final goal of fellowship among individuals, families, and peoples in history and is, therefore, the sphere for ethical, free activity of persons in society.[4] Historical preparation for accepting the Christian notion of the

---

3. *JR* 1:447. German original *RV* 1:491 (3rd rev. ed. [1889]). The translation here is mine.
    4. *JR* 1:448 (*RV* 1:492).

kingdom of God rests indirectly on "the moral fellowship of the family and that of the people in the state, and finally the joining of more peoples in the world [that is, the Roman] empire"; directly and religiously it rests on God's dealing with the chosen people as recorded in the Hebrew Scriptures.[5] Lest the point be overlooked, this means, for Ritschl, that the kingdom of God cannot be identified with any single state, empire, or political program.[6]

Similarly for Ritschl, the kingdom of God is not the church,[7] but is the creation of the loving fellowship of all persons in history. Creating this loving fellowship, nevertheless, is the church's task intended by the church's founder, Jesus. While both Jesus and the Hebrew prophets recognized the kingdom of God as the divinely intended task and goal of God's people in history, Jesus surpassed the Hebrew prophets and Judaism, in Ritschl's view, by elevating the injunction to love to the point where the political and cultic aspects of God's covenant relationship to the chosen people were eliminated. Together, Jesus and the prophets stressed the following themes: the importance of God's relation to a community, the ethical obligations inherent in the community's relation to God, the recurring necessity for the restoration of fellowship with God through the forgiveness of sins, and the method of such reconciliation through sacrifice. But Jesus drew attention to his own person as the bearer of God's ruling activity by purposefully carrying out his ethical vocation to inaugurate God's kingdom in history.[8] Indeed, Jesus exemplified God's will by perfectly fulfilling his ethical vocation, even to the point of death.[9]

Conceptually, then, Ritschl's theology of the kingdom of God would seem to provide a positive resource for liberationist developments. For him the kingdom is the transcendent goal of history. It is neither individualistic nor otherworldly, but becomes expressed in social relationships and counters collective expressions of evil. It implies a moral obligation to love even to the point of personal sacrifice. This view of the kingdom can be observed in various examples of liberation theology, including black theology. As we shall see, however, Ritschl's perspective also reflects certain limitations that render his kingdom theology problematic to African American liberationists—for example, a failure to achieve a

5. *JR* 3:309, 312 (*RV* 3:292–93, 295, respectively). The translation here is mine.

6. Many have criticized liberationist theologies for being "too political" or too tied to a particular program of political action. However valid the criticism, it seems not to touch Ritschl's position.

7. *JR* 3:289 (*RV* 3:275). The activity of Christians in ecclesiastical worship is reciprocally related to their activity in promoting love in the world, insofar as Christians must come to know one another in order to take advantage of occasions for mutual action in love.

8. *RV* 2 [3d rev. ed. (1889)], chap. 1; also 104–5 (no published English translation). See also *JR* 3:455, 458–59, 462–63 (*RV* 3:429, 432, 436).

9. *JR* 3:290–91 (*RV* 3:275–76).

systemic view of social analysis and change,[10] an inability to adopt an active resistance to evil, and a bias toward middle-class values.

THE SIGNIFICANCE OF WALTER RAUSCHENBUSCH
FOR MARTIN LUTHER KING, JR.

The thought of Martin Luther King, Jr., offers a good opportunity to assess the significance of Ritschl's theology of the kingdom of God in the context of the United States. Although King was martyred in the cause of religiously inspired social change and did not devote himself to academic theology, he was theologically informed. The sources of his theological position are, of course, multiple, and include the Evangelical piety of the black church, his socially concerned Christian mentors at Morehouse College, and Mohandas Gandhi's theory of nonviolent resistance. But in addition to these influences,[11] King's theology also reflects a Liberal understanding of the kingdom of God. For example, his notion of the "beloved community" can be traced to American Liberal theology's characteristic emphasis on building the kingdom of God in history. And if Ritschl's thought on this point influenced American Protestant Liberal theology's understanding of the kingdom of God, then at least an indirect relationship between Ritschl and King can be established.

In his published writings, King never mentions Ritschl or Ritschlianism explicitly; nor is there a reason, in the absence of an examination of King's unpublished papers, to suppose that Ritschl's writings influenced King directly. Nevertheless, one can identify channels of influence that flow from Ritschl to King. The most significant, by King's own testimony, was the theology of Walter Rauschenbusch.[12] Other relevant conduits of unabashedly Liberal views included George Davis, L. Harold DeWolf, Edgar Brightman, and Howard Thurman.[13] A second, corrective, influence was Reinhold Niebuhr. The latter, says King, "has refuted the false optimism characteristic of a great segment of Protestant liberalism" and "helped me to recognize the complexity of man's social involvement and the glaring reality of collective evil."[14]

10. It is useful to distinguish between "systemic" social analysis and more traditional, frequently individualistic, diagnoses of the human predicament. For example, one who adopts a "systemic" perspective would attribute human poverty to certain economic conditions of the relevant social system, rather than merely to individual sloth, and would recommend changes in that social system as the most effective way of addressing the problem.
11. For a detailed account of the intellectual sources of King's thought, see John J. Ansbro, *Martin Luther King, Jr.: The Making of a Mind* (Maryknoll, N.Y.: Orbis, 1982). For a well-written biographical account, see Taylor Branch, *Parting the Waters: America in the King Years, 1954–63* (New York: Simon and Schuster, 1988), chaps. 2 and 3.
12. See MLK, 91, where King explicitly cites WR and Rauschenbusch's understanding of the kingdom of God.
13. Cf. Ansbro, *Martin Luther King, Jr.*, chaps. 1 and 3.
14. MLK, 99. The gender-exclusive language appears in the original.

Two questions arise in assessing Rauschenbusch's role in mediating Ritschl's theology to King: First, was Rauschenbusch in any significant sense a Ritschlian? Second, did King accurately understand Rauschenbusch? The second question will be addressed in due course, but the first cannot be dodged, since it has been raised by two recent interpreters of Ritschl and Rauschenbusch.

In this vein, James Richmond asserts that at least some disciples of Rauschenbusch mistakenly identified the kingdom of God with "the geographical spread of American civilization, culture and Christianity, over the raw 'nature' of the untamed West." "This is *not* Ritschl," Richmond continues, "and great care must be exercised not to regard him through the eyes of latter-day 'disciples', some of whom in America had clearly never read him!"[15] While admitting the possible validity of Richmond's charge against certain unnamed "disciples," one may wonder if his brush actually tars Rauschenbusch as their "teacher." Did Rauschenbusch naïvely identify the kingdom with the progressive spread of American civilization so as to distort Ritschl's thought?

In his recent biography of Rauschenbusch, Paul Minus even more explicitly denies that Rauschenbusch is a Ritschlian:

> The Ritschlian influence was especially evident in his [Rauschenbusch's] final book, *A Theology for the Social Gospel,* but there WR also expressed regret that Ritschl's theological perspective had been developed without benefit of the insight generated by sociological analysis (pp. 138–39). In 1913 WR complained to a friend, "The Christian social thinkers in Germany . . . are rather tame and do not get beyond mild reform talk. Most of them are made conservative by their government positions" (WR to J. E. Franklin, 16 June 1913). In view of the non-Ritschlian origins of Rauschenbusch's thought and his continued ambivalence toward the German scholar and his disciples, it is misleading to label him a "Ritschlian."[16]

Minus is correct that Ritschl was probably not the primary, certainly not the only, source for Rauschenbusch's understanding of the kingdom of God. Tracing the influence of German Liberal theologians such as Ritschl on representatives of the social gospel, however, is not a simple matter. Rauschenbusch and the other social gospel theologians did not provide frequent citations of their sources, since they wrote in haste, with whatever materials that lay immediately to hand, for the common person in the pew.[17] Moreover, Rauschenbusch's notebooks and diaries do not re-

15. Richmond, 259.
16. Paul M. Minus, *Walter Rauschenbusch: American Reformer* (New York: Macmillan Publishing Company, 1988), 221, n. 11.
17. William R. Barnett, "Building the 'Whole Kingdom' in America: The Realization of a Systemic Social Perspective," in Marilyn Chapin Massey, Sheila Briggs, and Gerald W. McCulloh, eds., *Papers of the Nineteenth Century Theology Working Group,* American Academy of Religion Annual Meeting 1986 (Berkeley, Calif.: Graduate Theological Union, 1986), 12:117.

veal completely what he was reading at any given time: Ritschl's works,
for example, never appear in Rauschenbusch's private reading lists, but
we have Rauschenbusch's own published testimony that he had read
Ritschl!

Because Rauschenbusch's kingdom theology is unlikely to have
taken shape prior to 1886 (the year he became pastor of Second German Baptist Church in New York City), and because his reading lists
are incomplete, one cannot say with any confidence that he knew or
was influenced by Ritschl before that date. But during a trip to Germany in 1891, Rauschenbusch noted that he found the social views of
German pastors "too dated and too timid."[18] Certainly, Rauschenbusch had been influenced by British socialism by this time,[19] but in his
writing for the Brotherhood of the Kingdom (a group of Liberal pastors, founded no earlier than 1889) his views of the kingdom of God
also display a certain Ritschlian thematic flavor.

In 1891, Rauschenbusch began a lengthy monograph, "Revolutionary
Christianity," that focused on the kingdom of God as the central point of
the teaching of Jesus.[20] The themes of this book—that Jesus founded the
community of the kingdom, that the kingdom of God was the center of
Jesus' teaching, that the kingdom is God's intended goal for individuals
and nations, that the kingdom is social rather than pertaining merely to
individuals or to life after death, that the kingdom is resisted by socially
organized (and persisting!) forms of evil (the kingdom of evil), that the
members of the church are called to further the kingdom in this world by
following Jesus' ethical example—are all found in Ritschl's understanding
of the kingdom.[21] Of course, Rauschenbusch does move beyond these essentially Ritschlian positions to espouse a more direct transformation of
society, and this move reflects the influence of various socialist and non-
socialist thinkers. But that development hardly constitutes "rejection" of
Ritschl or Ritschlianism, as Minus claims.[22]

While moving beyond Ritschl to produce a systemic social analysis,
Rauschenbusch continues to endorse a theological approach that ensures
that the this-worldly nature of the kingdom can hardly be missed:

> It is true that any regeneration of society can come only through the act of
> God and the presence of Christ; but God is now acting, and Christ is now
> here. To assert that means not less faith, but more.[23]

    18. Walter Rauschenbusch, Diary, 20 May 1891, in Rauschenbusch Papers, American
Baptist Historical Society, Rochester, New York.
    19. Cf. Walter Rauschenbusch, "Noch einmal die soziale Frage," *Der Sendbote* (Cleve-
land, Ohio), 28 January 1891.
    20. This text as later revised was published by Max L. Stackhouse as *The Righteous-
ness of the Kingdom* (Nashville: Abingdon Press, 1968).
    21. Cf. Rauschenbusch, *Righteousness;* also see the summary in Minus, *Walter
Rauschenbusch,* 78–81.
    22. Cf. the discussion in Minus, *Walter Rauschenbusch,* 81.
    23. WR, 346. See also 246, 264–65, 271, and 359–60.

In a way that goes beyond Ritschl's understanding of the kingdom, Rauschenbusch's theology does not preclude an analysis of class conflict or even of a Christian's taking the side of the poor, the impartiality of Christian love to all notwithstanding:

> But if he [the Christian minister] really follows the mind of Christ, he will be likely to take the side of the poor in most issues. The poor are likely to be the wronged. . . . The strong have ample means of defending all their just interests and usually enough power left to guard their unjust interests too.[24]

Rauschenbusch's social gospel theology moves beyond Ritschl in another way: ethical obligations for the Christian are less passive. To be sure, Ritschl clearly emphasizes the Christian's duty to follow Jesus by fulfilling his or her ethical vocation. Indeed, for Ritschl, God's justification of the Christian aims at reconciliation, and reconciliation entails a certain ethical lifestyle that includes faith in God's providence, along with patience under suffering, humility, and prayer. Although one might admire much of what Ritschl says about such a lifestyle, patience, as he explains it, cuts the nerve of significant social change:

> Patience under the hampering limitations of the world, which arises from the judgment of faith in providence through the feeling of humble submission to God's fatherly guidance, accepts deserved evils as divine punishments and also as a means of education, undeserved evils as tests, or, perhaps at the same time, as the honor of martyrdom.[25]

For Ritschl, reconciliation essentially changes the way an individual *thinks* about himself or herself vis-à-vis evil and the world.[26] Such a view is utterly foreign to Rauschenbusch, who calls for *action* in behalf of social justice as the content of following the example of Jesus: "The championship of social justice is almost the only way left open to a Christian nowadays to gain the crown of martyrdom."[27]

On the basis of the thematic coherence between Ritschl and Rauschenbusch discernible by 1891, as well as Rauschenbusch's own testimony published later, we can conclude that his understanding of the kingdom of God reflects and was probably influenced by Ritschl's. We can also acknowledge that Rauschenbusch moved beyond Ritschl by employing a systemic social analysis and by calling for a degree of Christian action in behalf of social change that was practically revolutionary when compared

---

24. WR, 361.
25. *ICR* in *TE,* 244. (German original in *UCR* [5th ed., Bonn: Adolph Marcus, 1895], §53.) See also the more extended discussion of patience in *JR* 3:624–32 (*RV* 3:591–97).
26. See the discussion of this point in Richmond, chap. 6, especially 228–40.
27. WR, 418.

with Ritschl's conservative political and ethical positions.[28] We can therefore say that Rauschenbusch was a Ritschlian in his understanding of the
kingdom of God, but only with important modifications.

Having pointed out Rauschenbusch's modified affirmation of Ritschl's
notion of the kingdom of God, we can turn briefly to the question of
King's understanding of Rauschenbusch. King's positive remarks about
Rauschenbusch are worth quoting at length:

> Not until I entered Crozer Theological Seminary in 1948 . . . did I begin a
> serious intellectual quest for a method to eliminate social evil. Although
> my major interest was in the fields of theology and philosophy, I spent a
> great deal of time reading the works of the great social philosophers. I
> came early to Walter Rauschenbusch's *Christianity and the Social Crisis,*
> which left an indelible imprint on my thinking by giving me a theological
> basis for the social concern which had already grown up in me as a result
> of my early experiences. . . . Rauschenbusch had done a great service for
> the Christian Church by insisting that the gospel deals with the whole
> man, not only his soul but his body; not only his spiritual well-being but
> his material well-being. It has been my conviction ever since reading
> Rauschenbusch that any religion which professes to be concerned about
> the souls of men and is not concerned about the social and economic con-
> ditions that scar the soul, is a spiritually moribund religion only waiting
> for the day to be buried. It well has been said: "A religion that ends with
> the individual, ends."[29]

King's appreciation of Rauschenbusch's theology includes acceptance
of the latter's emphasis upon the this-worldly, social character of the
kingdom of God. That is, Rauschenbusch's reinterpretation of the kingdom of God in the history of Christian theology led him to deplore the
overweening concern with the salvation of the individual soul after
death.

Interpreting Jesus' teaching in the Synoptic Gospels in light of contemporary social problems, Rauschenbusch undertook an internal, historical critique of Christian theology. This critique emphasized not the
difficulties of the individual soul, but the social reality of the kingdom of
God, a social reality that meant, in turn, that Christians had to be concerned about human material well-being, about social and economic
conditions. In Rauschenbusch's words, "Love is the society-making
quality."[30] All of this King accepts into his program without difficulty.[31]
And yet, King finds it necessary to criticize Rauschenbusch:

---

28. See Janet Forsythe Fishburn, *The Fatherhood of God and the Victorian Family:
The Social Gospel in America* (Philadelphia: Fortress Press, 1981), for an argument that
Rauschenbusch's worldview, especially toward women and the family, was essentially Vic-
torian and middle class.

29. MLK, 91.

30. WR, 67.

31. See the summary discussion in Ansbro, *Martin Luther King, Jr.,* 167–72.

Of course there were points at which I differed with Rauschenbusch. I felt
that he had fallen victim to the nineteenth-century "cult of inevitable
progress" which led him to a superficial optimism concerning man's nature. Moreover, he came perilously close to identifying the Kingdom of
God with a particular social and economic system—a tendency which
should never befall the Church.[32]

THE "CORRECTIVE" INFLUENCE OF REINHOLD NIEBUHR

Martin Luther King became disabused of Protestant Liberal theology not
only because of his own experience, but also because of the critique by
Reinhold Niebuhr as found chiefly in *Moral Man and Immoral Society*.

> Niebuhr's great contribution to contemporary theology is that he has re-
> futed the false optimism characteristic of a great segment of Protestant lib-
> eralism. . . . Moreover, Niebuhr has extraordinary insight into human
> nature, especially the behavior of nations and social groups. He is keenly
> aware of the complexity of human motives and of the relation between
> morality and power. His theology is a persistent reminder of the reality of
> sin on every level of man's existence. These elements in Niebuhr's thinking
> helped me to recognize the illusions of a superficial optimism concerning
> human nature and the dangers of a false idealism. While I still believed in
> man's potential for good, Niebuhr made me realize his potential for evil as
> well. Moreover, Niebuhr helped me to recognize the complexity of man's
> social involvement and the glaring reality of collective evil.[33]

While not wishing to deny the originality and power of Niebuhr's social analysis, it is difficult to see how King could have overlooked the
persistence of sin and the reality of collective evil as major themes in
Rauschenbusch's thought. Indeed, Rauschenbusch knew well that the
kingdom of God is a transcendent ideal that can never be realized perfectly in history.[34] And he certainly described the reality of collective evil
on several occasions; his recognition of collective evil or social sin even
led him to espouse a rather mild form of socialism as a political prescription. Finally, Rauschenbusch himself expressed a version of the critique
of self-aggrandizing social institutions for which Niebuhr's book, *Moral
Man and Immoral Society*, later became famous:

> Theology has not given adequate attention to the social idealizations of
> evil, which falsify the ethical standards for the individual by the authority
> of his group or community, deaden the voice of the Holy Spirit to the con-
> science of individuals and communities, and perpetuate antiquated wrongs
> in society. . . . When the social group is evil, evil is over all.[35]

32. MLK, 91.
33. MLK, 99.
34. WR, 421: "At best there is always but an approximation to a perfect social order.
The Kingdom of God is always but coming."
35. Walter Rauschenbusch, *A Theology for the Social Gospel* (New York: The
Macmillan Company, 1917), 78, 81.

King, influenced by his teachers, may have misunderstood Rauschenbusch's theology as espousing the sort of Liberal progressivist optimism that surely characterized many representatives of the social gospel. But it also seems clear that King greatly admired Rauschenbusch and had read all his major works, including his later books, which certainly do not embody a "superficial optimism."[36]

King's misunderstanding of Rauschenbusch in reliance upon Reinhold Niebuhr's criticism of Liberal theology also raises a further intriguing possibility, namely, that Niebuhr himself may have served as a second channel through which Ritschl's theology influenced American Protestantism and King in particular. That is, however sharp Niebuhr's criticism of Liberal theology in general may have been, his thought may still have preserved many essential elements of Ritschl's (and, therefore, Rauschenbusch's) teaching on the kingdom of God. As jarring as the question may sound, was Reinhold Niebuhr himself, at least in some respects, a covert Ritschlian?

Regarding this question, Niebuhr's near silence about both Ritschl and Rauschenbusch turns out to be an intriguing bit of evidence. Nowhere in *Moral Man and Immoral Society,* for example, does he mention either by name. His criticisms of particular Liberal theologians are directed at Justin Wroe Nixon, William Adams Brown, or, most especially, the philosopher John Dewey.[37] Even in his volume *An Interpretation of Christian Ethics* (ironically, the Rauschenbusch Memorial Lectures delivered at Colgate-Rochester Divinity School in 1934), Niebuhr makes no explicit criticism of either Ritschl or Rauschenbusch and refers to the latter as "the real founder of social Christianity in this country" and "its most brilliant and generally satisfying exponent to the present day."[38]

Some years later, Niebuhr does criticize both Ritschl and Rauschenbusch as representatives of Liberal theology. Mistaking one aspect of Ritschl's understanding of the human predicament for the whole, Niebuhr rejects Ritschl's characterization of the fundamental religious problem as the relation between finitude and freedom. While admitting that the problem of human freedom in relation to the limitations of nature underlies all religion, Niebuhr continues:

36. Cf. the discussion of King's misunderstanding of Rauschenbusch by Ansbro, *Martin Luther King, Jr.,* 172, who also cites evidence (313, n. 66) that King knew the later Rauschenbusch corpus: "Kenneth Smith, King's professor and friend at Crozer, maintained that in his conversations with King as a student it had been evident that Rauschenbusch was King's favorite author in the field of ethics and that King had read and pondered all of his major works" ("Martin Luther King, Jr.: Reflections of a Former Teacher," *Bulletin of Crozer Theological Seminary* 57, no. 2 [Apr. 1965]: 3).

37. Niebuhr, *Moral Man,* Introduction.

38. Niebuhr, *An Interpretation of Christian Ethics* (New York and London: Harper & Brothers, 1935), Preface.

But Ritschl does not appreciate that the uniqueness of the Biblical approach to the human problem lies in its subordination of the problem of finiteness to the problem of sin. It is not the contradiction of finiteness and freedom from which Biblical religion seeks emancipation. It seeks redemption from sin.[39]

Similarly, Niebuhr criticizes Rauschenbusch for much the same reason, as representative of an evolutionary view of sin and human perfection in history:

The Bible becomes a library, recording in many books the evolutionary ascent of man to God. Sin becomes the provisional inertia of impulses, inherited from Neanderthal man, against the wider purposes of mind. Christ is the symbol of history itself, as in Hegel. The relation of the kingdom of God to the moral perplexities and ambiguities of history is resolved in utopia. The strict distinction between justice and love in Catholic thought is marvelously precise and shrewd, compared with the general identification of the agape of the New Testament with the "community-building capacities of human sympathy" in the thought of Rauschenbusch. This reduction of the ethical meaning of the scandal of the cross, namely, sacrificial love, to the dimensions of simple mutuality imparts an air of sentimentality to all liberal Protestant social and political theories.[40]

Niebuhr's twofold criticism is, first, that Ritschl fails to understand sin as the rebellion of humans against God, and, second, that Rauschenbusch compounds the error by interpreting the moral situation as one in which an earthly utopia can be constructed and sin can be overcome by applying the ethical principle of love. In both cases, Niebuhr abhors the lack of biblical realism regarding the radical nature of sin and regarding the dim prospects for achieving social/ethical perfection in this world.

Nevertheless, attention to Ritschl's own writings on sin provides ample reason to doubt the accuracy of Niebuhr's first criticism. Following Luther, Ritschl thinks of sin in both religious and moral categories. That is, sin is, first and foremost, opposition to the divine will; and *awareness* of sin emerges only in comparison with God's revelation in the divine law, with the ideal of Christ, with Jesus' fulfillment of his ethical vocation, and with the *summum bonum* as evident in the kingdom of God. Moreover, as already mentioned above, Ritschl follows Kant in pointing to the social character of sin in terms of a "kingdom of sin" opposed to the kingdom of God. Because of this sinful social context, the individual will can acquire an evil character. By this route, Ritschl essen-

---

39. Reinhold Niebuhr, *The Nature and Destiny of Man*, 2 vols. (New York: Charles Scribner's Sons, 1941), 1:178. Niebuhr cites *JR* 3:199 (*RV* 3:189).

40. Reinhold Niebuhr, "Coherence, Incoherence, and Christian Faith," *The Journal of Religion* 31 (July 1951): 162, as reprinted in Robert McAfee Brown, ed., *The Essential Reinhold Niebuhr* (New Haven and London: Yale Univ. Press, 1986), 227.

tially replaces the more traditional doctrine of original sin with a doctrine of social sin.[41]

Regarding Niebuhr's second criticism, recent scholarship has shown that Ritschl does not teach that the full perfection of the kingdom of God can be achieved in history.[42] But the matter may not be so easily settled in the case of Rauschenbusch. Niebuhr, in the passage quoted above, seems to think that Rauschenbusch's doctrine of the kingdom of God results in an uncritical application of the "law of love" to political and economic matters and that it therefore amounts to a naïve utopianism. But Daniel Day Williams, commenting upon this very passage, utterly rejects the accuracy of its description of Liberal theology, whether that of Ritschl or of Rauschenbusch:

> Now this paragraph tells us what Niebuhr sees in liberalism, especially its limitations. But what liberalism is he looking at? Hegel cannot be reduced to these dimensions. Neither can Rauschenbusch. Niebuhr himself once refers to Albrecht Ritschl as "the most authoritative exponent of liberal Christianity." But there is not a single statement in the above paragraph which can possibly be said to represent Ritschl's view.[43]

In his response to Williams, Niebuhr admits that his characterization of Liberal theology is too sweeping and too American. "In America liberalism was usually associated with a historical optimism which was not characteristic, for instance, of the theology of Albrecht Ritschl, who was a theological offshoot of Kantian philosophy."[44] Thus, while Niebuhr shrinks from calling Ritschl an optimist, he does not retract the charge against Rauschenbusch. But has Niebuhr correctly identified the difference between Ritschl and Rauschenbusch?

Admittedly, much of Rauschenbusch's theology of the kingdom of God appears to be optimistic and even evolutionary. This is especially the case with his historical analyses of political and economic problems and their solutions.[45] But his own statements demonstrate that he was not a *naïve* optimist:

> We know well that there is no perfection for man in this life; there is only growth toward perfection. . . . We make it a duty to seek what is unattain-

41. JR 3, chap. 5. Cf. also the discussion in Mueller, 70–77, 170–73. Mueller, in his critical remarks, grants that Ritschl does not adhere consistently to a description of sin in terms of human opposition to God and sometimes falls into speaking of the polarity between human freedom and natural limitation.

42. Cf. the discussion in Richmond, 259–60.

43. Daniel Day Williams, "Niebuhr and Liberalism," in Charles W. Kegley and Robert W. Bretall, eds., *Reinhold Niebuhr: His Religious, Social, and Political Thought* (New York: The Macmillan Company, 1956), 196.

44. Reinhold Niebuhr, "Reply," in Kegley and Bretall, *Reinhold Niebuhr*, 441. Mueller's discussion (see above, n. 38) gives ample reason to reject describing Ritschl's notion of sin in relation to the kingdom of God as simply Kantian.

45. See, e.g., Rauschenbusch, *Theology*, chaps. 8, 9, and 11.

able. We have the same paradox in the perfectibility of society. We shall
never have a perfect social life, yet we must seek it with faith.[46]

Such statements echo similar assertions by Ritschl and lend a note of realism to Rauschenbusch's theology that places him at odds with some
Liberals. No, contrary to Niebuhr's view, the difference between Ritschl
and Rauschenbusch does not lie here.

The most important difference between Ritschl and Rauschenbusch,
as suggested above, lies in the systemic social analysis that allows
Rauschenbusch to advocate more radical social change. Ritschl's description of the Christian lifestyle compels agreement with Philip Hefner
that, while "formally, there is no reason why his thought cannot be a
force for change and liberation, . . . he was almost totally captive to his
own elitist social class."[47] Rauschenbusch also reflects the influence of
his social class, but far less than does Ritschl. Indeed, as pointed out
above, Rauschenbusch transcends his own class to recommend what
some liberation theologians now call a "preferential option for the
poor." His prescription for a structural transformation of the political
economy of his time, instead of individual acts of charity, marks him off
from other representatives of the social gospel as well.

Whether Niebuhr recognized it or not, his own social thought reflects
many of the themes of Rauschenbusch's theology of the kingdom of God.
To be sure, Niebuhr's tone is more dialectical, more paradoxical, less optimistic about what ethical action can actually achieve by way of overcoming human sinfulness. But both Niebuhr and Rauschenbusch hold that a
perfect society is a transcendent ideal, that social change occurs through
conflict rather than through the preaching of platitudes, that Christian
faith is not merely a change in the believer's perspective or concept of self,
and that Christians ought not remain passive in the face of social evil.

What, then, was the impact of Niebuhr's criticism of Liberal theology
in general, and of Rauschenbusch in particular, upon Martin Luther
King's thought? King clearly thought that he agreed with Niebuhr's
criticisms of Liberalism. It is equally clear, however, that King probably
misunderstood Rauschenbusch's thought and therefore did not fully appreciate the Liberal (not to say, Ritschlian) roots of much of Niebuhr's
theological ethics. A correct view would be that Niebuhr's realistic,
socially concerned understanding of Christian faith reflects much of
Ritschl's theology of the kingdom of God. In addition, Niebuhr's theological ethics accepts Rauschenbusch's advance beyond Ritschl toward
systemic social analysis and change. Taking these two points together,
we can therefore conclude that King's thought is influenced indirectly by

46. WR, 420.
47. "Introduction," TE, 37–38. Cf. the confirmation of Hefner's conclusion in Richmond, 246.

Ritschl and directly by Rauschenbusch more than King either knew or acknowledged. In other words, King's thought represents a modified version of Ritschl's reinterpretation of Christian faith in history—the modifications coming chiefly at the hands of Rauschenbusch and Niebuhr.

DEVELOPMENTS AFTER MARTIN LUTHER KING, JR.

The foregoing discussion of Ritschl's significance for the theology of Martin Luther King, Jr., accomplishes three things. First, it demonstrates the continuing importance of Ritschl's social reinterpretation of the doctrine of the kingdom of God, over against an interpretation that focuses upon the fate of the individual soul after death. For Ritschl, the kingdom is the sphere of ethical activity, the development of socially organized opposition to evil, which, nevertheless, is not identified with any single political program or social institution. The kingdom is the ever-emerging final goal of history; it is the development of a community of love as inaugurated by Jesus, but is never to be simply identified with the institutional church. King's own vision of "the beloved community" retains many of these insights and cautions.

Second, the discussion demonstrates the lasting importance of the concept of social sin. Ritschl, following Kant and Schleiermacher, develops a notion of social sin that proves to be especially enduring despite Reinhold Niebuhr's criticisms of Liberal theology. This notion provides a vital corrective to eighteenth-century Enlightenment understandings of personal freedom that presume a morally neutral context for an individual's ethical decisions. Ritschl and those who follow him on this point contend that evil is socially organized, that ethical decisions are actually made in a morally tainted or distorted social context.[48] King's analysis of the power of racism in American society retains this theme.

Third, the discussion indicates the way in which the central figure of Jesus should be understood. For Ritschl, Jesus' fulfillment of his ethical vocation to found the community of the kingdom is the hallmark of his divinity. By carrying out his ethical vocation even to the point of suffering and death, Jesus not only provides an example of love, but also inaugurates a social force of love in history. In King's thought, as in Ritschl's, Jesus is not merely the figure who dies on the cross to repay our debt to God (a là Anselm or contemporary fundamentalism). Rather, Jesus is the one who pays the price that society exacts of those who love unconditionally; he is the one who attracts followers and founds the community of love in history. This sort of understanding of the figure of Jesus is frequently found in liberation theologians.[49]

---

48. It is perhaps helpful to observe in passing that this notion of social sin and its consequences is developed without resorting to a Marxist social analysis.

49. A good example of "Ritschlian" interpretation of Jesus in the context of liberationist themes can be found in Roger Haight, S.J., *An Alternative Vision: An Interpretation of Liberation Theology* (New York and Mahwah, N.J.: Paulist Press, 1985), chap. 7.

Of course, Martin Luther King, Jr., is not the only representative of black theology, much less of liberationist movements in general. And, as our discussion of Rauschenbusch has shown, Ritschl's thought itself is not above criticism. What follows is a brief assessment of Ritschl's strengths and weaknesses as a continuing resource for black and liberationist theologies.

Just as Martin Luther King, Jr., could accuse Rauschenbusch (incorrectly) of a naïve optimism, so have some leveled similar accusations against King, especially regarding his teaching of nonviolent social change and his goal of racial integration. Commenting on the high point of hope that came with King's "I Have a Dream" speech in Washington, D.C., in 1963—a hope that was dashed by subsequent events throughout the 1960s—James Cone observes:

> Unfortunately we did not listen to Malcolm X and his analysis of the depth of racism in American society. . . . The Watts riot [of 1965] and the other eruptions like it should have told black preachers something about the inadequacy of their analysis—both in terms of the method of nonviolence and the goal of integration.[50]

The subtleties of racism in the North, the realities of continuing oppression, and the eruptions of black frustration all posed the sharpest challenge to the traditional message of the black church.

In addition, the movement to understand and appreciate the African roots of black religion, black spirituality, and black social structures[51] has questioned the undue dependence of black religion and theology upon white, Western forms of Christianity. If Jesus, as the central figure of Christianity, is filtered through European/Western theology, how can he be expected to have any relevance to African Americans or to black persons in general? Moreover, to what extent and how might black experience result in a reinterpretation of the figure of Jesus? These questions are not simple, but they are included in the general question of whether Jesus can be expected to have universal significance for humankind.

Because of his own culture's influence on him, it is too much to say that Ritschl's theology provides a directly useful response to the issues of black power and the African American experience of oppression. As we have already seen, Ritschl himself stopped short of the systemic social analysis achieved by Rauschenbusch; and Ritschl's

50. James H. Cone, *For My People: Black Theology and the Black Church* (Maryknoll, N.Y.: Orbis, 1984), 55.

51. See Gayraud S. Wilmore, *Black Religion and Black Radicalism* (2d ed.; Maryknoll, N.Y.: Orbis, 1983); Albert Raboteau, *Slave Religion: The "Invisible Institution" in the Antebellum South* (New York: Oxford Univ. Press, 1978); and Charles H. Long, "Perspectives for a Study of Afro-American Religion in the United States," *History of Religions* 2 (1971): 54–66.

conservative politics would have made him hostile to those representatives of black power who, during the 1960s and 1970s, advocated
violence as a sometimes necessary means of social change. That Jesus
or his followers should take the side of the poor and oppressed in any
sort of class conflict would strike Ritschl as absurd and contrary to
the goal of universal love. And just as vehemently, Ritschl would have
denied any positive religious significance to African forms of spirituality or practice.[52]

Still, having acknowledged Ritschl's inadequacies, it must be recalled
that his theology of the kingdom supports a this-worldly, social emphasis
in Christian theology and proclamation. For example, slave songs (spirituals) can be interpreted to have double meanings insofar as they refer to
"stealing away" to a slave meeting or "following the drinking gourd [the
Big Dipper]" to freedom in the North. Such meanings are a legitimate expression of the Christian understanding of the kingdom of God and reflect the this-worldly, social themes of Ritschl's theology.[53] Of course, the
experience of the slaves who sang these spirituals is self-legitimating; the
blessing of a European theologian is not needed. But it might yet be important to recognize that a this-worldly understanding of the kingdom of
God constitutes an important bridge between rather widely differing cultural and religious perspectives.

The question of the possible inadequacy of the kingdom of God as
the universal goal of a community of love for all humankind is harder
to deal with. To be sure, Rauschenbusch, more than Ritschl, is willing
to urge the followers of Jesus to take the side of the poor and the oppressed in their struggles for justice. Rauschenbusch, more than
Ritschl, understands that necessary systemic social change will result
only from some measure of coercion as, for example, methods employed by the early twentieth-century labor movement. But neither
Rauschenbusch nor Ritschl is willing to give up on the ideal of the
kingdom of God as the universal goal for humankind. Given the controversy among black theologians over this very point during the past
thirty years,[54] what could Ritschl or Rauschenbusch possibly contribute to the discussion?

Whatever they contribute cannot be expressed from a position of
privilege; that much, at least, must be clear. If a privileged insistence

52. See William R. Barnett, "Historical Understanding and Theological Commitment:
The Dilemma of Ritschl's Christology," *The Journal of Religion* 59 (1979), 208–10, where
I show that Ritschl asserts the superiority of Christianity on the basis of a criterion of per-
fection drawn from within Christianity itself. See also *JR* 3:197–98, and Albrecht Ritschl,
*Schleiermachers Reden über die Religion und ihre Nachwirkungen auf die evangelische
Kirche Deutschlands* (Bonn: Adolph Marcus, 1874), 9–10, 12.

53. See, e.g., John Lovell, Jr., *Black Song: The Forge and the Flame* (New York:
Macmillan, 1972), and James H. Cone, *The Spirituals and the Blues* (New York: Seabury,
1972).

54. See Cone, *For My People*, chaps. 2 and 3.

upon an ideal of universal love becomes merely another tactic to delay justice, the ideal itself is contradicted. Rauschenbusch was able to see rather clearly the dangers of a socially privileged position. His work in behalf of the economically oppressed and, to some extent, the racially oppressed,[55] permitted him to develop the outlines of a theology "from below."

Still, Ritschl's and Rauschenbusch's understanding of Jesus' teaching as centering on the kingdom of God and of Jesus' activity as the founding of the community of love might give pause to those who would entertain a different teaching and a different activity.[56] The question here is not one of historical accuracy, but of a possible alternative. Even if the perfection of the community of love will not be realized in history, as both Ritschl and Rauschenbusch acknowledge, that ideal, as a goal for which Christians should strive, is perhaps preferable to any other. That one need not be naïve in calculating the means to achieve both ultimate and intermediate goals should be obvious after two decades of debate.[57]

CONCLUSION

One hundred years after Albrecht Ritschl's death, the threads of his historical legacy threaten to become tangled or lost altogether. It is still possible, though with some difficulty, to discern the significance of his theology of the kingdom of God in American liberation movements. Ritschl's legacy, to be sure, is ambiguous; but of whom could we say otherwise? His thought stimulated and confirmed Walter Rauschenbusch's theology of the social gospel, although Rauschenbusch found it necessary to move beyond Ritschl. Even Reinhold Niebuhr's thought reflects many of Ritschl's characteristic emphases, although in a more dialectical fashion. Influenced (sometimes unwittingly) by these Liberal and neoorthodox figures—and, of course, by other thinkers not named here—Martin Luther King, Jr., fashioned a theological rationale for a socially transformative movement. Tracing Ritschl's legacy in some detail shows why his

55. The complex story of the social gospel movement in relation to the struggle for racial justice in America has been recently told by Ronald C. White, *Liberty and Justice for All: Racial Reform and the Social Gospel* (San Francisco: Harper & Row, 1990).

56. Albert Cleage has offered perhaps the most controversial interpretation of Jesus' teaching and activity by referring to Jesus as "a revolutionary black leader, a member of the Zealots, . . . [who] sought to free Israel's black Jews from oppression and bondage, dying, not for the eternal salvation of the individual, but for the rebirth of the lost Black Nation." Quoted in Cone, *For My People*, 36.

57. J. Deotis Roberts can hardly be accused of overlooking the alienation of African Americans from white society. Yet, his writings consistently call for some sort of universal reconciliation as a goal to accompany and give direction to movements for liberation. See especially his *Liberation and Reconciliation: A Black Theology* (Philadelphia: Westminster Press, 1971), and *Black Theology Today: Liberation and Contextualization,* Toronto Studies in Theology, no. 12 (New York and Toronto: The Edwin Mellen Press, 1983).

thought deserves continued attention, both for historical and for constructive reasons.

But have we come to the end of this road? Are we so far removed from Ritschl in culture and time, and have so many modifications and corrections been introduced into his theological approach, that attempts to keep his memory alive are finally counterproductive? Most especially, as African American and other liberation theologians move forward, is time spent on Ritschl time wasted? "Knowing Ritschl's [conservative] political stance, why are we interested in this man?"[58] On the basis of the above analysis, perhaps a partial answer can be attempted.

As a reinterpretation of the Christian faith, Ritschl's theology of the kingdom of God expressed themes that continue to be relevant to any socially transformative theology today, including black theology. Sometimes it will be necessary to take into account his rather traditional expression of Christian doctrine. At other times, it will be necessary to move beyond him: even Rauschenbusch saw that at the turn of the century! But if we move beyond Ritschl, as we must, it is crucial to know at just which points and why. That his theology is not completely adequate for our time or situation should surprise neither us, nor, I suspect, Ritschl himself.

While we cannot uncritically accept all of his ideas, in an age marked by continuing oppression, by postmodern thought, and by resurgent fundamentalisms, it is important not to overlook the valuable and enduring aspects of his theology in stimulating socially relevant, realistic expressions of Christian hope. By rejecting an otherworldly escape from the concerns of human society on the one hand, as well as a despairing pessimism in the face of evil on the other, Ritschl professed a view of the kingdom of God as the goal for which Christians must struggle in history. Such a view, especially when coupled with a systemic understanding of society, carries enormous potential for social change. Whether that potential will be realized in Christian theology and action depends, at least in part, upon our remembering Ritschl's legacy and developing it appropriately and forcefully for our own time.

58. H. Martin Rumscheidt, during the Albrecht Ritschl Seminar at the Annual Meeting of the American Academy of Religion, Anaheim, California, 1988.

PART FOUR

Theology and Science

8

Ritschl's Doctrine of God

Its Significance for Twentieth-Century Theology

DARRELL JODOCK

This essay examines Ritschl's concept of God and its contemporary significance. Woven into its analysis are four interlocking questions: How did Ritschl respond to the cultural currents of his day? How did he assess the various parts of the Christian tradition that he inherited? How is today's setting different from or similar to Ritschl's? What can his theology contribute to constructive theological thinking today?

I

During the last three or four decades, theologians have devoted a good deal of their attention to the doctrine of God. In the late 1800s their predecessors focused on Jesus, history, Christ, and faith, and during the first half of the twentieth century, this Christocentricity continued into the neoorthodox theologies developed by Karl Barth, Emil Brunner, and Rudolf Bultmann. Several factors have helped to shift theologians' attention from "second-article" concerns to the character of the divine. One is the Holocaust, the massive suffering deliberately and systematically inflicted on approximately eleven million noncombatants during the 1940s: How is God to be understood in the face of such massive suffering? Another factor is the ecological crisis and the resulting concern for "first-article" issues regarding God's relationship to nature and the Christian's stance toward the physical and animal world. A third factor has been the influence of process philosophy (à la Alfred North Whitehead and Charles Hartshorne) with its revised concept of God and its critique of "classical theism" (its critique, that is, of the traditional Western assumptions that God is unchanging, the cause of all that happens, omnipotent while at the same time being benevolent, and omniscient in the sense of knowing the future as well as the past and the present).

In many striking ways Ritschl was clearly a nineteenth-century thinker. He endeavored, for example, to understand the historical context out of which church practices and teachings developed; for standards by which to evaluate these developments he appealed not to creeds and doctrines, but again to history, specifically to the apostolic witness to Jesus, and then, beyond that, witness to the person and teachings of the historical founder of Christianity. Moreover, Ritschl's *magnum opus* treated "justification and reconciliation." His own interest in "second-article" concerns is clearly reflected in the subject matter of this long-term project. However passé the traditional Protestant doctrine of justification by faith may have seemed to a variety of other nineteenth-century theologians, Ritschl's interest in faith, Christ, Jesus, and history is typical of nineteenth-century theology.

As much as Ritschl dealt with nineteenth-century issues, however, the problem of God was not peripheral to his work. During the 1860s he published a series of three articles entitled "Historical Studies on the Christian Doctrine of God."[1] The second of the four chapters in volume 2 of *Justification and Reconciliation* is devoted to "The Biblical Idea of God on Reconciliation and the Forgiveness of Sins."[2] The longest of the nine chapters in his third volume of *Justification and Reconciliation* is entitled "The Doctrine of God,"[3] and in 1881 he published a response to his critics entitled *Theology and Metaphysics,*[4] much of which is devoted to clarifying his concept of God.

As other essayists in this volume argue, Ritschl developed his own ideas primarily through historical study and biblical exegesis. What Ritschl had to say about God, however, arose in part from his own philosophical analysis of modern culture. His response to contemporary materialism became part and parcel of the constructive theological proposal he made to the church of his day. A revised understanding of God was necessary, he felt, in order to recapture essential biblical and Reformation insights regarding justification and reconciliation, to explain significant dimensions of the Christian message to his contemporaries, and to highlight a distinctively religious apprehension of the divine.

Not only did Ritschl give his attention to the concept of God, but in several significant ways he also anticipated the shape of the questions regarding God discussed in the latter half of the twentieth century. Ritschl's critique of what he called "metaphysics" (as applied to God and human beings) anticipates process theology's criticisms of classical theism. Likewise, Ritschl's emphases on an active God and on active human involvement (understanding religion as both gift and task) com-

---

1. Albrecht Ritschl, "Geschichtliche Studien zur christlichen Lehre von Gott," *Jahrbücher für deutsche Theologie* 10 (1865): 277–318, and 13 (1868): 67–133 and 251–302.
2. *RV* 2.
3. *JR* 3:193–326.
4. *TM* in *TE*, 149–217.

bine to anticipate the theme of "cocreatorship" so often found in post-Holocaust theology and in constructive proposals that address the ecological crisis. Finally, Ritschl effectively distinguished between the philosophical and the biblical elements in the traditional concept of God. In so doing, he pioneered a discussion that is still going on: How should one (re)construct a concept of God more adequate to the biblical witness and to our contemporary understanding of the world?

To be sure, I am not suggesting that Ritschl succeeded in formulating a view of God that is adequate for our own day. Nor am I claiming that he paid particular attention to questions raised by massive suffering, for he did not. Nor was he especially sensitive to the importance of preserving animal and plant life, for this contemporary issue certainly was not a main theme in his theology. (As we will observe below, his thought at this point actually moved in quite a different direction.)

For these and other reasons, I do not think that Ritschl succeeded in developing a concept of God that can be reproduced in our own day and regarded as adequate for our own post-Holocaust, ecologically sensitive setting. But his thinking can be instructive nonetheless. The problems Ritschl perceived in the traditional concept of God produced reflections that in some ways seem as much at home in the twentieth century as in the nineteenth. The issues with which he struggled when formulating his concept of God are similar enough to the questions confronting theology today, so that his successes and failures can be instructive for all who wrestle with this topic.

II

In order to understand Ritschl's concept of God, several preliminary observations about cognate themes are necessary.

1. *Value judgments.*   Ritschl strikes a very contemporary note when he insists that no knowledge is disinterested. The human spirit (*Geist*) is active (not passive) in all knowing, and all inquiries involve an evaluative judgment, a judgment at least that the information is worth pursuing. All knowledge is "interested," but not all knowledge is the same. According to Ritschl, human consciousness appropriates sensations in two ways: *either* as a feeling of pleasure or pain, which serves to heighten or depress the ego, *or* as the effect of a cause.[5] And this duality leads to differences of degree between religious-ethical insight, which grows out of the former, and scientific inquiry, which develops from the perception of cause and effect. Yet, because the two kinds of sensation occur simultaneously, religious-ethical insight and scientific inquiry can be distinguished but not separated. Feelings always accompany and guide even protoscientific and scientific cognition. When a desire for such knowledge prompts us to give our attention to something, the will

5. *JR* 3:203–4.

also enters the picture. Its attention is motivated by "the consciousness that a thing or an activity is worth desiring, or that something ought to be put away."[6] For Ritschl "value-judgments therefore are determinative in the case of *all* connected knowledge of the world, even when carried out in the most objective fashion."[7] No knowledge is disinterested; value judgments influence even the most objective endeavor to know and to understand.

This point of view does not imply, however, that value judgments are equally prominent in every search for knowledge. Ritschl distinguishes between "concomitant" and "independent" value judgments. "The former are operative and necessary in all theoretical cognition, as in all technical observation and combination,"[8] while independent value judgments are of at least two types: moral and religious. The scheme can be diagrammed in the following way:

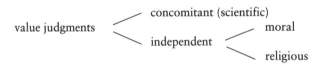

Or, perhaps, it can be diagrammed even better as a continuum, more like the following:

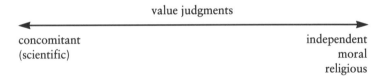

Moral value judgments concern moral ends or hindrances; they set the will in motion to pursue what is good or repel the opposite. Religious value judgments "relate to man's attitude to the world, and call forth feelings of pleasure or pain, in which man either enjoys the dominion over the world vouchsafed him by God, or feels grievously the lack of God's help to that end."[9] In other words, independent value judgments, while still involving cognition of the world, focus on the human spirit's response to or involvement in that world.

Living as he did in the second half of the nineteenth century, Ritschl was concerned to distinguish religious knowing from scientific knowledge. His brief discussion of value judgments enables him to articulate

6. *JR* 3:204.
7. Ibid. Emphasis added.
8. *JR* 3:204–5.
9. *JR* 3:205.

such a distinction, while still not separating religion and science into two isolated or conflicting spheres. Since both religious knowledge and theoretical knowledge are attempts to understand the world, they share a common object. As he says, "The possibility of both kinds of knowledge mingling, or, again, colliding, lies in this, that they deal with the same object, namely, the world."[10] "Thus no principle of discrimination between the two kinds of knowledge is, at least provisionally, to be found in the object with which they deal."[11] The scientific approach to the world differs from the religious approach in degree or emphasis, not in kind.

Ritschl thinks that epistemology (one's theory of how knowing takes place) plays a regulative role in theology; it helps to clarify the procedures that are used. "Every theologian, as a scientific worker, is under the necessity or obligation to proceed according to a certain epistemology of which he is himself aware and whose correctness he must demonstrate."[12] No *one* theory of knowledge is demanded by the contents of Christian theology, but every theology employs *some* kind of epistemology, and, as he acknowledges, these epistemological considerations become especially important when dealing with the concept of God. What Ritschl says about value judgments is an attempt on his part to spell out a portion of his own epistemology.

Ritschl's concept of value judgments has often been criticized as "subjective." Were he comfortable with a simple distinction between "facts" and "feelings," were he ultimately a relativist, such criticisms would perhaps be appropriate, but Ritschl is clearly *uncomfortable* with such a simple distinction. Religious knowledge, though arrived at differently, is not separate from theoretical knowledge, but part of it. In *all* learning, the perceiver has an active role to play. Therefore a continuum, not a division, exists between relatively objective issues, in which the perceiver's interests play a smaller role, and the relatively more existential issues, in which the perceiver's judgments play a larger role. Far from exalting a distinction between facts and feelings, he endeavors rather to overcome it.

Ritschl's discussion of value judgments is important for our topic, because for him the concept of God "can only be represented in value-judgments."[13] This observation is true for Christianity, where "religious knowledge consists in independent value-judgments, inasmuch as it deals with the relation between the blessedness which is assured by God and sought by man, and the whole of the world which God has created and rules in harmony with His final end."[14] But it is also true for other

10. *JR* 3:203.
11. Ibid.
12. *TM*, 187.
13. *JR* 3:225.
14. *JR* 3:207.

philosophies, even those that do not affirm the existence of a God, because such

> philosophical systems secure the unity of their view of the world either directly by introducing a tentative view of God or by employing conceptions of the world, which, being neither proved nor provable, belong to the imagination, and are therefore to be assigned to the sphere of religious knowledge rather than to that of theoretical cognition.[15]

Ritschl's discussion of value judgments is also important for our purposes because it affects his understanding of the role of theology. On the continuum from concomitant to independent value judgments, theological statements and religious statements fall at different points. In this connection, as he so often does in his writings, Ritschl appeals to Martin Luther. He cites a passage from Luther's explanation of the first commandment in his Large Catechism, in which Luther enunciates several ideas that Ritschl considers to be true and important. Among them is the observation that humans should not strive after "purely theoretical or 'disinterested' knowledge of God" as "an indispensable preliminary" for faith, because apart from the value judgment of faith, there is no religiously worthwhile knowledge of God.[16] "The truth rather is that we know the nature of God and Christ only in their worth for us. For God and faith are inseparable conceptions."[17] Religious knowledge involves value judgments. In the light of this insight drawn from Luther, Ritschl goes on to remark that

> theology is not devotion; as a science, rather, it is "disinterested" cognition. But as such it must be accompanied and guided by a sense of the worth of the Christian religion. The theologian, in his scientific work, must so far keep this degree of "interest" in sight as to conserve all those characteristics of the conception of God which render possible the trust described above.[18]

Theology is an organized, critical, internally consistent, "scientific" discipline. It makes room for the significance of religious value judgments and employs religious value judgments without itself being religious, without itself occupying the same point as religion on the continuum from independent to concomitant value judgments.

   2. *Religious knowledge.*   Religious knowledge is not an individual accomplishment, but grows out of a community and the way of looking at the world that can be found in that community. Indeed, it is not too much to say that for Ritschl God and community are correlative con-

15. *JR* 3:221.
16. *JR* 3:212.
17. Ibid.
18. *JR* 3:213–14.

cepts. More specifically, Ritschl objects to Eduard Zeller and Ferdinand Christian Baur, who describe the leading principle of the Reformation as "assigning value to the religious disposition, above every outward expression of it."[19] The principle of the "*Church*-reformation" championed by Luther and Zwingli cannot be understood as the "subjective consciousness of justification through Christ by faith," Ritschl says, "unless we take it in its close reciprocal connexion with that objective conception of the Church which regards it as being before everything, and before all legal ordinances, the divinely-founded community of believers."[20]

> In order to express accurately the one principle of the Church-reformation, we must take both these together in their inseparable connexion and reciprocal influence; on the one hand, the thought of the certainty of salvation in the individual believer . . . and, on the other hand, the thought of the community of believers under Christ—a community appointed and foreordained by God.[21]

For Ritschl Protestant theology ought to recognize the importance of the community of believers as well as the importance of justification by grace through faith. In an attempt to build this recognition into his own theology, he opens his *Instruction in the Christian Religion* with the following paragraph:

> Since the Christian religion has its origin in a special revelation, and exists in a special community of believers and worshipers, *its peculiar conceptions of God must always be interpreted in connection* (a) with the recognition of the one who bears this revelation and (b) *with the right appreciation of the Christian community,* if the total substance of Christianity is to be understood correctly. A system of doctrine which ignores either of these two elements will prove defective.[22]

And, as Ritschl goes on to say in the Introduction to the third volume of *Justification and Reconciliation,* the *significance* of the statements of Jesus "becomes completely intelligible only when we see how they are reflected in the consciousness of those who believe in Him."[23]

> Authentic and complete knowledge of Jesus' religious significance—His significance, that is, as the Founder of religion—depends, then, on one's reckoning oneself part of the community which He founded, and this precisely in so far as it believes itself to have received the forgiveness of sins as His peculiar gift.[24]

19. *JR* 1:157.
20. Ibid.
21. *JR* 1:157–58.
22. *ICR,* in *TE,* 221. Emphasis added.
23. *JR* 3:1.
24. *JR* 3:2.

Again:

> We are able to know and understand God, sin, conversion, eternal life, in
> the Christian sense, only so far as we consciously and intentionally reckon
> ourselves members of the community which Christ has founded.[25]

Christian theology is done adequately only by the theologian who recognizes him- or herself to be a part of the community of faith, because religious knowledge is community-based.

To come back to our topic, knowledge of God is also, therefore, based in a religious community. However much the procedures used by theology may be applicable in other areas of discourse, the content of a Christian view of God comes from the community in which the theologian participates and from the history of that community. If all knowing is "interested" knowing, religious knowledge is "interested" in the particular sense of emerging out of the context of a religious community.

Moreover, because theology emerges out of a religious community, its content cannot be corroborated by appeals to ideas borrowed from other philosophic or religious views of the world. Christian theology offers one paradigm of the world and of the place of the human spirit within that world. Other philosophies offer only alternative paradigms, and ideas found in one paradigm cannot confirm ideas in another.

The theologian of the 1990s can applaud Ritschl's attempt to articulate a community-based concept of God, since this approach is instructive for theological thinking undertaken in the social-cultural setting of a postmodern age. In a postmodern society no particular intellectual framework can be assumed. A theologian cannot suppose, as could be done in the "modern age," that some "givens" will be readily accepted, that people will agree, for example, that universality is a criterion of truth, that the objective is to be preferred, that technological progress is good, that rationality is the measure of all things, that human beings have the capacity to reform society in such a way as to improve it significantly, and that historicity is arbiter of reality. In a postmodern society, in which the assumptions and perspective of the thinker/perceiver are always up for scrutiny, it is appropriate to acknowledge that the Christian concept of God is not neutral, but is correlated with the context of the thinker, the context which is the Christian community. To be sure, Ritschl did not himself embody a postmodern outlook, but his correlation of theology and community continues to have value in a postmodern setting, because such a correlation acknowledges the status of the speaker/thinker and assumes no philosophical certainties upon which to establish a theological construct.

Not all contemporary theologians agree that the present cultural setting is best portrayed as "postmodern." However, even if they disagree

25. JR 3:4.

on this point, they can still, especially if they are Americans, benefit from Ritschl's emphasis on the central role of the Christian community, because it provides a much-needed antidote to the individualism that pervades most of our society and much preaching and church life within it. Individualism assumes that each person is an isolated atom, free to do whatever he or she wills, irrespective of that person's relationships, past and present. In such a setting Christianity becomes a "God and me" religion. A stress on the centrality of community pervades Ritschl's theology, from epistemology (as we will see below) through Christology to the overarching theme of the kingdom of God. He had a keen eye for those subtle, easily missed assumptions that contribute to individualism and detract from a recognition of the importance of community, and he formulated constructive alternatives. Because an emphasis on community is so germane to the setting in which contemporary American theology works, Ritschl's insights in this regard also remain valuable and useful.

3. *The distinction between "nature" and "spirit."* For Ritschl "nature" is that dimension of the world which is determined by mechanical laws of cause and effect. "Spirit" (*Geist*) is that dimension in which conscious self-direction and self-awareness occur. The "spiritual" includes freedom, understanding, volition, creativity, morality, and the capacity for personal relationships.

When talking about the world "out there," the distinction between nature and spirit is important, Ritschl believes, since human observation reveals that not all organisms can be exhaustively explained by mechanical laws. These organisms "demand, besides, the application of the idea of end."[26] However, the distinction between nature and spirit is also an important part of human experience. It arises even in the very act of knowing, where the human spirit treats nature as a means to its own end. The distinction between "nature" and "spirit" also forms the basis for religious awareness. Religion grows out of the internal conflict between "the downward pull of the 'world of nature'" and the "the upward pull" of the ethical and spiritual consciousness.[27] "In every religion," Ritschl says, "what is sought, with the help of the superhuman spiritual power reverenced by man, is a solution of the contradiction in which man finds himself, as both a part of the world of nature and a spiritual personality claiming to dominate nature."[28] The human being is part of nature and dependent on nature, yet "moved by the impulse to maintain his independence against [those other things which confine him]."[29] All religion "sustains or confirms for the personal spirit its own value over against the limitations imposed by nature or by the natural

---

26. *JR* 3:209.
27. The phrases come from Richmond, 86.
28. *JR* 3:199.
29. Ibid.

workings of human society."[30] Religion "springs up as faith in superhuman spiritual powers, by whose help the power which man possesses of himself is in some way supplemented, and elevated into a unity of its own kind which is a match for the pressure of the natural world."[31] The fundamental impulse undergirding religion is not "disinterestedly theoretical, but guided by practical ends."[32]

Ritschl is very cautious about proposing a definition of religion, because "language can furnish no terms sufficiently neutral and indeterminate to express the general conception of religion desired,"[33] and because a general conception of religion should be only regulative and not constitutive in theology,[34] but he suggests a definition, the terms of which retain a "directly Christian" stamp: Religion "is an interpretation of man's relation to God and the world, guided by the thought of the sublime power of God to realise the end of this blessedness of man."[35] In other words, religion involves a value judgment regarding the relationship of the spiritual and the natural, which asserts that the spiritual is not to be subsumed under the causal and that the divine supports the human spirit in its struggle to retain independent value over against the "downward pull" of nature. As Richmond remarks, "the 'general conception' of religion demonstrates that for Ritschl religion originates in the *human predicament* and that the 'postulate' of God arises in the attempt to resolve this . . . intolerable tension" of being "torn asunder" by the downward pull of nature which is in conflict with the upward pull of ethical and spiritual consciousness.[36]

Clearly, what motivated Ritschl to distinguish between spirit and nature was his generation's worry about materialism. Human beings seemed in danger of becoming mere "cogs in a machine." Society and nature were "not merely *apathetic* but even *hostile* to the attainment of those moral and spiritual ends encompassed in the divine and human end of the creation, the Kingdom of God."[37] "The world" was experienced as a threat—as so impersonal and mechanical as to doom human personality and its creative uniqueness.[38] Materialism was not merely an intellectual challenge, but an existential issue. As Richmond observes,

> by combating scientific materialism and naturalism, Ritschl was not unsuccessfully attempting to anchor his theology in the life-situation of nineteenth-century man. Had he been so unsuccessful as we have been

30. *TM,* 156.
31. *JR* 3:199.
32. *JR* 3:195.
33. Ibid.
34. *JR* 3:196.
35. *JR* 3:194.
36. Richmond, 86.
37. Richmond, 93.
38. Richmond, 92.

led to believe, it would be hard to account for the wide and deep influence his theology exercised over several generations.[39]

To summarize what has been said thus far in this section: If all knowledge is in some way "interested"—that is, motivated by a value consideration—and religious knowledge is "interested" in the particular sense of being community-based, religious knowledge is also "interested" in another special way: it emerges out of an existential dilemma and approaches God as that superhuman being who can undergird the self-conception of the human spirit as worthwhile and valuable and more than a cog in a machine. "Knowledge of God can be demonstrated as religious knowledge only when He is conceived as securing to the believer such a position in the world as more than counterbalances its restrictions."[40]

Viewed from the perspective of the 1990s, the distinction Ritschl draws between nature and spirit is troublesome, because it overlooks, or at least fails to emphasize, the interdependence of the human and the natural. Phrases such as "lordship over the world," "supremacy over the world," and "elevation over nature" seem to place religion on the side of those traditional and contemporary viewpoints which give the human spirit an unqualified priority. When confronting "scientific" determinisms and materialisms, it may well have been appropriate to emphasize that the spiritual is more important than the natural, but in the face of ecological insensitivity, a different word needs to be spoken, a word which emphasizes that the *shalom* of the kingdom includes the well-being of nonhuman creatures as well as the well-being of the human spirit. The *in*dependence of human beings should not be upheld at the expense of their *inter*dependence.

However, as long as the distinction between nature and spirit is understood to be only a distinction and not a separation that renders humans insensitive to their interdependence with nature, it remains an important part of contemporary thinking. Without some room for human freedom, a covenantal relationship with God would not be possible. However much this insight may need to be redefined in the light of twentieth-century developments, it remains an important distinction with which theology continues to work.

Moreover, to the degree that the "dominion" over nature promised by religion encourages human beings to take appropriate responsibility for conditions in society and the harmful effects of society upon nature, to the degree that this view encourages an activist stance vis-à-vis society and nature, Ritschl's perspective also remains helpful at the end of the twentieth century. Only if human beings understand that God will not act unilaterally, that they share responsibility for preventing another

39. Ibid.
40. *JR* 3:212.

Holocaust, a nuclear catastrophe, or an ecological disaster, will life on
this planet be saved.

   4. *The exclusion of metaphysics from theology.*   As is well known,
Ritschl sought to exclude metaphysics from theology. But what exactly
was he excluding? Were "metaphysics" to be understood as the "branch
of philosophy that investigates ultimate principles of reality,"[41] such investigations would not themselves be troublesome for Ritschl. Nor does
he object to philosophical reasoning; it plays an important role in his
theology. He is constantly trying to avoid and/or overcome contradictions and inconsistencies in order to formulate an internally *coherent*
view. Moreover, he is quite ready to bring up philosophical issues and
problems as part of his evaluation of other theologians, past and present, and as part of his own theological proposals. Thus "it would be
ill-considered and unthinkable to assert that I would eliminate *all* metaphysics from theology. . . . The question at issue . . . can be formulated
correctly only in the following manner: '*Which* metaphysics is justified
in theology?'"[42]

   To what, then, did Ritschl object? First, he objected to any metaphysics that did not take into account the distinction between spirit and
nature but tried to use "being" (in the sense of "thing-ness") as the basic
category. (In what follows, "metaphysics" and "metaphysical" in quota-
tion marks will designate this particular understanding.) "Metaphysics"

> devotes itself to the investigation of the universal foundations of all being.
> Now the things that our cognition concerns itself with are differentiated as
> nature and spiritual life [*geistiges Leben*]. Therefore, any investigation of
> the common foundations of all being must set aside the particular charac-
> teristics by which one represents the difference between nature and spirit
> and the means by which one knows that these groups of things are dissim-
> ilar entities. Thus natural and spiritual manifestations or entities occupy
> the attention of metaphysical knowing only insofar as they are to be
> grasped generally as "things."[43]

For Ritschl, such "metaphysical" cognition is not without value, but it
does not deal with reality as exhaustively as do modes of apprehension
that recognize the distinction between spirit and nature. "Compared
with natural science and ethics, metaphysics yields elementary and
merely formal knowledge."[44]

   Ritschl states his objection very carefully. The metaphysics that has
value investigates the forms that guide the spirit in conceptualizing objects. So long as this knowledge of things in general does not displace at-

----

   41. *Funk and Wagnalls Standard Dictionary* (New York: New American Library,
1980), 498.
   42. *TM*, 187. Emphasis added.
   43. *TM*, 154.
   44. *JR* 3:16.

tention to the distinction between spirit and nature but precedes or follows such attention, it causes Ritschl no problems. He objects only when
the added claim is made that metaphysical analysis yields a "more basic
and more valuable cognition of spiritual entities than would be the case
through psychology and ethical examination of those entities."[45]

In theology false "metaphysics" uses categories of causation to seek
independent access to God and claims to arrive at a definition of God
more basic or more encompassing than one derived from a theological
analysis of revelation. It erroneously applies to God categories appropriate to things in general; there results an image of God not as spirit,
but as part of a world system.[46] However glorified and exalted, the construct remains a thing rather than a spiritual being; the resulting image
of God is devoid of religious value, so Ritschl calls it an idol. Ritschl
proposes to subordinate everything in theology to revelation and in so
doing to restrict the role of metaphysics in that discipline to appropriate
boundaries; theology borrows from metaphysics but does so on its own
terms, as a separate discipline functioning with its own priorities and
procedures.

To Ritschl's way of thinking, classical doctrines of God are "metaphysical." The idea of God found in Aristotle and the Platonists "either
does not transcend the world or it merely represents the idea of the
world."[47] Ritschl thus rejects the portrait of the divine operative in traditional cosmological and teleological proofs of God's existence, "because
they disregard the difference between nature and spirit, since they regard
the content of the world [as a whole] as a chain of effects and causes."[48]
Since "in all of its forms, the religious world view is established on the
principle that the human spirit differentiates itself to some degree in
value from the phenomena within its environment and from the workings of nature that press in upon it," in the final analysis the Aristotelian
portrait of God "is the denial of religion altogether."[49]

Ritschl likewise rejects the view that God is "absolute," because he
considers the idea to be "an unseemly mingling of metaphysics with revealed religion."[50] So far as Ritschl is concerned, the concept implies a
being who can exist as a unity apart from relationships, and he does not
see how this fits with the Christian notions of love and personhood,
both of which imply relationships. He does not think some attributes of
God should be drawn from "metaphysical" speculation, while other attributes are drawn from revelation. The mixture is "unseemly" and betrays epistemological confusion. Nor does he think that Christian
theology should seek to prove the truth of its own view of God by show-

45. *TM,* 155.
46. *JR* 3:215.
47. *TM,* 158.
48. Ibid.; see also *JR* 3:214–16.
49. *TM,* 156–57.
50. *TM,* 164.

ing that it agrees with some philosophical or juridical view of the world. The proof of the truth of Christianity comes via praxis.[51]

Ritschl's objection to "metaphysics" (as he understands the term) is essentially the same as Martin Luther's objection to Aristotle: The interpersonal character of religion is obscured by a "thing-oriented" metaphysics. One is not surprised, then, when Ritschl perceives parallels between Luther's struggle against scholasticism and his own against "metaphysics."[52] (The corresponding dissimilarity is that the main opponent in his nineteenth-century context is materialism.)

> Now, if the Absolute is to be taken as real, and yet not to be taken as spirit, it must be a material thing. And this shows all the more clearly that the Absolute, which [the confessionalist theologian Franz Hermann] Frank posits as God, has the form and impress of an idol. I do not say that Frank has any inkling that this is implied in his position; but to my mind there is an element of materialism in his view.[53]

A "thing-oriented" metaphysics opens the door for materialism.

Ritschl also objected to any epistemology or metaphysics that claimed to be able to know something "more real" "behind" what we experience of another person or of God. Classical conceptions of God employ a Platonic or an unexamined commonsense epistemology, either of which assumes knowledge of things in themselves spatially "behind" and temporally "before" appearances.[54] These views mistakenly assume that the provisional distinction between the memory image we construct and the appearances we experience is a distinction between cause and effect, between the thing in itself and the sensations it produces. "A contradiction results when a thing, presupposed to be placid, indifferent, and powerless in our recollection, is at the same time represented as moved and moving, changing and alterable."[55]

One problem, according to Ritschl, is that such a view misunderstands the human soul. "We know nothing of a self-existence of the soul, of a self-enclosed life of the spirit above or behind those functions in which it is active, living, and present to itself as a being of special worth."[56] "The relation of the soul to all the causes which work upon it is not one of simple passivity: all actions upon it, rather, it takes up in its sensation as a reaction in which it manifests itself as an independent cause."[57]

Another problem with the commonsense view is that it introduces a pernicious disjunction between revelation and "God in himself." Ritschl's

51. *JR* 3:24–25.
52. Cf., e.g., *JR* 3:226 and 212.
53. *JR* 3:238.
54. *TM*, 182–83.
55. *TM*, 182.
56. *JR* 3:21.
57. Ibid.

objection at this point is similar to Martin Luther's opposition to a "theology of glory." Ritschl's own view is that "a thing 'exists' in its relationships and it is only in them that we can know the thing and only by them that we can name it."[58] A correct epistemology enables us to locate God *in* God's revelation:

> Only in . . . the actuality of the spiritual life can one understand the actions of God which furnish the basis for religion. But since we can only perceive God in his actions toward us, which correspond to his public revelation, so it is that we perceive God's presence for us precisely *in* these actions [and not "behind" them].[59]

According to Ritschl we have no unmediated knowledge of either human beings or God. As active spiritual beings, the personality and character of God and humans are evident in their actions. Our knowledge of them comes exclusively through their behavior. Over against classical conceptions of God that employ a Platonic or commonsense epistemology, Ritschl insists that God is to be known through divine activity—in revelation and in the Christian community.

III

In the light of the foregoing, how does Ritschl develop his own concept of God?

1. *God's existence.* Although he does not put a great deal of stock in its importance, he is able to formulate a modified moral argument for the existence of God. (The cosmological, teleological, and ontological arguments are all dismissed.)[60] The moral argument alone begins with a distinction between nature and human spirit. Drawing on the philosophy of Immanuel Kant, Ritschl argues that the hope of felicity entails the coming together of the independent realms of morality and nature. The moral agent necessarily postulates a God who, as moral Creator, insures the congruence of virtue and happiness.[61] The result is a practical conviction that God exists.

This argument is acceptable to Ritschl for at least two reasons: Its appeal to morality preserves the distinction between spirit and nature, and the appeal to morality employs data from outside the specifically religious view of the world.[62] It is neither circular in its reasoning nor incompatible with religious trust.

However, Ritschl does not find Kant's moral argument entirely satisfactory. He believes that Kant failed to grant practical reason its right-

---

58. *TM*, 184.
59. *TM*, 194. Emphasis added.
60. *JR* 3:214–19; *TM*, 156–57.
61. *JR* 3:219.
62. *JR* 3:224.

ful value when it and its God-postulate are excluded from theoretical cognition.

> Knowledge of the laws of our action is also theoretical knowledge, for it is knowledge of the laws of spiritual life. Now the impulse of knowledge, of feeling, and of aesthetic intuition, of will in general and its special application to society, and finally the impulse of religion in the general sense of the word, all concur to demonstrate that spiritual life is the end, while nature is the means. This is the general law of spiritual life, the validity of which science must maintain if the special character of the spiritual realm of existence is not to be ignored.[63]

Although the laws of spiritual life differ from the laws of mechanics operating in nature, they, too, can be known by theoretical reason. "If the exertion of moral will is a reality, then the practical Reason is a branch of theoretical cognition."[64]

> Since men, as spiritual beings who exercise through their natural organism particular effects on nature and on one another, constitute a special realm of reality in the world, and since the moral goods they call into existence are no less real than the natural world, therefore knowledge of the practical laws obtaining in this sphere falls under theoretical cognition no less than natural science does.[65]

One set of laws operates in nature, another in morality and the life of the spirit. Not only must theoretical reason acknowledge the reality of these two dimensions of life, it must also "seek for a law explaining the coexistence of these two heterogeneous orders of reality."[66]

The only way Ritschl sees to explain this coexistence is to postulate the Christian conception of God as a benevolent Divine Will. Though revelation and not theoretical reason is its source, the Christian concept of God can nonetheless be acknowledged as suitable for theoretical purposes; the notion of Divine Will both explains the natural world and satisfies the religious principle that a world-transcending spirit endorse and undergird the value of human spirits. In Christianity the value of human spirit is confirmed by the "consciousness of blessedness—a consciousness conditioned by the idea of the purely spiritual God, Who as Creator of the universe governs all things on the principle that mankind are ordained to be the final end of the world, through trust in God as members of His spiritual kingdom."[67]

> Now we must either resign the attempt to comprehend the ground and law of the coexistence of nature and spiritual life, or we must, to attain our

63. *JR* 3:222.
64. *JR* 3:221.
65. *JR* 3:222–23.
66. *JR* 3:223.
67. Ibid.

end, acknowledge the Christian conception of God as the truth by which our knowledge of the universe is consummated. . . . Nothing remains but to accept the Christian idea of God, and that, too, as an indispensable truth.[68]

In other words, either morality and religion are baseless illusions, and we are back to materialism, or one must postulate a divine will in order to achieve a coherent view of the universe and our place in it.

Because Ritschl's concept of God as loving will respects the distinction between spirit and nature, because it respects the independent value of science, morality, and religion, this understanding of God is, in his judgment, more comprehensive and exhaustive than theisms rooted in classical "metaphysics." Spirit has not been reduced to nature; God has not been made part of a world system; God transcends both human spirit and nature but unifies them by guiding both toward a goal or final purpose.

One could object that Ritschl has not proved the existence of God, at least not in any way that is universally compelling. But such objections would not distress Ritschl, because there exists for him no language neutral enough to prove a God in general. In order for Ritschl's argument to be convincing, one must, among other things, accept his reading of religious consciousness. In this reading, religion involves a value judgment that a superhuman power is supporting the human spirit against the deterministic forces of nature and society. Kant's argument, Ritschl acknowledges, betrays the influence of a Christian conception of God and the world, as does his own even more. What Ritschl believes he has shown is the compatibility of a concept drawn from Christian revelation with a modern scientific outlook and a post-Kantian understanding of philosophy and of human life. Belief in God remains a judgment, but not an absurd one, and not one based on feelings alone. The judgment arises from persons within the community of faith but is amenable to theoretical cognition. We may ask whether, in the final analysis, any other Christian theologian can legitimately claim to have proven more.

2. *Personality and loving will.*   Ritschl goes on to endorse the divine attributes of "personality" and "loving will," which simultaneously (*a*) satisfy the desire for a comprehensive view of spirit and nature and (*b*) correspond to the character of the God revealed in Jesus and witnessed to by the Scriptures.

Personality and loving will are not equivalent notions. Personality has to do with form and loving will with content.[69] When applied to God in isolation from Christian revelation, personality is an empty, formal concept capable of several quite different meanings.

---

68. *JR* 3:223–24.
69. *JR* 3:274.

But, is the form itself applicable to God? Since human personality is conditioned by so many environmental factors, can God be understood as a person without committing the theologian to an internal contradiction? Yes, Ritschl argues, if one adopts an appropriate model of human personality as the analogue of God. "The conceivability of the personality of God is to be reached . . . through the study of what is so worthy of esteem among men—independent personality."[70] Ritschl pursues the analogy in the following way:

> Developed personal individuality consists in the power to take up the inexorable stimuli of the environment into one's plan of life, in such a way that they are incorporated in it as means under firm control, and no longer felt as obstacles to the free movement of the self.[71]

Although God is a person, what distinguishes God from human personality is the lack of restraint that God experiences. "As the cause of all that happens, God is affected only by such forces of influence as He has conferred upon His creatures, and as He sees transparently to be the effects of His own Will. Nothing which affects the Divine Spirit is originally alien to Him."[72] Humans experience an environment not of their own making, but the world God experiences is the product of God's own creation and governance.

The analogy of developed personal individuality has several advantages for Ritschl. In the first place, it satisfies his desire that God be conceived as a personal being. In the second place, it removes from the idea of personality the limitation that would otherwise preclude its application to God. God is not defined by the environment, that is, by the world, as are human beings. Third, it avoids the problems and contradictions encountered when Christian theology attempts to use the traditional scholastic metaphysical view of God. Postulating a divine substratum behind appearances may make God "absolute" but permits no relation to the world. So far as Ritschl can see, the alternatives, in that case, are always either separation from the world or identification with it—in short, deism or pantheism. Fourth, the analogy of developed individual personality ascribes individuality to God, the individuality necessary to distinguish God from human creatures who are also personal.

By choosing "person" as his primary category for understanding God, Ritschl breaks with the classical tradition. The

> full conception of God as a Person, Who establishes the Kingdom of God as the final end of the world, and in it assures to every one who trusts in Him supremacy over the world . . . may be differentiated without further

70. *JR* 3:233.
71. *JR* 3:234.
72. *JR* 3:236.

remark from limitless being, regarded as the substance of the universe, from the idea of a First Cause which need not be personal, and from the self-conscious but self-enclosed Final End of the world. The conception of God thus set up is of such a nature that it simply cannot be distorted into Pantheism or Deism.[73]

Other theologians thought they could begin by conceiving of God as limitless being and add on to that concept the attribute of personhood found in Christian revelation. Ritschl disagrees, and with that disagreement he unravels the centuries-old assumption that the classical philosophic and biblical portraits of God are compatible. Ritschl arrives at this conclusion, in large part at least, because he wants to avoid pantheism and deism, which in his mind are variations on the same themes that he finds in materialism—namely, that humans are but pieces of the world or the world soul and not properly valued as free beings with independent worth.[74]

Ritschl's objection to a "mixed" concept of God is evident at other places as well—in his rejection of predestination, for example. "Eternal election of individuals is neither a Biblical idea nor a religious conception, but merely a deduction of Augustine's from his abstract idea of God—an idea which makes all temporal history nothing but unreal appearance."[75] In this regard Ritschl finds an inconsistency in Luther's concept of God (especially as expressed in *The Bondage of the Will*). Alongside his Reformation insight into the revealed will of God, Luther retained the idea of the hidden will of God. According to Ritschl the latter was a carryover from medieval nominalism.[76] The combination of these two alien notions is what Ritschl labels "inconsistent," for the "secret will" of God is then allowed to limit God's openly expressed will that in the gospel salvation is offered to all. To this undercutting of the gospel with the "secret will" of God he objects, as he does to any representation of the elect or the human race as sums of individuals subject to God's eternal decree.

In order to overcome the inconsistency of "mixed" understandings of God, Ritschl reconsiders God's role in election. For him election applies to the community founded by Christ and relates to the revealed will of God. It "is an idea which the common Christian feeling applies to all who are already within the circle over which the influence of Christ's work extends, or who may hereafter enter into that circle."[77] "A judgment on the eternal and unconditioned reprobation of individuals, therefore, cannot possibly be deduced from this idea of election, but only the

73. JR 3:228.
74. JR 3:211.
75. JR 3:121–22.
76. Ritschl, "Geschichtliche Studien," *Jahrbücher für deutsche Theologie* 13 (1868): 78–88.
77. JR 3:129.

judgment that certain individuals have not yet been brought within the sphere of the operations of Divine grace."[78]

This advance beyond Luther is consistent with Ritschl's approach to the doctrine of God, but, as I will discuss later, it is in other ways a costly step, because the consistency he eventually achieves irons out some of the tensions and complexities found in the biblical portrait of God. The problem is not with his procedural objectives, for to retain the tensions and the complexity one need not return to "alien" notions drawn from philosophical theism, but one does need to rethink Ritschl's understanding of the content of the biblical portrait of God.

To recapitulate, what Ritschl has accomplished by considering God to be a person is the following: He has avoided pantheism and deism. He has employed a concept drawn from Christian revelation, which is consistent with the portrait found in the Scriptures. He has formulated a "positive" concept—that is, one drawn from a religious community and its history rather than the product of sheer speculation. Because it is positive, and because it coheres with other concepts in an ordered view of the world, it is scientific/academic/scholarly (*wissenschaftlich*). The view of God as person is also consistent with the essential Reformation insights celebrating the gospel of a God active in love *pro me* (for me). The concept of God as person moves beyond the understanding of God found in Kant and Schleiermacher. And, most important perhaps, to conceive of God as person undergirds the spiritual (*geistlich*) dimension of the human being, which Ritschl finds so threatened by practical and theoretical materialism.

3. *Loving will.* The attribute of "loving will" comes directly from the New Testament, where Jesus extends to the community of faith the right to participate in his own relationship with God. God in Christ embraces the community and thereby reveals himself as loving will.[79] Jesus also extended this understanding of God to include the whole of creation, thus embracing Son, community, and world.[80]

That God is love could not have been deduced from philosophical analysis, but once revealed, Ritschl says, the concept of a loving God does explain the world as a connected whole, thereby satisfying the desires of both religion and theoretical cognition. God is not to be conceived first, in general, as personality and second, in particular, as loving will. "What I mean is rather this, that the conception of love is the only adequate conception of God, for it enables us, both to understand the revelation which comes through Christ to His community, and at the same time to solve the problem of the world."[81] "Even the recognition of the personality of God does not imply independent knowledge apart

78. Ibid.
79. JR 3:273.
80. Clearly, Ritschl did not intend his theology to be antithetical to an appropriate stewardship of the environment.
81. JR 3:274.

from our defining Him as loving Will. It only decides the form to be given to this content, for without this content of loving Will the conception of spiritual personality is not sufficient to explain the world as a connected whole."[82] As a glove sliding on a hand, form and content here come together in Ritschl's concept of God.

Ritschl's definition of love is "will aiming either at the appropriation of an object or at the enrichment of its existence, because moved by a feeling of its worth."[83] This understanding, he goes on to say, means that only persons (not things) are loved. It also implies consistency on the part of the lover. Moreover, understood in this way, love does not simply render assistance, but promotes the personal end of the one loved. And love makes the end of the loved one part of its own.

The final, revealed goal for this loving will is the kingdom of God. As love, God guides all things toward the kingdom in such a way that human beings, whose end is also God's kingdom, thereby receive and achieve their full stature as human spirits. And this achievement for humans, rather than denying divine self-fulfillment, actually affirms it. Like all who love, God achieves a measure of self-completion by granting perfection to another through his love. Thus, because God wills for humans their highest good, divine and human fulfillment coalesce. The kingdom becomes for Ritschl the substantive link holding together his doctrine of God, his insistence upon human participation, his Atonement theory, his conception of the unity of the world, his emphasis on the community, and the religious character of all theological knowledge.

To summarize: Ritschl has argued that our human experience of setting ourselves above nature despite our involvement in it is buttressed by religion. This experience can be accounted for, in any integrated and integrating way, only by affirming the existence of God as a personal spirit, analogous to ourselves, whose creative and redemptive activity assures the legitimacy of our high self-evaluation. In Christianity we are both assured of our spiritual freedom and drawn into a transcendent project that is universal in scope and self-transforming in significance. The content supplied by Christian revelation combines with the formal analysis of philosophical reflection to create a more comprehensive and adequate view of reality than any other metaphysical system, all of which are rivals. By comparison, classical theism is reductionistic and unsuited to sustain human freedom and personhood in the late nineteenth century from the threat of secularism and materialism and from the tendency among Christians toward quietism.

IV

What can Ritschl's theology contribute to constructive theological thinking today? The answer has to be dialogical and dialectical. When recon-

---

82. Ibid.
83. *JR* 3:277.

textualizing a century-old theology one needs to identify what to avoid as well as what to pursue more deeply. When this particular contemporary looks back at Ritschl's concept of God, he finds things to applaud and things to question or, in some cases, even to lament.

As a contemporary I can applaud the magnificent way in which Ritschl's sensitivity to historical development, his attention to the biblical portrait of God, his understanding of church history, and his critical appreciation of Martin Luther came together to help him discern the uncomfortable mixture of classical philosophy and biblical themes resident in the dominant Western tradition. Anyone who listens carefully to Ritschl can no longer endorse the too-easy assumption that the traditional view of God is uniformly biblical in origin. Ritschl's questions about some traditional assertions regarding God were and are unsettling enough to prompt further research and constructive formulations, including ones that move beyond his own.

As a contemporary I can applaud Ritschl's embryonic quest for an ontology of relationship, his intuitive awareness that the human being is so defined by relationships that, reconciled to God, one is a significantly different person from what one was unreconciled to God. Likewise, the human being who is part of a community sees things differently from the person uninfluenced by these communal ties. Ritschl's preference for "person" language when speaking of God is consistent with this insight and with this quest for an ontology of relationship. So, too, are his objections to "absolute" as an attribute ascribed to God.

As a contemporary I can lament Ritschl's undialectical understanding of the ontology of relationship. His portrait of God comes out unnecessarily "flat," as does his portrait of the human being who lives in faith. However much Ritschl's God may move and grow and change, God seems always in control of the process, taking up the "stimuli of the environment" into God's plan of life, in such a way that they are incorporated into it as a "means under firm control, and no longer felt as obstacles to the free movement of the self."[84] However much God is active in revelation, God still seems "above it all" rather than involved in the fray; God seems undeterred and unscarred by evil. Given the massive, intentionally inflicted suffering of the twentieth century, it is hard to picture God in this way. It is equally difficult to picture the Christian living the kind of life in which stimuli are incorporated in a plan that keeps them "under firm control." Under contemporary conditions a Christian who affirms the call to be with and identify with the suffering person is likely to find himself or herself crossing social boundaries and swimming in the uncertainties of quite unfamiliar situations; such a life seems full of unforeseen, ambiguous developments not at all under one's control. Ritschl's God and Ritschl's Christian were both patient, well-modulated, unrebellious personalities. From the perspective of the

84. Cf. JR 3:234.

1990s, when Christianity is more clearly a countercultural movement, a more colorful, vulnerable portrait of God and of the Christian seems appropriate for theology.

As a contemporary I can wish that Ritschl had understood the theology of the cross more clearly, so that he could have written more forthrightly about God's capacity to suffer, to coexperience the anguish of human failure and the dehumanization caused by oppression. Such insights would have been compatible with his readiness to revise traditional modes of thinking and compatible with his critical admiration of Luther's religious outlook. The result would have been a more dynamic sense of God at work in the world and a more profound sense of how love works from within to break open human life to its own radically creative possibilities.

As a contemporary I can appreciate Ritschl's understanding of religion and the task of theology. We know far more today than Ritschl knew about the non-Christian religions of the world. We therefore need a definition of religion different from the one he offered and himself recognized to be inadequate. But his understanding of Christian theology as an internally consistent paradigm of the world and his understanding of the place of the human spirit in that world continue to recommend themselves. For theology, any definition of religion remains a regulative principle rather than a constitutive one. And the same is true for the role served by epistemology and metaphysics. They are important and should be used carefully and creatively within theology, but—as feminist theologians, black theologians, liberation theologians, and others have in recent times so clearly reminded us—no claims should be made regarding the universal validity of a particular epistemology or metaphysics employed by a contemporary theology. The task of theology is not to formulate universally recognized truths, but to awaken the community to the gifts it enjoys and the tasks it needs to accomplish.

9

Religious Cognition in Light of Current Questions

Does Albrecht Ritschl's theory of religious cognition have any relevance for the contemporary dialogue between science and religion? Can Ritschl's theory of knowing (his epistemology) be seen as an initial plank in building the stage for this discussion? Are his ideas represented in any of the current science-religion theoreticians? Can Ritschl be seen as a resource for the contemporary science-religion dialogue?

In a strict sense, the answer to all the questions raised above is no. Ritschl was a historian concerned with interpreting Christianity for his church. His theological method was based on historical criticism and guided by loyalty to dogmatic principles articulated by the Protestant reformers. One regulating principle for Ritschl was Christ as the sole revealer of God's will and only source of knowledge of God. Another was Ritschl's concept of the Christian "style of living" (*Lebensführung*) by which he sorted out "correct" conduct from the variety of ways people have, in fact, lived out their Christianity. The historical approach guided by dogmatic principles does not suggest that Ritschl would have much to offer to the current science-religion dialogue.

However, if we draw out implications of ideas latent in his epistemology, the Ritschlian legacy is relevant to some current issues in science and religion. I am arguing not that Ritschl directly *influenced* the contemporary interchange between scientists and religious thinkers, but that some of his ideas surprisingly show up in their thought. I am suggesting that the seasonal relevance of his epistemology may be more germane to the late twentieth century than to his own era. Ritschl was perhaps ahead of his time with his theory of religious cognition, and only now can we perceive its relevance. Admittedly, this rather loose kind of argument assumes that ideas have a life of their own; they emerge on the stage of history, have an impact or fail to do so, lie dormant, and then reemerge in later periods. Thus I use the categories of "themes" and "modes" of thought to make comparisons between Ritschl and the current science and religion forum.

I want to argue that Ritschl's method is relevant to the contemporary science-religion discussion, but that the justification he offers in support of his theory of religious cognition is not. He makes an important methodological contribution by arguing for the cognitive validity of faith, or that faith is the foundation of rationality. This reintegration of spirituality with rationality takes Ritschl a step beyond the Kantian bifurcation of practical and pure reason, in which knowledge is denied in order to make room for faith. But his justification for faith's cognitive validity is finally too anthropocentric: nature exists for the purpose of spirit. This means that the created order itself serves the purpose of human salvation. Of course, Ritschl's justification is finally theocentric, because he places human salvation in the context of the kingdom of God, which for him is the ultimate destiny of existence. Christian revelation "saves" humanity from the mechanistic determinism of nature's causal order. However, the anthropocentric focus of God's salvation is seen now, a century after Ritschl, as a problem instead of a solution. Humanity's disregard for the natural world is expressed in the idea that humans are superior to nature in the "Great Chain of Being."[1] Furthermore, Ritschl's justification rests on a principle of dogmatic theology: that the destiny of existence is revealed in Jesus Christ.

PLACING RITSCHL IN THE SCIENCE-RELIGION DIALOGUE

Ian Barbour follows standard interpretations of Ritschl by placing him in the Kantian tradition. According to Barbour, Ritschl sets forth a "theology of moral values."[2] Barbour presents a succinct summary of the main methodological issues that need to be discussed in assessing Ritschl's relevance to the science-religion dialogue:

> Ritschl agreed with Kant that no knowledge of God can be achieved by "theoretical reason" or philosophical speculation; religion is a matter of "practical reason," inseparable from conscience and judgments of value. Ritschl, like Schleiermacher, looked to the experiential basis of religion, but he interpreted it primarily as man's ethical will. . . .
>
> Ritschl pictured a sharp contrast between the *human sphere* and the *sphere of nature*. In part this was a continuation of the Kantian distinction between the objective realm which science investigates, and the realm of man's history and culture in which there is freedom and value. But it was

1. John Carmody, *Ecology and Religion: Toward a New Christian Theology of Nature* (New York: Paulist Press, 1983), 46.
2. Ian G. Barbour, *Issues in Science and Religion* (New York: Harper & Row, Harper Torchbooks, 1966), 107.

also a reaction to the image of evolution as a process of conflict and struggle. The liberals were concerned to rescue man from nature; they did this
not by denying evolution but by affirming the victory of spirit over nature.
They defended man's free ethical personality from mechanical or materialistic interpretations. Religion could aid their cause by asserting the infinite
value of the human soul and the spiritual supremacy of man over the impersonal natural order.[3]

The main methodological issue here is that nineteenth-century Liberal
theologians based their theology on human experience. Schleiermacher
began his *Glaubenslehre* with an analysis of the human psyche and "discovered" the *religious a priori* (the feeling of absolute dependence) at the
base, root, or ground of human consciousness. Ritschl followed Schleiermacher's appeal to human experience but broadened the category to
include moral and social experience. As Barbour says, Ritschl sharply con-
trasts the human sphere and the sphere of nature; for him religious knowing is confined to the personal, existential, ultimate concerns of human
beings trying to find meaning in the natural world. Nature, however, offers no clue to the meaning of life, no message of hope, no revelation. The
legacy of the Liberal theological tradition for the science-religion dialogue,
then, is that religious knowing is quite different from scientific knowing.
Science investigates the "factual" processes of nature, and religious knowing becomes a matter of personal valuation, attempting to orient oneself
meaningfully in an opaque universe.

Ritschl's theory of religious knowledge does seem to provide a basis
for existential theology, which splits apart nature and spirit. For Ritschl,
"we never exercise religious cognition in merely explaining nature by a
First Cause, but always only in explaining the autonomy of the human
spirit over and against nature."[4] He did not, however, intend religious
knowledge to be confined to the sphere of the personal isolated from the
rigors of scientific methodology. Ritschl makes the more interesting
claim that religious knowledge, which is a matter of "practical reason,"
is a "branch" (*Zweig*) of "theoretical reason."[5] Religious knowledge is
that dimension of theoretical knowledge which explains the purpose of
gaining any kind of knowledge at all:

> Now the impulses of knowledge, of feeling, and of aesthetic intuition, of
> will in general and in its special application to society, and finally the im-
> pulse of religion in the general sense of the word, all concur to demon-
> strate that spiritual life is the end, while nature is the means. This is the
> general law of spiritual life, the validity of which science [*Wissenschaft,*

3. Ibid.
4. *JR* 3:218–19. *Selbständigkeit* has been translated as "autonomy" instead of "independence" as in the Mackintosh-Macaulay translation.
5. *JR* 3:221.

that is, scholarship in general] must maintain if the special character of the spiritual realm of existence is not to be ignored.[6]

Thus for Ritschl, nature and spirit are not separate realms with specific kinds of knowledge pertinent to each domain, but are two aspects of a unified reality. Ritschl offers an important modification of Kant's epistemology which is often overlooked in the characterization of Ritschl as a "neo-Kantian" theologian. Ritschl's point is that Kant divided reality into two spheres: nature and spirit. The "really real," for Kant, is nature and her laws. The "subjectively real" is spirit with its laws of morality and aesthetic judgments. The result of the Kantian bifurcation of reality, Ritschl recognized, is that faith, morality, and aesthetics become *mere* matters of personal conviction, affairs of the heart, which have subjective value, but no cognitive significance. According to Ritschl, Kant's split of theoretical and practical reason, of knowledge about nature and spiritual knowledge, does not adequately account for the fact that the spiritual life is something just as real as the laws of nature. Ritschl does not deny that religious knowledge is a subjective matter, but claims that personal conviction is just as significant, just as real, as physical laws. While Kant divided reality into two orders, Ritschl thought his Christian view of the world held the two orders together.

For Ritschl, nature and spirit are knowable as coexisting to attain "knowledge of the universe," and this knowledge is "consummated" in the Christian conception of God.[7] Ritschl most likely got the idea that nature exists for the purpose of spirit from Rudolf Hermann Lotze, who was his colleague at Göttingen. Lotze argued that the mechanisms of the causal orders of reality existed for the purpose of enhancing value.[8] Lotze apparently convinced Ritschl that Kant did not give religious cognition the status it deserved. Philosophically, Kant did not give equal weight to theoretical and practical reason. Theologically, Kant based religion on morality, while Ritschl based morality on religion.[9] Ritschl's more general point is that whenever philosophy (specifically the philosophy of materialism) sets out on a search for the "wholeness" of things, it becomes caught up in a religious mode of thought. When theoretical

6. *JR* 3:222. It should be noted that science (*Wissenschaft*) refers to the discipline of scholarship itself and not to the "hard" or natural sciences, as we use the term today. Ritschl refers to "theoretical reason" and philosophy in the sense in which we refer to science.

7. *JR* 3:223.

8. Rudolf Hermann Lotze, *Microcosmos: An Essay Concerning Man and His Relation to the World*, 3d ed., trans. E. Hamilton and E. E. C. Jones (New York: Scribner and Welford, 1888), 1:343.

9. Ritschl criticizes Kant in *JR 1* for turning practical reason into an "arbitrary kind" of knowledge (403); for basing religion on morality, not morality on religion (409); for not giving Christ's satisfaction a "constitutive influence on the moral life" (414); and for "dogmatizing . . . the critical principles of his doctrine of ethics" (416). Ritschl thought Kant's mistake was that he did not give the same cognitive significance to religion as he gave to theoretical reason (knowledge).

cognition seeks to discover a "supreme universal law of the world" that explains the "differentiated orders of nature and the spiritual life," theoretical cognition "betrays rather an impulse religious in its nature" (*aber veräth sich vielmehr ein Antrieb religiöser Art*).[10] This search for the Whole, which is a "religious impulse," is at the core of Ritschl's theory of religious cognition. Instead of describing Ritschl's project as a "theology of moral values," one might equally call it a theology of "intuitive imagination" (*der anschauenden Phantasie*), because when philosophy attempts "to deduce the world as a whole," it "betrays itself as being quite as much an object of the intuitive imagination, as God and the world are for religious thought."[11] The specific kind of knowledge that Ritschl describes as religious cognition is concerned with representations (*Vorstellungen*) of intuitive imagination. Philosophical first principles, as well as the idea of God, can never be proved (*erweisen*), but are "anticipatively assumed" (*vorgreifender Weise angenommen*).[12] Thus, religious cognition is a highly intuitive form of cognition, which must be recognized as just as significant as theoretical reason in order to establish the cognitive validity of faith. Ritschl does not deny reason to make room for faith, as does Kant, but presents the stronger claim that faith ultimately is the foundation of reason, since philosophical first principles are based upon religious impulses. Where, then, might Ritschl be placed in the contemporary science-religion dialogue?

Instead of placing Ritschl in the neo-Kantian tradition of existential theology that separates the orders of nature and spirit, I want to suggest that Ritschl can be seen as a precursor to the vision of the Cosmic Christ/Omega Point found in Teilhard de Chardin's *The Phenomenon of Man*. Both Ritschl and Teilhard argue that nature exists for the purpose of spirit. However, Teilhard personalizes the natural world in a way foreign to Ritschl's thinking. To make this point we need to review Ritschl's train of thought.

How does Ritschl support the claim that nature exists for the purpose of spirit? Ritschl makes the case through his interpretation of the doctrines of justification (that is, the forgiveness of sins) and reconciliation (of humans with God). Ritschl argues that his theological project is firmly rooted in *historical* revelation. Significant information—yes, information in terms of knowledge—is contained in that revelation which tells us (1) what God is like (love), and (2) what the divine purpose for the world is (enhancement of love). Christ creates a community founded on the premise that humanity is no longer separated from the love of God, in spite of the fact that the community is still sinful (that is, not always trusting or believing in God). The revelation of God's love in Christ is the moment of grace, the gift of the forgiveness of sins, and this

10. *JR* 3:207.
11. Ibid.
12. *JR* 3:208.

gift is the import of the theological doctrine of justification. However, the simultaneous result of living in communion with God ("religious intercourse with God") is the "exercise of that freedom" in accordance with God's purpose for the world.[13] Exercising freedom in accordance with God's will is reconciliation. The impact of reconciliation is none other than the "moral organization of mankind." But the moral organization of humanity is set in the context of the "Whole," which includes both nature and spirit:

> The assertion that the religious view of the world is founded on the idea of a whole (1) (*Vorstellung von einem Ganzen*) certainly holds true of Christianity: as regards the other religions it must be modified thus far, that in them what is sought is a supplementary addition to human self-feeling or to human autonomy (*Selbständigkeit*) over against and above the restrictions of the world. For in order to know the world as a totality, and in order himself to become a totality in or over it by the help of God, man needs the idea of the oneness of God, and of the consummation (*Geschlossenheit*) of the world in an end which is for man both knowable and practicable (*erkennenbaren und ausführbaren*). But this condition is fulfilled in Christianity alone.[14]

Thus the Christian idea of God enables human beings to discern the nature of reality itself ("the world as a totality"), a claim more in line with philosophical realism, rather than the Kantian limitation of reason. Ritschl might be called a "religious-philosophical realist," because his theory of religious cognition is based on the claim that nature exists for the purpose of spirit. For Ritschl, however, this claim is sanctioned by the "fact" of faith (an experience) that stems from the original community of Jesus ("the apostolic circle of ideas"). When the experience gets expressed through ideas, the faith then points beyond the original community, since the message of Jesus is universal. The claim that nature exists for the purpose of spirit invokes a fundamental teaching of Christianity and is therefore a dogmatic claim; it does not fall within sense perception or the realm of Kant's theoretical knowledge.

Methodologically, then, Ritschl begins with faith, which means his starting point is human subjectivity, human experience. However, and this is what the Kantian-existentialist line of interpretation misses, from the starting point of faith Ritschl proceeds to succeeding levels of generality. The initial perspective of the self in relation to God occurs because that self is a member of a community that has arisen in response to Jesus of Nazareth. This relation of self-in-community is further expanded in that the same relationship applies to the culture at large ("the moral or-

---

13. *JR* 1:1.
14. *JR* 3:199–200. Ritschl's footnote refers to Lotze's *Microcosmos*. *Selbständigkeit* has been translated here as "autonomy" instead of "independence" and *ausführbaren* as "practicable" instead of "realizable." *Vorstellung* remains translated as "idea," but with the understanding that it is a representation of intuitive knowledge.

ganization of mankind"). The self, now understood as the community of faith, has an impact on the community, now understood as the culture at large. The modulation from the individual in the community of faith in relation to the culture at large gains even more generalization in the perception of the God-world relationship. The historical revelation of Jesus becomes the clue to Ritschl's most general concept—the kingdom of God, which is the *telos,* the purpose, the end of the creation. Nature exists for the purpose of spirit and the Christian doctrine of atonement becomes the most general statement of the ontological significance of Christ. Ritschl's method proceeds through experience, community story, and ethical code, to the point of lifting up doctrine as the basis of a complete worldview.

The justification (in the sense of how can we know) of Ritschl's "view of the whole" is transrational. The kingdom of God is the unifying and guiding principle in Ritschl's theological system, the intuitive apex of the system. There is no rational way of establishing that the creation exists for the purpose of establishing God's kingdom or that nature exists for the purpose of spirit. This is a transrational presupposition which the individual, as a member of the community of Christ, hopes and believes to be the case. Such is the *existential* and *dogmatic* thrust of Ritschl's system.

Although Ritschl denies he is doing metaphysics, a metaphysical explanation emerges when Ritschl links self-Christ-God-community-culture-kingdom. He begins with a specific set of concepts (the individual related to God through Christ) and from these derives generic concepts that apply to the development of human culture guided by a transcendental aim. Theologically he begins with faith and ends with the kingdom of God. Philosophically he begins with human subjectivity and ends with the idea that nature exists for the purpose of spirit. Not only does Ritschl's theology spell out the personal and social significance of Christianity, but that significance finally is of cosmic importance. The doctrine of the kingdom of God contains the vision of the whole of reality, which is knowable and becomes the guide for life itself. The kingdom of God reveals the nature of ultimate reality (Personal Love)[15] and the position of the human being in relation to that reality. The existential thrust of Ritschl's theology has taken on cosmic significance.

If it is the case that Ritschl's interpretation of Christianity does take on a cosmic dimension, especially in the doctrine of the kingdom of God, the existential focus of his system must be placed in a larger context. Ritschl countered the materialistic philosophy of his day not by rejecting it out of hand, but by transforming the causal, impersonal, theoretically reasonable science with the "faith" that the natural world is here for the purpose of enhancing the love of God: the natural world is the means by which the spiritual life develops.

15. *JR* 3:237–38.

As already suggested, Ritschl's perspective anticipates that of Teilhard de Chardin. To be sure, they do not share similar understandings of nature. Their similarity instead concerns the goal or *telos* of the created order, as reflected in Teilhard's vision of the "within of things" progressing toward the cosmic Omega Point. As he wrote at the end of *The Phenomenon of Man:*

> I have tried to show that we can hope for no progress on the earth without the primacy and triumph of the personal at the summit of mind. And at the present moment Christianity is the unique current of thought, on the entire surface of the noosphere, which is sufficiently audacious and sufficiently progressive to lay hold of the world, at the level of effectual practice, in an embrace, at once already complete, yet capable of indefinite perfection, where faith and hope reach their fulfilment in love. Alone, unconditionally alone, in the world today, Christianity shows itself able to reconcile, in a single living act, the All and the Person. Alone, it can bend our hearts not only to the service of that tremendous movement of the world which bears us along, but beyond, to embrace that movement in love.
>
> In other words can we not say that Christianity fulfils all the conditions we are entitled to expect from a religion of the future; and that hence, through it, the principal axis of evolution truly passes, as it maintains?
>
> . . . In the impetus which guides and sustains its [Christianity's] advance, this rising shoot implies essentially the consciousness of being in actual relationship with a spiritual and transcendent pole of universal convergence.[16]

These thoughts from Teilhard, coupled with Ritschl's doctrine of the kingdom of God, suggest a kind of existentialism with a cosmic vengeance. Both see the personal love of God revealed in Christ as the key to reality itself. In both, nature exists for the purpose of spirit/noosphere.[17]

When Teilhard discusses the "convergence of science and religion," one can perceive the same type of discussion that Ritschl carried on with Kant. When science reaches the limits of its explanatory powers, it becomes "charged with faith."[18] The scientific "belief" in progress and

---

16. Teilhard de Chardin, *The Phenomenon of Man,* trans. Bernard Wall, intro. Julian Huxley (New York: Harper & Row, Harper Torchbooks, 1959), 297–98.

17. The Teilhard-Ritschl comparison can be seen in the work of Philip Hefner, who began his career with Ritschl scholarship and has moved into the heart of the science-religion dialogue. Between these two foci is a book on Teilhard, in which Hefner states: "The promise of Teilhard for the churches, therefore, is a challenge whose future is not fully certain. In terms of practice, it is the vision that the exercise of the Christian faith— love for God and for neighbor—is earth-building, and this may be the most decisive innovation that confronts Christianity in our time" (*The Promise of Teilhard* [Philadelphia: J. B. Lippincott Co., 1970], 117–18). Hefner has reinterpreted the Ritschlian "moral organization of mankind" with the Teilhardian conceptions of "personalizing the universe" and "building the earth."

18. De Chardin, 284.

unity is finally based on a "super-rational intuition."[19] Considering the "Whole," Teilhard says:

> When, in the universe in movement to which we have just awakened, we look at the temporal and spatial series diverging and amplifying themselves around and behind us like the laminae of a cone, we are perhaps engaging in pure science. But when we turn towards the summit, towards the totality and the future, we cannot help engaging in religion.
>
> Religion and science are the two conjugated faces or phases of one and the same complete act of knowledge—the only one which can embrace the past and future of evolution so as to contemplate, measure and fulfil them.[20]

The significance of religious cognition, which Ritschl sought to articulate in conversation with Kant, is given further expression in the thought of Teilhard de Chardin.

Placing Ritschl in this trajectory of intellectual history is an implication drawn from his epistemology, whereas his own intentions do lean in the direction of neo-Kantian existentialism. If the Ritschlian legacy ends in existentialism, then his theory of religious cognition makes sure that the integrity of the two disciplines is maintained by their separation.[21] I am suggesting that the Ritschlian legacy does not end in existentialism, but that his theory of religious cognition seeks a unified theory of knowledge in which science and religion are seen as two aspects, two branches, of the one tree of knowledge. Methodologically, then, Ritschl's thought can be seen as an initial step in promoting dialogue between science and religion, since he took the science of his day seriously, although he perceived it as a threat to and not a resource for theology. He integrated science into his theology with the argument that nature exists for the purpose of spirit. An extension of this mode of thought is seen in the work of Teilhard de Chardin.

RITSCHLIAN THEMES IN CONTEMPORARY THOUGHT

A number of themes found in Ritschl's criticism of the materialistic science of his day are relevant to the contemporary dialogue between science and religion:[22] (1) a critique of reductionistic modes of explanation; (2) the reintroduction of the notion of end, or purpose, or final cause, to scientific explanation; (3) the world as the basic datum of both science

---

19. Ibid.
20. Ibid., 285.
21. See Karl Heim, *Christian Faith and Natural Science* (New York: Harper & Row, 1953).
22. For a more expanded discussion see Richard P. Busse, "Ritschl's Critique of Materialism," *Papers of the Albrecht Ritschl Seminar, American Academy of Religion Annual Meeting*, 1988 (Syracuse, N.Y.: Le Moyne College, 1988), 40–54.

and religion; (4) intuitive imagination at the heart of religious cognition; and (5) the place of the human being in nature. An exhaustive survey cannot be presented here, but a representative selection of contemporary thinkers illustrates the point that Ritschl's theory of religious cognition does have relevance for the current discussion.

1. *Reductionism.* "Reductionism is the belief that a whole may be represented as a function (in the mathematical sense) of its constituent parts, the functions having to do with the spatial and temporal ordering of parts and with the precise way in which they interact."[23] This issue of reductive analysis is far from settled in the current science-religion dialogue. "Hard" scientific analysis uses and is successful in using reductionism. Francis Crick and J. D. Watson, famous for their "discovery" of DNA and RNA, agree that "the ultimate aim of the modern movement in biology is in fact to explain all biology in terms of physics and chemistry."[24] It is not unreasonable to say that the materialism of mid-nineteenth-century Germany is alive and well in the most respected scientific circles of the twentieth century. Trained scientists who take an interest in religious-theological issues perceive they must fight the same battle that Ritschl fought with the materialists of his day.

Ritschl's main objection to the materialist point of view is its reductionistic mode of explanation, and his objection is similar to F. A. Lange's analysis of materialism.[25] Ritschl asserts that the materialist critique of Christianity stems "from the fact that the law of a particular realm of being is set up as the law of all being."[26] Ritschl does not deny the validity of the causal method of explanation used by natural science, which "is right and consistent in explaining the mechanical regularity of all sensible things by the manifold movement of simple limited forces or atoms."[27] However, "the idea of end" is missing from detailed causal explanation; the category of final cause, or teleology, is not part of the scientific method.

For Ritschl, materialism stems from a "confused religious impulse."[28] On the one hand, materialism is derived from "cosmogonies of heathenism." (At this point Lange's critique is similar, because for him the roots of materialism lie in Greek atomism.) On the other hand, materialism "can only suggest chance as the moving force of the ultimate causes

23. P. B. Medawar and J. S. Medawar, *Aristotle to Zoos: A Philosophical Dictionary of Biology* (Cambridge: Harvard Univ. Press, 1983), 227.

24. Francis Crick, *Of Molecules and Men* (Seattle: Univ. of Washington Press, 1966), 10. See also James D. Watson, *Molecular Biology of the Gene,* 3d ed. (Menlo Park, Calif.: W. A. Benjamin, 1976), 54: "Complete certainty now exists among essentially all biochemists that the other characteristics of living organisms . . . will all be completely understood in terms of the coordinative interactions of small and large molecules."

25. See F. A. Lange, *The History of Materialism,* trans. E. C. Thomas and intro. Bertram Russell (New York: Humanities Press, 1950).

26. *JR* 3:208.

27. *JR* 3:209.

28. Ibid.

of the world."[29] Ritschl does not consider the possibility that chance may be the "supreme law of things." But even if chance is the ultimate principle of the universe, his argument still stands: such a notion is derived from a religious impulse rather than from the scientific method itself, which can say nothing about ultimate, final causes. The materialist critique of religion, then, is really a conflict between two competing religious viewpoints: the naturalistic religion of Greek atomism and Christianity.

So materialism fails, according to Ritschl, because by depending on a religious impulse for its first principle it is not true to the scientific method. But it fails also as a religious worldview because it does not distinguish between nature and spirit. For Ritschl, Christianity is the most adequate worldview because it offers a complete picture of the "whole." Notice that Ritschl does not deny the validity of science, but simply says it does not present the whole picture. Theoretical/scientific knowledge and materialism (and other philosophies that Ritschl discusses, such as Platonism, Aristotelianism, pantheism, Hegel's Absolute) do not account for the worth and value of the individual. The distinctive feature of Christianity, however, is the religious "estimate of the self." Christianity answers the problem of human being, that is, as a creature dependent on nature, yet free from nature.[30] Ritschl's critique of materialism is one segment of his extended argument concerning the cognitive validity of faith.

A similar critique of materialism is very much part of the contemporary science-religion discussion. For example, Arthur Peacocke and Holmes Rolston, both trained in physics and theology, contest adamantly against reductionistic "nothing buttery" (Peacocke's phrase), that is, against the view that mind or spirit is nothing but a unique configuration of neurological cells and processes. Psychology is thus reduced to neuroscience.[31] Peacocke argues in the other direction, toward a "hierarchy of natural systems" in which each system of nature (from subatomic to the psycho-social-ecological levels) builds upon the level of complexification present in the immediately "lower" level.[32] Scientists do not dispute that a hierarchy of natural systems exists in nature. The disagreements occur on how to conceive of the relationship between systems. Peacocke argues for "theory autonomy" at different levels of systemic analysis. Reductive analysis is not denied within system analysis, but each level of complexification attains a certain autonomy. Thus, brain processes do account for consciousness, but the "I" of self-consciousness is more than neurological components. Similarly, a system of theology, which is a theory about religious life, cannot be reduced to a "subsystem" of analysis such as psy-

29. Ibid.
30. *JR* 3:211, 218.
31. See Patricia C. Churchland, *Neurophilosophy: Toward a Unified Science of the Mind/Brain* (Cambridge: MIT Press, A Bradford Book, 1986), 399.
32. Arthur R. Peacocke, *Creation and the World of Science* (Oxford: Clarendon Press, 1979), 112–19.

chology or sociology. Peacocke, in effect, is arguing for the autonomy of the human being and theological "science." Peacocke says that "theology should neither be immune from the changing outlook of the sciences of man nor should it be captive to them."[33] Ritschl might have said the same.

Holmes Rolston weaves an antireductionist theme into his reflections on religion and science. Human experience itself tells us that science has no "natural" explanation for the emergence of mind and spirit. Is spirit epiphenomenal? For Rolston: "To the contrary, it [the phenomenon of spirit] is faithful to experience, more so than are simplistic reductions of everything to matter and energy."[34] And in a very Ritschlian sense Rolston says that "the scientific method can teach us much but not all about nature. Philosophical and religious judgments are required positively to evaluate its meanings."[35] Religious judgments evaluate the meaning of scientific discoveries? This is precisely Ritschl's point with regard to the materialists of his day.

Ritschl, Peacocke, and Rolston argue that reductionism must be circumscribed as the most powerful mode of explanation if the spiritual life is going to receive any recognition as a "real" factor of existence. Spiritual life is an "autonomous theory," as Peacocke might explain, necessary to evaluate the "meaning" of nature for Rolston, and is the goal of nature itself for Ritschl. Both Peacocke and Rolston argue that religious value judgments add a significant component to the scientific analysis of nature; their argument is consistent with Ritschl's theory of religious cognition.

2. *Causality and purpose.*   Purpose (final causation) is another issue at the heart of the science-religion dialogue. Whitehead suggests that "the function of reason is to promote the art of life."[36] For Whitehead, reason functions to direct the "attack" on the environment in a threefold manner: "(i) to live, (ii) to live well, (iii) to live better."[37] In other words, there is an urge to live in such a way that satisfaction will increase. "This conclusion amounts to the thesis that Reason is a factor in experience which directs and criticizes the urge towards the attainment of an end realized in imagination but not in fact."[38] The issue debated in science and religion circles is whether or not purpose is inherent in the structure of existence. Final cause was displaced by the ef-

---

33. Ibid., 371.
34. Holmes Rolston, III, *Science and Religion: A Critical Survey* (New York: Random House, 1987), 303.
35. Ibid., 254. Rolston uses this summary statement to describe "soft naturalism," a romantic view of nature expressed in American Transcendentalism, Pragmatism, and many current environmentalists. See note 17, 294.
36. Alfred North Whitehead, *The Function of Reason* (Boston: Beacon Press, 1958), 4 (italics omitted).
37. Ibid., 8.
38. Ibid.

ficient causal explanations of nature put forth by Galileo and Newton. In contrast, Whitehead argues that in order to make sense of the course of evolution, the category of final cause (the third function of reason) must be included in the explanation.

Ritschl's religious epistemology introduces purpose via the category of the "religious impulse," which is an "object of intuitive imagination." If we substitute Whitehead's "Reason" for Ritschl's "religious impulse," the effect of the arguments is the same: the idea of purpose is necessary for a complete view of existence. Ritschl's point is that Christians know this, philosophers doubt it, and scientists deny it. In terms of a methodological contribution, Ritschl's thought is relevant for reinserting the category of purpose into the science-religion dialogue.

Causality and purpose are categories that have been used to divide science and religion into separate domains. I have argued that Ritschl does not make such a tidy division in his formulation that nature exists for the purpose of spirit. The "whole" picture is incomplete without a notion of the end, which for Ritschl is, of course, the kingdom of God. The epistemological claim is that theoretical and practical reason are combined in a unified act of knowing.

Ritschl reasoned intuitively that the idea of *telos* was crucial for religious cognition and, in fact, was the primary function of religious knowing. Since the time of Newton, physics employed only the material and efficient causes of Aristotle's four causes. Matter in motion explained everything. Ritschl's critique of materialism called into question the limitation of knowledge to material and efficient cause and in effect (not in actual terminology) reintroduced the formal and final causes: the plan and the aim of existence are found in the Christian worldview.

3. *The world.* It is clear from what has been said so far that Ritschl was concerned to interpret Christianity in terms of "one world."[39] For Ritschl, the materialists and theologians of his day were concerned with the same "reality," not two orders of being such that science produces knowledge of the natural world and religion pertains exclusively to knowledge of the spiritual life. Ritschl's argument with Kant and the materialists sought to include the spiritual life within the context of the natural world, although it seemed to him that, for the sake of the integrity of human freedom, spirit must oppose itself to nature. But remember: nature is the means by which spiritual life develops, spirit being the goal of nature itself. Thus, Ritschl claims, science and religion are concerned with "one world." Science is mistaken in thinking it presents the "whole picture." Religions formulate worldviews, and for Ritschl, Christianity presents the most complete picture of the world.

At this point we need to consider another "placing" of Ritschl, but now in terms of the relationship between science and religion. Pea-

---

39. The same concern is expressed by physicist John Polkinghorne in *One World: The Interaction of Science and Theology* (London: SPCK, 1986).

cocke proposes an eight-point, two-dimensional grid that is helpful in locating Ritschl's understanding of the relationship between science and religion.[40]

(1) "Science and theology are concerned with two distinct realms." For our purposes this would mean that science investigates nature and religion discloses spirit. This option is attractive for an interpretation of Ritschl if the existential thrust of his thinking is seen as the key. Points 4 and 5 on Peacocke's grid are versions of this relationship: (4) "Science and theology constitute two different language games" (Wittgensteinian forms of life); (5) "Science and theology are generated by quite different attitudes" (objective, logical vs. subjective, committed). However, if I am correct in suggesting an alternative interpretation of Ritschl's relationship to Kantian epistemology, the categories of nature and spirit do not constitute two distinct realms, languages, or attitudes, but suggest variations on a continuum of "one reality."

Points 2, 7, and 8 on Peacocke's grid seem not to apply to Ritschl: (2) "Science and religion are interacting approaches to the same reality." Ritschl, however, did not believe that science could actually modify theological assertions. Point 7, "Science and theology may be integrated," suggests that science and theology may be "consonant"[41] in that some scientific insights such as "open systems" might illuminate Christian doctrines such as eschatology (Pannenberg and Moltmann move in this direction). But it seems that Ritschl placed no "value" in nature itself, except the utilitarian value that the natural machine produced valuing creatures, while simultaneously threatening their existence. For Ritschl, nature was not consonant with, but a tool for, human beings to use in accomplishing God's purposes. Certainly point 8, "Science generates a metaphysic in terms of which theology is then formulated," is contrary to Ritschl's purposes, because the metaphysics of materialism was not the framework from which Ritschl developed his theology, but was one opposing pole against which his theology took shape. However, it cannot be denied that his modification of Kantian epistemology did provide a framework for his interpretation of Christian doctrine. So while point 8 is contrary to Ritschl's purposes, he implicitly employed philosophy in his theological constructions.

Points 3 and 6 from Peacocke's grid are helpful in "placing" Ritschl on the science-religion matrix. Point 3, "Science and theology are two distinct non-interacting approaches to the same reality," returns to the causality/purpose debate mentioned above. For Ritschl, science does describe long chains of causal interactions that occur in nature. But the ultimate goal, the purpose for which nature's causal system operates (exercising freedom in accordance with God's will), is found in theology

40. See the introduction to *The Sciences and Theology in the Twentieth Century,* ed. A. R. Peacocke (Notre Dame: Univ. of Notre Dame Press, 1981), xiii–xv.
41. See Ernan McMullin, "How Should Cosmology Relate to Theology?" in *The Sciences and Theology in the Twentieth Century,* 51.

(Christian theology) alone. Yes, science and theology consider "one world," but the destiny of the world, the why of existence, the view of the "whole," is found in Christianity. It offers the most complete knowledge of the world. Thus, point 6, "Science and theology are subservient to their objects and can only be defined in relation to them," indicates that science and theology are both "confessional enterprises." Science is subservient to the causal machine of nature and describes its processes, while theology is subordinate to the will of God as revealed in Jesus of Nazareth.

It seems that the modern theologian who is perhaps most in line with Ritschl's intentions is Thomas F. Torrance:

> It is my intention to clarify the process of scientific activity in theology, to throw human thinking of God back on him as its direct and proper Object, and thus to serve the self-scrutiny of theology as a pure-science. At the same time it is the aim of the argument to draw out the implications for the human subject of the fact that he is addressed by God and summoned to faithful and disciplined exercise of his reason in response to God's Word, and therefore to call a halt to the romantic irrationality and bloated subjectivity with which so much present-day theology is saturated. This is an essay in philosophical theology calling for objectivity and rationality within the positive and constructive task of theological science.[42]

Torrance places rationality in God's service. Ritschl would agree.[43]

Now, what about my earlier placing of Ritschl in the direction of Teilhard's and even Whitehead's thought? I see this direction as an implication of Ritschl's epistemology, but if we consider Ritschl's own intentions, we return to a very traditional and, yes, Barthian kind of theology as represented in Torrance. So it seems that the existential dimension of Ritschl's theology does hold sway if we are concerned to interpret Ritschl in line with his own intentions. I think the more interesting aspects of Ritschl's thought, however, stem from speculations as to how one might expand upon some latent and implicit ideas within Ritschl's theology. This is the "loose" form of argument I mentioned at

---

42. T. F. Torrance, *Theological Science* (London: Oxford Univ. Press, 1969), xvii–xviii.

43. The rationality of theology is certainly the theme of Wolfhart Pannenberg's *Theology and the Philosophy of Science,* but I have chosen not to discuss this important work due to limitations of space and because Pannenberg gives ontological priority to the future. The latter seems antithetical to Ritschl's notion of historical development on a linear scale from past to present, and then on to the future, although Ritschl's notion of first principles being "anticipatively assumed" is suggestive of some comparison. Wentzel van Huyssteen argues for the "justification of cognitive claims in theology" in *Theology and the Justification of Faith* (Grand Rapids, Mich.: Eerdmans, 1988). Like Ritschl, van Huyssteen argues that faith (religious experience) is not devoid of reason and is subject to explanation and reference, as is science. Also, commitment and rationality are intertwined, since claims based on religious commitment are open to rational criticism. He argues for the cognitive validity of faith in that commitment is foundational to all forms of explanation, both theological and scientific.

the beginning of the chapter. Why should we feel bound to replicate in today's circumstances what Ritschl said or even intended in response to the problems of his day? Rather, why not explore the provocative, the implied, the insinuations and intuitions that emerge from reading Ritschl in a very different historical context? That is why I find his method interesting but his justification not convincing.

4. *Intuitive imagination.*   As outlined above, the phrase *intuitive imagination (die anschauende Phantasie)* occurs in the context of Ritschl's claim that philosophers in search of first principles do so out of a "religious impulse." Philosophical first principles are the result of the intuitive imagination, just as God and the world are for religious thought! This is perhaps the most tantalizing phrase in Ritschl's argument against materialism. Methodologically Ritschl here suggests that knowledge springs from experience,[44] prelinguistic experience, intuitions of "deep structures" that make life what it is. As Mary Gerhart has said, "The place to begin a study of the relationship between science and religion is found . . . not in the book of language but at the door of experience."[45] The fundamental relationship of science and religion, following Gerhart, stems from the fact that they are both activities of human consciousness. Philosophical/scientific/religious principles emerge from the depths of the "intuitive imagination."

What kind of general intuitions or "religious impulses" do science and religion share? First, one general intuition is of a reality outside us upon which humans are dependent and that arouses awe, fear, and reverence. A second general intuition is of a reality inside us that we call the self, consciousness, the "I." The outside reality, the Other, is felt to be the source of power, the power to be, as Paul Tillich, Shubert Ogden, and Langdon Gilkey argue in various ways. That reality is the ground of order, of life, and means something, but exactly what, we do not know. These intuitions are manifold, and science depends on primal intuitions such as "order" and "unity within diversity." The sense of self in relation to the Other gives rise to further cardinal intuitions such as moral obligation and responsibility, guilt, humility, and acceptance of forgiveness—intuitions at the base of religious experience.

Ritschl's point about primary intuitions is a theme that runs through Langdon Gilkey's extensive conversation with scientists:

> These intuitions, for example that of order, the order within continuing experience, are not discovered by science, nor are they validated by induction. Rather they too are the presuppositions that make science possible and make inductions logically valid. They represent another example of

___

44. The phrase comes from Ian Barbour's discussion of religious experience in *Issues in Science and Religion*, 208ff.

45. Mary Gerhart and Allan Russell, *Metaphoric Process: The Creation of Scientific and Religious Understanding* (Fort Worth: Texas Christian Univ. Press, 1981), 11.

extra scientific knowledge or *cognition* necessary for there to be modern empirical science at all. To me—as to the entire tradition of religion—they also represent traces of the sacred, that is of the sacred as a unity of reality, order, meaning, or value.[46]

Such foundational presuppositions that pertain not only to science and religion, but to all of life as we know it, provide the justification for Ritschl's concern with the cognitive validity of faith. As Bernard Meland has said in line with Gilkey, faith in "order" is the foundation of science, whereas faith in the meaningfulness of life is the foundation of religion: two presuppositions for the possibility of any knowledge at all. Faith is thus not a secondary hope that order and meaning exist. Faith is not a "practical knowledge" that prevails "as if" order and meaning were true. Faith, says Meland, is the foundation of rationality itself.[47] These arguments are similar to Ritschl's critique of Kant.

Thomas F. Torrance makes the same argument apropos faith by relying upon Michael Polanyi's contention that all knowledge is "personal knowledge":

No human intelligence, Polanyi claimed, however critical or original, can operate outside such a context of faith, for it is within that context that there arises within us, under compulsion from the reality of the world we experience, a regulative set of convictions or a framework of beliefs which prompts and guides our inquiries and controls our assessment of the evidence. They are the ultimate beliefs or normative insights grounded in reality on which we rely as premises in any authentic thrust toward truth, and which finally give our arguments any persuasive power they may have. Unless our minds are informed by prior intuitive contact with reality which we have in this way through our basic beliefs they flounder about in fruitless surmises and irrelevant interpretations and theories.[48]

Ritschl's claim that "intuitive imagination" is the most fundamental kind of knowledge is perhaps the most relevant contribution of his theory of religious cognition to the current science-religion dialogue. Our discussion of this topic also reveals the difficulty in placing Ritschl firmly in any one theological framework. Gilkey the existentialist, Meland the Whiteheadian, and Torrance the Barthian all appeal to a similar style of

46. Langdon Gilkey, "The Influence of Science on Theology," Presbyterian Task Force, Jacksonville Beach, Florida, May 6, 1989, p. 17 (italics mine). The idea that science depends on extrascientific presuppositions occurs in all of Gilkey's books that address science and religion issues: *Naming the Whirlwind; Religion and the Scientific Future; Society and the Sacred; Creationism on Trial.* For a succinct statement of Gilkey's position see "What of Value Does Religion Have to Say to Science?" *The Center for Theology and Natural Sciences Bulletin* 10 (Autumn 1990): 6–9.
47. For a similar mode of argument see Bernard E. Meland, *The Realities of Faith: The Revolution in Cultural Forms* (New York: Oxford Univ. Press, 1962), 137ff.
48. Thomas F. Torrance, *Christian Theology and Scientific Culture* (New York: Oxford Univ. Press, 1981), 64.

argument with respect to the cognitive validity of faith. Faith is the foundation of rationality.

5. *Human being in nature.* The final theme seeks to delineate the role of the human being in the natural order. For Ritschl, humans have a very important role to play, if not the most important role. Nature exists for the purpose of spirit, and it is the human spirit, responding to the grace of God, that furthers God's actualization of the kingdom, the goal and destiny of life itself. The famous elliptical poles of Ritschl's theology illustrate this interpretation. Grace is the gift from God that enables the human task of reconciliation, and this is the basis of all Christian vocation, no matter what concrete form that vocation takes. Justification and reconciliation are the two primary, interrelated Christian doctrines that set forth the most complete vision of life.

Ritschl's view of the place of human being in the natural order manifests itself in Philip Hefner's conception of the human being as "created co-creator." Hefner, a Ritschlian scholar, has transposed the implication of Ritschl's epistemology in the following way:

> Is nature friend or foe? Friend, we can say theologically. Nature in its entirety—from its original singularity 18 billion years ago, through the Big Bang, through the formation of planet earth, through the appearance of primordial soup and the flourishing of animate life, through the long genetic history of biological development, through the appearance of human culture, through the history of Hebrew and Christian religions, and through chapters in our future story that have yet to be written—is being guided by the eschatological purpose of the one God who is the creator of all things. And this purpose is to perfect all that constitutes the creation, human beings included. More than that, we humans created in the image of God are participants and co-creators in the ongoing work of God's creative activity. We are being drawn toward a shared destiny that will ultimately determine what it means to be a true human being.[49]

Such is Hefner's reformulation of Ritschl's notion that nature exists for the purpose of spirit, and further, that human beings have the unique role as participants, as cocreators in God's plan for the universe, as cobuilders of God's earth and kingdom. Hefner re-presents a twentieth-century imagination of Ritschl's "moral restoration of mankind." The understanding of nature is different, but the Christian principles are similar.

CONCLUSION

Now what justifies the claim, or how can we say that we know, that nature exists for the purpose of spirit, and that human beings have such an

---

49. Philip Hefner, "The Evolution of the Created Co-Creator," in *Cosmos as Creation: Theology and Science in Consonance,* ed. Ted Peters (Nashville: Abingdon Press, 1989), 231–32. See also Hefner on "The Creation," in *Christian Dogmatics,* 2 vols., ed. C. E. Braaten and R. W. Jenson (Philadelphia: Fortress Press, 1984), 1:323–41.

important role to play in the cosmic process? At this point the circularity of the argument becomes apparent. We know that nature exists for the purpose of spirit because of our primal intuition (our faith) about the universe and our place in it. The "objective" claim about reality is based on a "subjective" intuition. If primal intuitions are the foundation of rationality, then it makes sense to speak of a "friendly" universe that wants and needs human cooperation in perfecting its development. Ritschl did not think of nature as friend, but as a vast causal machine that threatened human freedom. But the end of the argument for Ritschl and the scientists/theologians we have discussed is the same, in that life's purpose receives a unique configuration in Jesus Christ. Human beings either respond to or deny the spiritual goal discerned in Christ. Religious truth, then, as Ritschl maintained a century ago, is a matter of value judgments. The circle of faith is complete. We know that nature exists for the purpose of spirit because of a primal faith that is the basis of all knowledge. Ritschl's theory of religious cognition is very much a part of the contemporary science-religion dialogue.

However, the problems with Ritschl's theory are twofold. First, the truth disclosed in Christian revelation is finally based not on primal intuitions of order and meaning, but on the dogmatic principle that Jesus Christ is the locus of all truth concerning the creation, its destiny, and the role of human beings in that destiny. We know this only if we are Christians. Second, that nature exists for the purpose of spirit is a highly anthropocentric view of the created order. Is not such an idea the source of the intense ecological damage that we now inflict on nature? I am not charging the scientists and theologians with disregarding ecological issues, since they are extremely sensitive to the problems. The question, rather, pertains to the "high" view of the human in the Great Chain of Being that we now call the "hierarchy of natural systems." Why should we assume that humans, instead of plants and animals, are more important for the destiny of the universe?

Finally, is there a destiny, a purpose to life, or not? This question is the relocation of the God question from existence to purpose. It is the question that haunts all discussions between theologians and scientists. It is the question on which Ritschl focused in his interpretation of the kingdom of God. Ritschl's method places the science-religion dialogue in the depths of epistemology and ultimately ontology, which is where the current discussion takes place also. One hundred years later, it seems, we are lost in those depths, but perhaps we are learning how to swim within nature, learning what it means to be part of the flow of life, instead of procuring nature for the purpose of spirit.

Justifying a method via appeals to Christian dogmatics will inevitably end the conversation between theologians and scientists. But justifying a method via appeals to primal intuitions of order and meaning—intuitions that receive a unique configuration in the Christian matrix of meaning known as Jesus the Christ—leaves open the possibility for dialogue and perhaps even an integration of theological claims with scientific rationality. The search for common ground continues.

Ritschl's theory of religious cognition can be seen as an important resource in the contemporary quest for foundational truth and meaning in both religion and science. The other initial questions posed in this chapter also have been answered affirmatively. Ritschl's theory of religious cognition can be seen as an initial formulation of problems addressed in the current science-religion dialogue. And Ritschl's ideas are represented in recent science-religion thinkers. The seasonal relevance of Ritschl's method is the integration of spirituality with rationality. Much of the present discourse on science and religion attempts the same reconciliation.

Epilogue

A Reevaluation

 CLAUDE WELCH

Several times the preceding chapters refer to Karl Barth's famous remark in his chapter on Ritschl in *Die Protestantische Theologie im 19. Jahrhundert* that, unlike Schleiermacher, Ritschl cannot be considered the founder of an epoch but is only an "episode" in the history of theology. This is a pejorative comment, found in a disgracefully cursory chapter on Ritschl. It may well reflect the not uncommon Germanic tendency to rebel against one's immediate theological forebears. It completely (and deliberately?) ignores the many ways in which Barth actually follows in the footsteps of Ritschl. But irrespective of the fact that in the late twentieth century Barth himself may need to be judged only an episode, this is an interesting type of statement. Barth's comment is essentially a *systematician's* judgment of value for constructive theological efforts, rather than a *historian's* judgment of impact or influence.

The latter is the kind of estimate to which I shall want to return, as I consider myself essentially a historian rather than a systematician. For the moment, however, it may be worth recalling an important difference in the ways in which Ritschl and Schleiermacher were brought into the English-speaking world. Schleiermacher's *Speeches* (*On Religion*) were indeed translated into English in 1893 by John Oman, but the *Glaubenslehre* (*The Christian Faith*) did not appear in English until 1928 in the H. R. Mackintosh translation (following the *Soliloquies* in 1926). On the other hand, as noted in earlier chapters in this volume, the first (historical) volume of Ritschl's *Justification and Reconciliation* was translated as early as 1872, and the third (constructive) volume in 1900, along with Swing's translation of the *Instruction* in 1901. It remains an oddity, since Ritschl thought of himself as essentially a biblical theologian (see especially the chapter above by Clive Marsh), that *RV 2*, on the biblical foundation of the doctrine, has not yet been published in English. What this history of translations says is that the direct influence of Ritschl on the British and American scene antedated that of Schleiermacher, and this helps to account for the important Ritschlian dimensions of the Liberal theologies of Britain and America in the early decades of the twentieth century—whereas one might argue that it was really the work of Barth (and perhaps of Rudolf Otto) that brought Schleiermacher to the fore and that this, together with the shocks of the First World War to late nineteenth-century optimism, had something to do with the more than forty-year hiatus in extended treatments of Ritschl (see the chapter by David Lotz).

But let us come back to the question of Ritschl's value for systematic theology, which is a main concern of the other contributors to the present volume, as part of the effort to recover the importance of Ritschl's work and to overcome the many misinterpretations of what he was about. Without attempting to recapitulate, or even to summarize, the contents of the excellent preceding chapters, let me simply identify in an unscientific way what I judge to be some of the most significant elements in those arguments, particularly as they have succeeded in correcting common misunderstandings of Ritschl.

One of the major contributions of this volume is the insistence on viewing Ritschl's work in the light of his entire corpus of writings, instead of focusing almost entirely on the third volume of *Justification and Reconciliation* and on the *Instruction in the Christian Religion*. See particularly the chapter by Lotz, stressing Ritschl's lifelong concern for continuation of the Reformation begun by Luther, as well as Wall's relating of Ritschl's idea of the kingdom of God to his (earlier and larger) notion of *Gemeinde*. And we may recall Philip Hefner's argument[1] for the importance of Ritschl's study of Pietism, particularly as part of his emphasis on the new *Lebensideal* as the real core of Luther's Reformation.

Second, we have here a convincing rejection of the tendency to write Ritschl's work off as mere reflection of late nineteenth-century *Kulturprotestantismus*, or even of H. R. Niebuhr's (carefully qualified) identification of Ritschl as a classic illustration of the "Christ of Culture" kind of thinking. (See especially Rich Wall's chapter; also William Barnett's discussion of Ritschl's relation to Rauschenbusch, to Reinhold Niebuhr, and to Martin Luther King.) Granted that Ritschl tended to interpret the idea of Christian vocation largely (and not uncomfortably) within the parameters of the contemporary German social structures, it is not the case (pace Otto Ritschl's biography) that after the unhappy outcome of the Frankfurt Assembly, Ritschl simply withdrew from concern for social reform. He did continue to protest against the kind of political encroachment represented by the Catholic church, and in his polemic

---

1. See Hefner's introduction to *TE* as well as his *Faith and the Vitalities of History* (New York: Harper & Row, 1966).

against Lutheran Confessionalism he abandoned the "two kingdoms" approach. But his insistence on the morally educative role of the church was, as Wall puts it, an identification of "the practical means by which it [the church] is to become the premier reforming agent within society."

Ritschl's conception of the kingdom of God was, indeed, not one that led to the social radicalism of the Swiss religious socialists or even of some of the British and American social gospelers, but his concerns certainly cannot be written off as the uncritical ethics of bourgeois society. If he could not accept a Catholic approach to the relation of church and state, neither could he allow simple withdrawal from the world. And, in Wall's language, his attempt to balance an "inner autonomy of the Christian community with its moral and ethical tie to the state" may well be of positive continuing value for theology.

Further, we have in these chapters a most important reconsideration of Ritschl's view of the relation of theology and science (note particularly the chapters by Busse and Jodock). Ritschl was not responsible for the radical separation of religious and scientific judgments, the "loss of nature" that did appear in Wilhelm Herrmann.[2] Ritschl is rightly well known for his insistence that religious knowledge consists in independent value judgments, and here, as I have argued elsewhere,[3] he stands squarely in the nineteenth century's emphasis on the role of the subject and its valuing in any account of religious apprehension. Religion was for him more a matter of doing than of feeling or of thinking. But that does not make religious knowledge noncognitive. Jodock and Busse have shown admirably that while religious and scientific (or theoretical) knowing are distinct, in that for the latter value judgments are only concomitant, both kinds of knowing are "interested." They are not separate or antithetical. They are both attempts to understand the world. Kant's sharp separation of the theoretical and the practical reason was not acceptable. Ritschl was thus no mere Kant redivivus.

Indeed, and just because of the intrinsic valuational character of religious affirmations, and with a better epistemology that recognizes that the reality of God or of the self is indeed given in its relationships, Ritschl proposes that the religious view of the world is philosophically/theoretically more adequate than a merely scientific view. Knowledge of the universe is "consummated" in the Christian idea of God.[4] Thus, despite Ritschl's dependence on a more mechanical conception of "nature's" laws than is acceptable in the twentieth century and his concern to distinguish spirit from nature, whose dominance is to be "overcome," he cannot be blamed for the kind of theological loss of nature

2. See, e.g., the recent volume by Frederick Gregory, *Nature Lost? Natural Science and the German Theological Tradition of the Nineteenth Century* (Cambridge, Mass.: Harvard Univ. Press, 1992).
3. Welch 2
4. *JR* 3:223.

that did appear in Herrmann and in a good deal of the subsequent "dialectical theology."

Fourth, in relation to both the preceding kinds of observations, Ritschl can be more positively viewed as participant in the great inclusive problem of both nineteenth- and twentieth-century theology, namely, the problem of church and society (or Christ and culture). Ritschl's search for the right envisioning of the church as community not only led him to oppose the Catholic kind of imperialism with respect to the state (whose other side was the move toward the creation of a Catholic subculture). He also fought the Throne and Altar ideas of confessional Lutheranism, the individualism of the Rationalists, and the cultural isolationism of neo-pietists. One dimension of this struggle was for a different understanding of religious authority, of a nondogmatic sort, which was widely taken up in Liberal Protestant theologies in Germany, Britain, and America, and which might even be said to be reflected later in post–Vatican II Roman Catholic theology. Ritschl's concern with authority was expressed largely in relation to ecclesiastical authority, but this was also always a question of the right understanding of the Christian community, biblically and historically grounded, and its relation to the "world." Though one may not feel that Ritschl achieved a finally correct balance in these areas (and I do not now judge that Ritschl was as comfortable about the relations of faith, history, and ethics as I once thought), his search for a balance is surely one to be affirmed in theology that wants to repudiate churchly authoritarianism without falling into mere private judgment.

Finally, in relation to the question of Ritschl's enduring value for systematic theological construction, it may be worth noting his decisive importance for a number of Barthian themes, many of which are mentioned in the other chapters in this volume and some of which have entered into the warp and woof of theology through the twentieth century. One of these is the necessary character of theology as *church* theology, which must arise out of and be responsible to the community of Christians (note Barth's change in title for his dogmatics from *Christian* to *Church* Dogmatics). A second is the importance of the idea of the kingdom of God, which, though with a quite different notion of the kingdom, nevertheless lies behind Barth's early insistence that a Christianity that is not utterly eschatological has nothing to do with Jesus Christ and has led to an almost universal emphasis on an eschatological character of theology. A third is the conception of ethics as integral to theology. A fourth is Ritschl's notion of love as central to the Christian idea of God, which has much in common with Barth's demand for the utter priority of grace, his reversal of the law-gospel dialectic, and his rejection of the *decretum absolutum* and the double will in the reformulation of the doctrine of election, and which may well be reflected in Barth's definition of God as the loving in freedom and his insistence that

God *is* in God's works and ways. Finally, we may note the turn to radical Christocentricity in theology, and the rejection of natural theology, where Barth follows clearly in the footsteps of Ritschl. Nowhere does Barth give credit to Ritschl for this sort of dependence, but any sophisticated reader of the two is compelled to recognize the profound affinities at such crucial points.

This sort of acknowledgment leads to the other kind of question I mentioned at the outset, namely, the question of the *historian's* rather than the systematician's judgment about Ritschl's significance. I must confess that with respect to Ritschl's direct value for present-day theological construction, Barth's description of him as an "episode" is not altogether wrong. Ritschl is not a thinker of the stature of Augustine or Aquinas or Luther or Calvin or Schleiermacher, or even Barth, to whom one is drawn to return regularly with excitement and enthusiasm as conversation partners and aids to theological reconstruction. He is not, at least to me, that "interesting." But as a force in the reshaping of modern theology, Ritschl was unquestionably a figure of first-rate importance.

A decade ago, in writing on Ritschl in my history of Protestant thought in the nineteenth century, I described him as more a representative than a creative figure. I still think that judgment not incorrect. Ritschl was, in fact, a herald of a new mood and style in theology (the new mood that Isaac Dorner rather plaintively noted in his own systematic theology as one in which Dorner's kind of thinking would be left behind), and Ritschl's new directions were carried far beyond him by disciples and successors. I thus said that Ritschl "provided a new theological impulse and an alternative for his time, and set the tone for Protestant theology in imperial Germany."[5] Yet, I would now be inclined to credit Ritschl himself with a more decisive role than I previously implied.

A better historical judgment would be to describe Ritschl as a crucial agent in the transition from the kinds of mediating theologies of the early and middle nineteenth century that sought to bring the Christian tradition into vital relation to modern culture and science, efforts that largely reflected impulses from Schleiermacher or Hegel. Ritschl, too, was a mediator who wanted to reestablish the practical relevance of justification (in particular) as the center of Protestantism and, indeed, of all religion. But he was a mediator of a new kind, cutting loose from the speculative and the metaphysical (as represented by such thinkers as Dorner and Richard Rothe, Julius Müller and F. C. Baur), as well as the neo-pietists, and turning to the practical and the historical as a new foundation and form for theology. Thus his work was critical to the emergence of a variety of modes of twentieth-century thought. Or, bet-

5. Welch 2:2.

ter, one might describe him as a lens through which the light was re-
fracted in a new way. He not only represented the transitions, he initiated many of them—though, as I shall want to say, in a paradoxical way.
I note a half-dozen such areas of change.

The first is Ritschl's move to recover the notion of the kingdom of
God as a central theological theme. Here, as Ritschl insisted, was a
major advance upon Schleiermacher, one fraught with immense consequences for the understanding of Christian community, especially of its
origins in Jesus' proclamation of the kingdom. This was to be of great
potential for altering the course of subsequent theology, so that for many
later thinkers the eschatological motif could become not only the central
but the first doctrine in a theology oriented to the future.

Closely related was a second element, the demand that the ethical (the
"teleological" character of the Christian religion which Schleiermacher
had included in his definition, but had then forgotten) be elevated to a
status equal to the "religious," as in Ritschl's figure of the ellipse with
two foci, or, to put it better, that the thoroughgoing ethical character of
this religion be made explicit. There follows the "practical" turn in theology, the recognition that discussion of the Christian faith cannot be
separated from attention to the Christian life—a move that is reflected in
such diverse ways as Barth's incorporation of ethics into dogmatics and
liberation theology's emphasis on praxis, as well as the widespread
recognition that the important thing in Christology is not theories about
Christ's person but following Christ.

A third major element in the transition was Ritschl's demand for a
historical perspective. As I have put it elsewhere, whereas Schleiermacher made a half turn to history, Ritschl wanted to make a full turn, and
he was the critical figure through whom the historical impetus of Strauss
and Baur was transmitted and transfigured into the seminal work of
Johannes Weiss and Albert Schweitzer (in their stress on the apocalyptic
nature of the kingdom in Jesus' preaching), of Adolf Harnack in the history of doctrine, of Ernst Troeltsch in the history of social teachings in
Christianity as well as in the idea of modern historical consciousness as a
whole, and of Karl Holl in a new phase of Luther research. (I could wish
that the other contributors to this volume had made more of this side of
Ritschl's work, since history was for him fundamental to the nature of
community.)

A fourth area of focus was the overthrow of Confessionalism in theology, which was to be reflected in the attack by both Wilhelm Herrmann
and Troeltsch, as well as by Harnack, on the "dogmatic" principle, and
even in the conception of dogma in Karl Barth (for whom the decisions
of the past may well be reaffirmed, but only after the most searching
reconsideration from the ground up). It cannot be said that Ritschl
succeeded wholly in defeating the Lutheran Confessionalism that so
strongly opposed him, for that continued to cast a heavy shadow in sub-

sequent German Lutheranism. Nor did his work have any impact on Roman Catholic theology. But it did have a decisive influence on the views of religious authority that came to characterize the Liberal theologies of the late nineteenth and early twentieth century, and that have been recovered in the late twentieth century.

Further, we may recall Ritschl's rejection of natural theology, which led directly to Barth's extreme hostility. Recent years have seen a new interest in theology of nature, often coupled with ecological concerns, and even renewed support for some kind of "natural theology." But the latter has had to be quite different among theologians (though, oddly, not so much among some philosophers of religion) from the sort of thinking that preceded Ritschl's time. And the face of nature as presented by twentieth-century natural science is not seen as the threat posed by mid-nineteenth-century materialism (see the chapters above by Jodock and Busse).

Finally, one must think of Ritschl's recovery of the Old Testament witness as an essential part of the biblical theology he wanted to defend. Certainly, he was not alone in this in his own time, but his principle and his method were a marked contrast to the limbo into which Schleiermacher seemed to cast the Old Testament.

In at least all these ways, Ritschl's work has entered into the warp and woof of twentieth-century theology and to this extent Ritschl can have a fresh pertinence for theological reconstruction.

But at the same time, it must be said that in precisely such areas, Ritschl's influence was paradoxical, or at least ambiguous. I note two areas in particular. Ritschl recovered the theological importance of the kingdom of God, but his own idea of the kingdom in the teaching of Jesus was quickly to be overthrown in the work of Weiss and Schweitzer (see, *inter alia,* the chapter above by Hans Schwarz). The eschatological motif was thereafter to become a dominant strain in theology, but it was in quite different ways than Ritschl could have envisaged and with unresolved disputes about the role and even meaning of the eschatological. And in the radical social gospels of Ragaz and Kutter in Switzerland, even in Rauschenbusch who was deeply indebted to Ritschl, the idea of the kingdom had a quite different shape, with a much stronger sense of tension between the transcendent and the immanent, between the divine act of inauguration and fulfillment and the human response of "kingdom work."

Of equal importance was the inherent ambiguity, or instability, in Ritschl's stress on the historical foundation and character of the Christian religion, especially on the "canonical picture" of the earthly Jesus that was given in the Gospels. Within three years of his death there emerged, in Martin Kähler's *Der sogennante historische Jesus und der geschichtliche, biblische Christus* (The so-called Jesus of history and the historical biblical Christ) the controversy over the distinction between the *historisch* and the *geschichtlich*. The debate opened with Wilhelm Herrmann's attack on Kähler and continued well into the twentieth century, being reflected, for example, in Rudolf Bultmann as well as in Karl Rahner and Eduard Schillebeeckx. This was a problem of which Ritschl seemed to have had no inkling. Even though he could distinguish sometimes between the "historical" and the "ideal" Christ, he regularly used *historisch* and *geschichtlich* interchangeably. Yet, the extended debate over the distinction and the relation between the two terms led to the powerful tensions in the relation of faith and history that came quickly to light, perhaps supremely in Ernst Troeltsch, and are far from being resolved in the "new" quests for the historical Jesus, in contemporary christological debates, and in the massive preoccupation with hermeneutics.

In these as well as other areas, one might say that Ritschl was both a lens through which theological problems became focused in a new and decisive way and a refractor or prism through which the light of the gospel came to be distributed in a variety of directions and colors. Thus one has to recognize the several ways in which Ritschl's impulses were carried on in more productive and decisive modes by his disciples and successors: by Adolf Harnack in the history of doctrine, by Karl Holl in Luther research (see Lotz, above), by Johannes Weiss and others in the idea of the kingdom of God, by the "history of religions school" in the question of the social context of both Old and New Testaments, by Wilhelm Herrmann and Ernst Troeltsch on the authority of confessions and dogma, by Troeltsch on the question of the finality of the Christian religion and on the relativity of all historical judgments, and even by Karl Barth on the nature of christological affirmation.

In sum, then, when one returns to the question of the value of Ritschl for late twentieth-century theologizing, an ambiguous answer is unavoidable. The contemporary scene is so different from the situation of the third quarter of the nineteenth century. The relation of Christianity to other religions, by which Ritschl was quite untroubled (here he was a fairly parochial Lutheran Protestant), has emerged as one of the great and unavoidable questions. Two world wars and a Holocaust have intervened to destroy the confidence that seemed to prevail in the late nineteenth century. There has been a kind of rapprochement of Catholic and Protestant theology that would have stunned Ritschl. Liberation theologies, whether Latin American or African American or feminist, have emerged that have fundamentally altered the ideas of praxis and of social location in theology.

Such dimensions of the confused, even chaotic, present theological situation, along with the ambiguities noted above in some of Ritschl's most cherished positions, immensely complicate the question of Ritschl's direct values for present theological construction. Yet, whatever answers may be given to that sort of query—and my colleagues have made inter-

esting and significant suggestions for answers, which go far to rehabilitate Ritschl's theological positions—it must also be said that contemporary theologizing cannot be carried on in an intelligent way without
recognizing the critical role that Albrecht Ritschl played in shaping the
possibilities for modern (or postmodern) Christian theology.

Index